The Undergraduate's Companion to African Writers and Their Web Sites

Recent Titles in the Undergraduate Companion Series
James K. Bracken, Series Editor

The Undergraduate's Companion to American Writers and Their Web Sites
James K. Bracken and Larry G. Hinman

The Undergraduate's Companion to Women Writers and Their Web Sites
Katharine A. Dean, Miriam Conteh-Morgan, and James K. Bracken

The Undergraduate's Companion to English Renaissance Writers and Their Web Sites
Steven Kenneth Galbraith

The Undergraduate's Companion to Women Poets of the World and Their Web Sites
Katharine A. Dean

The Undergraduate's Companion to Arab Writers and Their Web Sites
Dona S. Straley

The Undergraduate's Companion to African Writers and Their Web Sites

Miriam E. Conteh-Morgan

Undergraduate Companion Series
James K. Bracken, Series Editor

LIBRARIES
U N L I M I T E D
A Member of the Greenwood Publishing Group

Westport, Connecticut • London

Library of Congress Cataloging-in-Publication Data

Conteh-Morgan, Miriam.
    The undergraduate's companion to African writers and their web sites / Miriam E.
  Conteh-Morgan
        p. cm. — (Undergraduate companion series)
        Includes bibliographical references and index.
        ISBN 1–59158–116–8 (pbk. : alk. paper)
        1. African literature—Computer network resources. 2. African literature—
  Bibliography. I. Title. II. Series.
      PL8010.C63   2005
      025.06'809896—dc22   2005016078

British Library Cataloguing in Publication Data is available.

Library of Congress Catalog Card Number: 2005016078
ISBN:1–59158–116–8

First published in 2005

Libraries Unlimited, 88 Post Road West, Westport, CT 06881
A Member of Greenwood Publishing Group, Inc.
www.lu.com

Printed in the United States of America

The paper used in this book complies with the
Permanent Paper Standard issued by the National
Information Standards Organization (Z39.48–1984).

10   9   8   7   6   5   4   3   2   1

To my departed parents, KJM and AJM,
for the legacy of memories.

Contents

Acknowledgments

Many thanks to the Series Editor, Jim Bracken, for encouraging me to undertake this project, and to the Director of The Ohio State University Libraries, Joseph Branin, for granting me research leave to work on the manuscript of this book. My appreciation also goes to the editorial staff who worked on various stages of the publication process with me. And of course there's also John to thank for his unwavering support.

Introcduction

The need for the study of Africa in institutions of higher learning in the United States came in the wake of some parallel and interconnected developments of the 1960s. These include the Black Consciousness Movement in the US that led to the creation of Black Studies departments and courses about the black world, and the decolonization of Africa, which spawned new alliances among nations and altered the dynamics of Cold War politics.

This period was also marked by an increase in the publication of literary texts by Africans, and consequently by a growing body of critical literature devoted to it. Today, with four Nobel prizewinners—Wole Soyinka, Naguib Mahfouz, Nadine Gordimer, and J. M. Coetzee—African literature has not only gained high global recognition, but it has become a firmly established part of non-Western or world literature course offerings in many general education curricula across the United States.

No longer exclusively housed within Black/Africana studies programs, African writers are now read in English, French, Portuguese, women's studies, and comparative studies departments, for example, making African literature a broader part of the undergraduate experience.

Many undergraduates typically come to these courses with little or no prior exposure to African writers, and, therefore, with no experience doing research on them. Numerous introductions to the literature and works of criticism on specific writers are available in most academic libraries. There are also bibliographies and reference resources such as *African Authors,* by Donald Herdeck (Washington DC: INSCAPE, 1974), and Bernth Lindfors's cumulative series, *Black African Literature in English* (1987, 1995, and 2000). Others include Virginia Coulon's *Bibliographie francophone de littérature africaine* (1994), *The Companion to African Literatures,* by Douglas Killam and Ruth Rowe (Bloomington, IN:

Indiana University Press, 1999), Pushpa Parekh and Siga Jagne's *Postcolonial African Writers* (Greenwood Press, 1998), and the more recent *Encyclopedia of African Literature* (Routledge, 2003), edited by Simon Gikandi. Like many literary reference works, however, they do not include Web resources.

Given that Web sites have been cited in many studies as the primary and preferred reference source for today's undergraduates, *The Undergraduate's Companion to African Writers and Their Web Sites,* like other companions in the series, seeks to meet a need for literary reference works that would steer students toward useful information on the Web. Conceived and compiled with undergraduates' research needs and tool preferences in mind, this book brings together carefully selected Web and print resources deemed useful for researching specific African writers.

Featured Writers and Their Works

The writers featured in this companion were selected based on two criteria: that there is material on them in an easily available reference work, and that there is some information of research value on free Web sites. Fee-based online databases are excluded because of the disparities in access that may exist among academic libraries. The research materials that I consider of value include biographies, bibliographies of primary and secondary works, excerpts from, or electronic full text of, writers' works, critical essays, and interviews (including audio and video clips of them).

Writers who meet only one or neither of these two criteria are not included. For example, for known writers like James Ene Henshaw (Nigeria) and Fatima Dike (South Africa), I found no research Web site; and the more contemporary Ingrid de Kok and Karen Press (South Africa) have a significant Web presence, but they do not seem to have yet made it into the reference books I consulted. In the end, the book contains entries on just over 300 writers from thirty-nine countries. About a quarter are women, and each of their names is marked with an asterisk in the country list of writers.

I also had to determine a working definition of the terms "Africa" and "African writer." Instead of going by the familiar division of the continent into sub-Saharan and North (or Maghrebian) Africa, I adopt a whole-continent approach, to also include the Indian Ocean islands. I include major writers from North Africa, who either write in French, or whose original Arabic works are available in English. Students will therefore find in this companion entries on writers from Algeria, Morocco, and Egypt, from the Indian Ocean islands of Mauritius and the Comoros, and from sub-Saharan countries such as Djibouti (east), Sierra Leone (west), and Zimbabwe (south). The rationale for being all-inclusive rests mainly on the view that many survey courses on African literature try to be representative, and they typically feature writers from around the continent.

On the question of defining an African writer, I follow established practice. The most common characteristic is being African-born, regardless of country of later residence. In this category would be a writer like Ben Okri, born in Nigeria, now living in Britain, and who is also classified as a British writer. I also include in this category Albert Camus, who was born and raised in Algeria, though he is best known as a French writer. Another reference work, *African Writers* (Charles Scribener's, 1997), has an entry on him. Authors such as Doris Lessing, who moved to South Africa with her British parents at an early age (she is also part of British literary tradition), or British-born Kenyan-transplant, Marjorie Oludhe Macgoye, have also been considered African, and both are listed in this book as such.

For other writers, though, the description of African writer may be debated because neither the country of birth nor the residence criterion holds true for them. For example, Azouz Begag and Marie Ndiaye were both born in France to African immigrant parents; they continue to live there, but they are identified as African writers because of their heritage. Clearly, classifications are not always neat or easy, and that is why some writers straddle two literary traditions. For such African writers, I have included in this book references from both traditions.

Another central issue in African literature is language. There is no single one that characterizes the literature because the works are written in a variety of languages. The majority of modern African writers use one of three European languages of colonization—English, French, or Portuguese—giving rise to descriptions for such writing and writers as "anglophone," "francophone," and "lusophone" respectively. Others write in African languages such as Gikuyu, Swahili, Afrikaans, Hausa, Amharic, or Zulu. Although the references cited in the book are predominantly in English, they describe writers who use a wide variety of languages.

All the authors in this book belong to the late 19th century and the 20th-century. One notable exception is Olaudah Equiano, an eighteenth-century African, whose slave narrative is sometimes considered the first work of African literature. Their writing covers all the genres, with some creating works across different genres and forms. Examples include Flora Nwapa and Chinua Achebe, who write novels and children's stories; Ousmane Sembène who is a writer and filmmaker; and Francis Bebey, a writer and musician. Realizing that undergraduates will gain a more complete picture of writers' creativity, and that these authors can be researched under each of these genres and modes of expression, I have tried where possible to include reference sources for each of the categories.

Selecting Web Sites

It is a cliché to say that the World Wide Web throws too much information at a searcher, both good and useless. In the process of whittling down the hits to reliable and research-worthy ones, I have eliminated those whose pages have too many distractions, especially when the information they contain is found elsewhere, and with some value-added features.

Most of the sites I selected fall into one of four categories. First, there are Web projects created by members of academic institutions. These tend to be stable, and they feature multiple writers; most importantly they are designed specifically either for students as complements to African literature courses, or as instructor-supervised student projects. One is more likely to find bibliographies of critical works, in addition to the usual biographies and lists of writers' works on such sites.

I also relied on Web projects hosted by cultural and research institutions, major newspapers, and professional organizations. Examples of the former include the Africa Centre and the British Council, both in the United Kingdom. The newspapers I cite include the *New York Times, The Guardian* (UK), and *The Mail and Guardian* (South Africa), and they typically provide book reviews, interviews with writers, and obituaries.

A third category of Web site selected is the kind embedded within country or region projects. Some such as The KwaZulu-Natal Literary Map are sponsored by government agencies, and others are hosted by commercial Internet service providers. Such projects are intended to showcase a country or region's diverse assets, including the literary. Then there are projects developed by literature enthusiasts. They are most often dedicated to single authors or to authors who write a certain kind of literature. Although the sites tend to be of unequal value, the ones deemed good enough to be included normally have brief biographies and links to other Web sources on a writer.

Not all the sites are researcher friendly. A number of them do not rigorously conform to Web editing protocols. On some sites, for example, it is impossible to identify their creators, and they contain neither revision dates nor clear statements of objective. In other instances, sites may provide the full text of poems and short stories without always citing their source materials. However, I do not consider some of these contraventions major enough to warrant rejecting the site, especially when the information a site contains withstands some basic reliability tests. Where they occur, the shortcomings are acknowledged in my citations (as in "update unavailable") or in annotations.

Another point worth mentioning is that the sites in the book are not always in English, given the linguistic diversity of the literature noted earlier. If there are two language versions of the site, I systematically choose the English language one. But when a site is in French, or, in a few cases, in Portuguese, I still include it because some upper-level students would have a high enough language proficiency to understand the information provided.

Generally every Web site has a full bibliographic citation, with an indication of the date I last visited it, the URL, and a descriptive annotation. An exception is made for sites with multiple author pages. In such cases where the main projects are referred to many times throughout the book, and each author page follows the same template, the complete citation is not repeated, nor is an annotation given. Instead, the "Frequently Cited Web Sites" section of this book provides the full bibliographic details and site description.

Print Sources

The references cited in the non-Web categories are all taken from the many print sources I personally consulted. The majority of these books are standard reference material found in many academic libraries, so most undergraduates should have access to them. Among these are the multi-volume Gale series: *Dictionary of Literary Biography, Contemporary Literary Criticism, Twentieth Century Literary Criticism,* and *Black Literature Criticism.* Many of the literary criticism works repackage the same information in the different series, so I selected only those that provide a chronological flow without much overlap. Other reference works on African literature, postcolonial literature, and world writers were also used.

For selections from multivolume sets with various editors, I provide only the name of the editors of the specific volume, the series titles, and volume numbers. Where multiple entries are drawn from one volume, I give partial bibliographic information, just as in the case of Web projects with multiple author pages. The full citations for all these books appear in the "Frequently Cited References" section.

In a few instances I have used book chapters and journal articles to flesh out bio-critical entries and interviews. This occurred when I could find no substantial entry in the reference books I consulted, but I felt the writer had to be included in the book.

Organization of Entries

The writers are listed in alphabetical order. Each entry is headed by the writer's full name, including variant forms and pseudonyms, and the date of birth, and death, where applicable. The canonical reference books, and sometimes obituaries in newspapers, have served as the authorities for these biographical details.

Pre-eminence is given to Web sites, so that is the category listed first after each writer's name. This section is not broken down by content type, unlike the print resources, which are subdivided into biographies and criticism, and any of the following where they apply: dictionaries, encyclopedias and handbooks, bibliographies, and interviews.

The entries follow MLA citation style.

Using the Companion

This book is meant to serve as a resource for introductory material on African writers, so it is by no means an exhaustive guide to the literature. The references provided should serve well in cases where what the undergraduate student needs is material for a short research paper. In cases where more extensive research is called for, I highly recommend working with reference and African Studies librarians for more in-depth searches in journal databases and online catalogs for critical articles and books. This book will also be a useful guide for the casual reader of African literature with a need for information on writers.

The Undergraduate's Companion to African Writers and Their Web Sites

Alphabetical List of Authors

Abbas, Ferhat, 1899–1985

Abrahams, Lionel, 1928–2004

Abrahams, Peter, 1919–

Achebe, Chinua, 1930–

Acholonu, Catherine, 1951–

Adedeji, Remi, 1937–

Adiaffi, Anne-Marie, 1951–1995

Agualusa, José, 1960–

Ahmed, Leila, 1940–

Aidoo, Ama Ata, 1942–

Aiyejina, Funso, 1949–

Alkali, Zaynab, 1950–

Aluko, T. M., 1918–

Amadi, Elechi, 1934–

Amrouche, Jean, 1907–1962

Amrouche, Marguerite, 1913–1976

Angira, Jared, 1947–

Anyidoho, Kofi, 1947–

Appiah, Peggy, 1921–

Armah, Ayi Kwei, 1939–

Asare, Meshack, 1945–

Assaad, Fawzia, 1929–

Awoonor, Kofi, 1935–

Bâ, Amadou Hampaté, 1901–1991

Bâ, Mariama, 1921–1981

Baccouche, Hachemi, 1917–

Badian, Seydou, 1928–

Bakr, Salwa, 1949–

Bandele-Thomas, Biyi, 1967–

Barry, Kesso, 1948–

Bebey, Francis, 1929–2001

Begag, Azouz, 1957–

Behr, Mark, 1944–

Békri, Tahar, 1951–

Bemba, Sylvain, 1934–1995

Ben Jelloun, Tahar, 1944–

Berliner, Janet, 1939–

Berrada, Mohammed, 1938–

Beti, Mongo, 1932–2001

Beyala, Calixthe, 1961–

Bhêly-Quénum, Olympe, 1928–

Biyouala, Daniel, 1953–

Black, Stephen, 1880–1931

Blixen, Karen, 1885–1962

Boni, Tanella, 1954–

Bosman, Herman, 1905–1951

Boudjedra, Rachid, 1941 –
Bouraoui, Hédi, 1932–
Bouraoui, Nina, 1967–
Brew, Kwesi, 1928–
Breytenbach, Breyten, 1939–
Brink, André, 1935–
Brutus, Dennis, 1924–
Bugul, Ken, 1948–
Butler, Frederick, 1918–2001

Campbell, Roy, 1901–1957
Camus, Albert, 1913–1960
Casely-Hayford, Adelaide, 1868–1960
Casely-Hayford, Gladys, 1904–1950
Casely-Hayford, Joseph, 1866–1930
Chedid, Andrée, 1920–
Cheney-Coker, Syl, 1945–
Chimombo, Steve, 1945–
Chinodya, Shimmer, 1957–
Chinweizu, 1943–
Chipasula, Frank, 1949–
Choukri, Mohamed, 1935–2003
Chraïbi, Driss, 1926–
Clark, John Pepper, 1935–
Clouts, Sydney, 1926–1982
Coetzee, John Michael, 1940–
Collen, Lindsey, 1948–
Conton, William, 1925–2003
Cope, Jack, 1913–
Couchoro, Felix, 1900–1968
Couto, Mia, 1955–
Couzyn, Jeni, 1942–
Craveirinha, José, 1922–2003
Cronin, Jeremy, 1949–

Dadié, Bernard, 1916–
Dangarembga, Tsitsi, 1958(9)–
Dangor, Achmat, 1948–
de Graft, Joe, 1924–
d'Erneville, Annette Mbaye, 1926–

Devi, Ananda, 1957–
Dhlomo, Herbert, 1903–1956
Diallo, Nafissatou, 1941–1982
Dib, Mohammed, 1920–2003
Diescho, Joseph, 1955–
Dikobe, Modikwe, 1913–
Diop, Birago, 1906–1989
Diop, Boubacar, 1946–
Diop, David, 1927–1960
Dipoko, Mbella Sonne, 1936–
Djaout, Tahar, 1954–1993
Djebar, Assia,1936–
Djoleto, Amu, 1929–
Dongala, Emmanuel, 1941 –

du Plessis, Menan, 1952–
Easmon, Raymond Sarif, 1913–1997
Effa, Gaston-Paul, 1965–
Efoui, Kossi, 1962–
Ekué, Christiane, 1954–
Ekwensi, Cyprian, 1921–
Emecheta, Buchi, 1944–
Equiano, Oulaudah, 1745–1797
Essop, Ahmed, 1931–

Fagunwa, Daniel, 1903–1963
Fall, Aminata Sow, 1941–
Farah, Nuruddin, 1945–
Fofana, Aicha, 1957–2003
Freed, Lynn, 1945–
Fugard, Athol, 1932–
Fugard, Sheila, 1932–

Gabre-Medhin, Tsegaye, 1936–
Gabre-Tsadick, Marta, 1932–
Gordimer, Nadine, 1923–
Gurnah, Abdulrazak, 1948–
Gwala, Mafika, 1946–

Hazoumé, Flore, 1959–

Head, Bessie, 1937–1986
Honwana, Luis Bernardo, 1942–
Hope, Christopher, 1944–
Hove, Chenjerai, 1956–
Hussein, Ebrahim, 1943–

Ike, Chukwuemeka, 1931–
Ilboudo, Monique, n.d.
Imbuga, Francis, 1947–
Isegawa, Moses, 1963–
Iyayi, Festus, 1947–

Jabès, Edmond, 1912–1991
Jacobson, Dan, 1929–
Joachim, Paulin, 1931–
Johnson, Lemuel, 1941–2002
Joubert, Elsa, 1922–

Ka, Aminata Maïga, 1940–
Kachingwe, Aubrey, 1926–
Kagame, Alexis, 1912–1981
Kamanda, Kama, 1952–
Kane, Cheikh Hamidou, 1928–
Karodia, Farida, 1942–
Kateb, Yacine, 1929–1989
Kayira, Legson, 1942–
Kellas, Anne, 1951–
Kgositsile, Keorapetse, 1938 –
Khair-Eddine, Mohamed, 1941–1995
Khosa, Ungulani, 1957–
Kibera, Leonard, 1942–1983
Kimenye, Barbara, 1930?–
Kourouma, Ahmadou, 1923–2003
Kunene, Mazisi, 1930–
Kuzwayo, Ellen, 1914–
Kwahulé, Koffi, 1956–
Kyomuhendo, Goretti, 1965–

La Guma, Alex, 1925–1985
Ladipo, Duro, 1931–1978

Laing, Kojo, 1946–
Laye, Barnabé, 1941–
Laye, Camara, 1928–1980
Lessing, Doris, 1919–
Likimani, Muthoni,
Liking, Werewere, 1950–
Livingstone, Douglas, 1932–1996
lo Liyong, Taban, 1939–
Lopes, Henri, 1937–

Mabanckou, Alain, 1966–
Macgoye, Marjorie Oludhe, 1928–
Maddy, Yulisa Amadu, 1936–
Magona, Sindiwe, 1943–
Mahfouz, Naguib, 1911–
Maillu, David, 1939–
El Maleh, Edmond, 1917–
Mammeri, Mouloud, 1917–1989(88?)
Manaka, Matsemala, 1956–1998
Mapanje, Jack, 1944–
Maraire, J. Nozipo, 1966–
Marechera, Dambudzo, 1952–1987
Marouane, Leila, 1960–
Mattera, Don, 1935–
Maunick, Edouard, 1931–
Mbuli, Mzwakhe, 1959–
Mda, Zakes, 1948–
Memmi, Albert, 1920–
Meniru, Theresa, 1931–
Miller, Ruth, 1919–1969
Millin, Sarah Gertrude, 1888–1968
Mimouni, Rachid, 1945–1995
Mnthali, Felix, 1933–
Modisane, Bloke, 1923–1986
Mofolo, Thomas, 1876–1948
Mollel, Tololwa, 1952–
Monénembo, Tierno, 1947–
Moore, Bai, 1916–1988
Mopeli-Paulus, Atwell Sidwell,
    1913–1960

Mphahlele, Ezekiel, 1919–
Mpina, Edison, 1942?–
Mqhayi, Samuel E. K., 1875–1945
Mtshali, Oswald Mbuyiseni, 1940–
Mudimbe, Valentin, 1941–
Mugo, Micere, 1942–
Mulaisho, Dominic, 1933–
Mungoshi, Charles, 1947–
Munonye, John, 1929–1999
Mwangi, Meja, 1948–
Mzamane, Mbulelo, 1948–

Nazareth, Peter, 1940–
Nazombe, Anthony, 1955–2004
Ndao, Cheikh Aliou, 1933–
Ndebele, Njabulo, 1948–
Ndiaye, Marie, 1967–
Ndu, Pol, 1940–1976
Neto, Agostinho, 1922–1979
Ngandu-Nkashama, Pius, 1946–
Ngcobo, Lauretta, 1931–
Ngugi wa, Thiong'o, 1938–
Nicol, Abioseh, 1924–1994
Njami, Simon, 1962–
Njau, Rebeka, 1932–
Nkosi, Lewis, 1936–
Nortje, Arthur, 1942–1970
Ntiru, Richard, 1946–
Nwankwo, Nkem, 1936–
Nwapa, Flora, 1931–1993
Nzekwu, Onuora, 1928–

Oculi, Okello, 1942–
Odaga, Asenath, 1938 –
Ogot, Grace, 1930–
Ogundipe-Leslie, Molara, 1949–
Ogunyemi, Wale, 1939–2001
Ojaide, Tanure, 1948–
Ojo-Ade, Femi, 1941–
Okai, Atukewi, 1941–

Okara, Gabriel, 1921–
Okigbo, Christopher, 1932–1967
Okoye, Ifeoma, n.d.–
Okpewho, Isidore, 1941–
Okri, Ben, 1959–
Omotoso, Kole, 1943–
Onadipe, Kola, 1922–
Onwueme, Tess, 1955–
Osofisan, Femi, 1946–
Osundare, Niyi, 1947–
Ouologuem, Yambo, 1940–
Oyono, Ferdinand, 1929–
Oyono-Mbia, Guillaume, 1939–

Palangyo, Peter, 1939–1993
Paton, Alan, 1903–1988
p'Bitek, Okot, 1931–1982
Pepetela, 1941–
Peters, Lenrie, 1932–
Plaatje, Sol, 1876–1932
Pliya, Jean, 1931–
Plomer, William, 1903–1973
Pringle, Thomas, 1789–1834

Rabearivelo, Jean-Joseph,
    1901–1937
Rabémananjara, Jacques, 1913–
Rafenomanjato, Charlotte, 1938–n.d.
Rakotoson, Michèle, 1948–
Rawiri, Angèle, 1954–n.d.
Rifaat, Alifa, 1930–1996
Rive, Richard, 1931–1989
Robert, Shaaban, 1909–1962
Roberts, Sheila, 1937–
Rooke, Daphne, 1914–
Rotimi, Ola, 1938–2000
Rubadiri, David, 1930–
Ruganda, John, 1941–
Ruhumbika, Gabriel, 1938–
Rui, Manuel, 1941–

el-Saadawi, Nawal, 1931–
Salih, Tayeb, 1929–
Sall, Amadou Lamine, 1951–
Sallah, Tijan, 1958–
Saro-Wiwa, Ken, 1941–1995
Sassine, Williams, 1944–1997
Schreiner, Olive, 1855–1920
Sebbar, Leila, 1941–
Segun, Mabel, 1930–
Sekyi, Kobina, 1892–1956
Selormey, Francis, 1927–1983
Sembène, Ousmane, 1923–
Senghor, Léopold Sédar, 1906–2001
Sepamla, Sipho, 1932–
Serote, Mongane, 1944–
Serumaga, Robert, 1939–1980
Smith, Pauline, 1882–1959
Smith, Wilbur, 1933–
Sofola, Zulu, 1935–1995
Sousa, Jamba, 1966–
Sowande, Bode, 1948–
Soyinka, Wole, 1934–
Stockenström, Wilma, 1933–
Sutherland, Efua, 1924–1996

Tadjo, Véronique, 1955–
Tansi, Sony Labou, 1947–1995

Tati-Loutard, Jean-Baptiste, 1938–
Tenreiro, Francisco, 1921–1963,
Themba, Can, 1924–1968
Tlali, Miriam, 1933–
Toihiri, Mohamed, 1955–
Tutuola, Amos, 1920–1997

Ulasi, Adaora, 1932–
U Tam'si, Tchicaya, 1931–1988
Uys, Pieter-Dirk, 1945–

van der Post, Laurens, 1906–1997
Vera, Yvonne, 1964–
Vieira, José, 1935–
Vilakazi, Benedict, 1906–1947

Waberi, Abdourahman, 1956–
Wachira, Godwin, 1936–
Waciuma, Charity, 1936–
Wangusa, Timothy, 1942–
Wicomb, Zoë, 1949–
Worku, Daniachew, 1936–1995

Zaourou, Zadi, 1938–n.d.
Zeleza, Tiyambe, 1955–
Zimunya, Musaemura, 1949–
Zinsou, Senouvo, 1946–

Authors by Nationality

* = women writers

Algeria

Ferhat Abass

Jean Amrouche

*Marguerite Amrouche

Azouz Begag

Rachid Boudjedra

Hédi Bouraoui

*Nina Bouraoui

Albert Camus

Mohammed Dib

Tahar Djaout

*Assia Djebar

Yacine Kateb

* Leïla Marouane

Rachid Mimouni

*Leila Sebbar

Angola

Jose Eduardo Agualusa

Sousa Jamba

Agostinho Neto

Pepetela

Manuel Rui

Jamba Sousa

José Luandino Vieira

Benin

Olympe Bhêly-Quénum

Felix Couchoro

Paulin Joachim

Barnabé Laye

Jean Pliya

Burkina Faso

Monique Ilboudo

Cameroon

Francis Bebey

Mongo Beti

*Calixthe Beyala

Mbella Sonne Dipoko

Gaston-Paul Effa

*Werewere Liking

Simon Njami

Ferdinand Oyono

Guillaume Oyono-Mbia

Comoros

Mohamed A. Toihiri

Congo (Brazzaville)

Sylvain Bemba

Daniel Biyouala

Emmanuel Dongala

*Flore Hazoumé

Henri Lopes

Alain Mabanckou

Sony Labou Tansi

Jean-Baptiste Tati-Loutard

Felix Tchicaya U'Tamsi

Congo (formerly Zaire)

Kama Kamanda

Valentin Mudimbe

Pius Ngandu-Nkashama

Djibouti

Abdourahman Waberi

Egypt

*Leila Ahmed

*Fawzia Assaad

*Salwa Bakr

*Andrée Chedid

Edmond Jabès

Naguib Mahfouz

*Alifa Rifaat

*Nawal el-Saadawi

Ethiopia

Tsegaye Gabre-Medhin

Daniachew (Dannyacchew) Worku (Werqu)

Gabon

*Angèle Ntyugwetondo Rawiri

Gambia

Lenrie Peters

Tijan Sallah

Ghana

*Ama Ata Aidoo
Kofi Anyidoho
*Peggy Appiah
Ayi Kwei Armah
Meschack Asare
Kofi Awoonor
Kwesi Brew
Joseph Ephraim Casely-Hayford

Joe de Graft
Amu Djoleto
Kojo Laing
Atukewi Okai
Kobina Sekyi
Francis Selormey
*Efua Sutherland

Guinea

*Kesso Barry
Camara Laye

Tierno Monénembo
Williams Sassine

Ivory Coast

*Anne-Marie Adiaffi
*Tanella Boni
Bernard Dadié
Ahmadou Kourouma

Koffi Kwahulé
*Véronique Tadjo
Zadi Zaourou

Kenya

Jared Angira
*Karen Blixen
Francis Imbuga
Leonard Kibera
*Muthoni Likimani
*Marjorie Macgoye
David Maillu
*Micere Mugo

Meja Mwangi
*Rebeka Njau
*Asenath Odaga
*Grace Ogot
Ngugi wa Thiong'o
Godwin Wachira
*Charity Waciuma

Liberia

Bai T. Moore

Madagascar

Jean-Joseph Rabearivelo
Jacques Rabémanajara

*Charlotte-Arrisoa
   Rafenomanjato
*Michéle Rakotoson

Malawi

Steve Chimombo
Frank Chipasula
Aubrey Kachingwe
Legson Kayira
Jack Mapanje

Felix Mnthali
Edison Mpina
Anthony Nazombe
David Rubadiri
Tiyambe Zeleza

Mali

Amadou Hampaté Bâ
Seydou Badian

*Aicha Fofana
Yambo Ouologuem

Mauritius

*Ananda Devi

Edouard Maunick

Morocco

Tahar Ben Jelloun
Mohammed Berrada
Mohamed Choukri
Driss Chraïbi

Mohamed Khain-Eddine
Edmond Amran El Maleh
Moloud Mammeri

Mozambique

Mia Couto
José Craveirinha

Luis Bernardo Honwana
Ungulani Khosa

Namibia

Joseph Diescho

Nigeria

Chinua Achebe
*Catherine Acholonu
*Remi Adedeji
Funso Aiyejina
*Zaynab Alkali
T(imothy) M. Aluko
Elechi Amadi
Biyi Bandele-Thomas
Chinweizu
John Pepper Clark
Cyprian Ekwensi
*Buchi Emecheta
Oulaudah Equiano

D(aniel) O. Fagunwa
Chukwuemeka Ike
Festus Iyayi
Duro Ladipo
*Theresa Meniru
John Munonye
Pol Nnamuzikam Ndu
Nkem Nwankwo
Flora Nwapa
Onuora Nzekwu
Molara Ogundipe-Leslie
Wale Ogunyemi
Tanure Ojaide

Femi Ojo-Ade
Gabriel Okara
Christopher Okigbo
*Ifeoma Okoye
Isidore Okpewho
Ben Okri
Kole Omotoso
Kola Onadipe
*Tess Onwueme
Femi Osofisan

Niyi Osundare
Ola Rotimi
Ken Saro-Wiwa
*Mabel Segun
*Zulu Sofola
Bode Sowande
Wole Soyinka
Amos Tutuola
*Adaora Ulasi

Rwanda

Alexis Kagame

Sao Tomé and Principe

Francisco José Tenreiro

Senegal

*Mariama Bâ
*Ken Bugul
*Annette Mbaye d'Erneville
*Nafissatou Diallo
Birago Diop
Boubacar Diop
David Diop
*Aminata Sow Fall

*Aminata Maïga Ka
Cheikh Hamidou Kane
Cheikh Aliou Ndao
*Marie Ndiaye
Amadou Lamine Sall
Ousmane Sembène
Léopold Sédar Senghor

Sierra Leone

*Adelaide Casely-Hayford
*Gladys Casely-Hayford
Syl Cheney-Coker
William Conton

Raymond Sarif Easmon
Lemuel Johnson
Yulisa Amadu Maddy
Abioseh Nicol

Somalia

Nuruddin Farah

South Africa

Lionel Abrahams
Peter Abrahams
Mark Behr

*Janet Berliner
Herman Charles Bosman
Breyten Breytenbach

André Brink

Dennis Brutus

Frederick Guy Butler

Roy Campbell

Sydney Clouts

John M. Coetzee

*Lindsey Collen

Jack Cope

Jeni Couzyn

Jeremy Cronin

Achmat Dangor

Herbert Dhlomo

Modikwe Dikobe

*Menan du Plessis

Ahmed Essop

*Lynn Freed

Athol Fugard

*Sheila Fugard

*Nadine Gordimer

Mafika Gwala

*Bessie Head

Christopher Hope

Dan Jacobson

*Elsa Joubert

*Farida Karodia

*Anne Kellas

Keorapetse Kgositsile

Mazisi Kunene

*Ellen Kuzwayo

Alex La Guma

Douglas Livingstone

*Sindiwe Magona

Matsemala Manaka

Don Mattera

Mzwakhe Mbuli

Zakes Mda

*Ruth Miller

*Sarah Gertrude Millin

Bloke Modisane

Thomas Mofolo

Atwell Sidwell Mopeli-Paulus

Oswald Mbuyiseni Mtshali

Ezekiel Mphalele

S(amuel) E(dward) K(rune) Mqhayi

Mbulelo Vizikhungo Mzamane

Njabulo Ndebele

*Lauretta Ngcobo

Lewis Nkosi

Arthur Nortje

Alan Paton

Sol Plaatje

William Plomer

Thomas Pringle

Richard Rive

*Sheila Roberts

*Daphne Rooke

*Olive Schreiner

Sipho Sepamla

Mongane William Serote

*Pauline Janet Smith

*Wilma Stockenström

Can Themba

Miriam Tlali

Pieter-Dirk Uys

Lauren van der Post

Benedict Vilakazi

*Zoë Wicomb

Sudan

Taban lo Liyong

Tayeb Salih

Tanzania

Abdulrazak Gurnah
Ebrahim Hussein
Tololwa Mollel

Peter Palangyo
Shaaban Robert
Gabriel Ruhumbika

Togo

*Christiane Akoua Ekué

Kossi Efoui

Tunisia

Hachemi Baccouche
Tahar Békri

Moloud Mammeri
Albert Memmi

Uganda

Okot p'Bitek
Moses Isegawa
*Barbara Kimenye
*Goretti Kyomuhendo
Peter Nazareth

Richard Carl Ntiru
Okello Oculi
John Ruganda
Robert Serumaga
Timothy Wangusa

Zambia

Dominic Mulaisho

Wilbur Smith

Zimbabwe

Shimmer Chinodya
*Tsitsi Dangarembga
*Bessie Head
Chenjerai Hove
*Doris Lessing
*J. Nozipo Maraire

Dambudzo Marechera
Charles Mungoshi
*Yvonne Vera
Tiyambe Paul Zeleza
Musaemura Zimunya

Frequently Cited Web Sites

African Children's Literature. Ed. Lilian Temu Osaki. 28 May 2004. U. of Florida
   Libraries. 20 Jul. 2005, http://www.uflib.ufl.edu/cm/africana/children.htm.
   This Web site provides short biographies of nine writers of children's literature, with a list of their published works. The main page of the Web site has a
general introduction to the literature and uses the same chronological classification as for Africa's other literary works: precolonial, colonial, and postcolonial.
A bibliography of relevant Web sites and print resources rounds out the rest of the
site.

African Letters. Eds. Chimdi Maduagwu and Bode Osanyin. Copyright 2002–4.
   US–Africa Literary Foundation. 20 Jul. 2005, http://www.bowwave.org/
   AfricanWriters/africanletters.htm.
   African Letters is one of the projects of the US–Africa Literary Project,
whose aim is to give wider visibility to African poets and their diverse works.
The site lists more than one hundred writers, but only about one-third so far have
the full text of their poems available. The main page with the list of poets needs
more careful editing because there are typographical errors in some writers'
names.

African Literature in English: Five Women Writers. Ed. Ingrid Kerkhoff. Copyright 2001. Universität Bremen. 20 Jul. 2005, http://www.fb10.uni-bremen
   .de/anglistik/kerkhoff/AfrWomenWriters/index.htm.
   Developed for a course on Anglophone women writers, Kerkhoff's initial
project now includes links to seven authors: Aidoo, Dangarembga, Emecheta,
Head, Magona, Nwapa, and Vera. For each writer, there are links to a biography,
a bibliography of secondary literature, study questions on the work being read in
the class, the full text of articles and reviews contained within the project
archives, and external Web sites on the author. Also available behind the "Reading

Lounge" links for each author are excerpts from selected works. See also *Post-colonial African Literatures in English* later in this section.

African Poetry. Ed. Eric Aghadiuno. Update unavailable. Aghadiuno.com. 20 Jul.
        2005, http://www.geocities.com/eaghadiuno/poetry/african/.
        Hosted by a poetry enthusiast, this site has the full text of selected poems by
ten published poets.

African Writers: Voices of Change. Ed. Dan Reboussin. 26 May 2004. U. of Florida
        Libraries. 20 Jul. 2005,, http://web.uflib.ufl.edu/cm/africana/writers.htm.
        A Web project of the University of Florida Libraries that contains bio-critical
information on seventeen writers. It also includes links to relevant African-literature
Web sites and a bibliography of reference works.

Anglophone and Lusophone African Women's Writing. Ed. Tony Simoes da Silva.
        Update unavailable. U. of Exeter. 20 July 2005, http://www.ex.ac.uk/~ajsimoes/
        aflit/.
        Dedicated to African women writers whose literary language is English or
Portuguese, da Silva's site complements another site dedicated to African women
writing in French (described later in this section). Both projects rely on each
other for English and French translations of author pages through the links created between the two. For easy navigation purposes, *Anglophone and Lusophone
African Women's Writing* is divided according to language, with each section
providing a general introduction to the subject, an alphabetical list of authors, and
a bibliography of secondary sources. Each author page provides a short biography and a list of related Internet sites. Of added value is the list of links to African publishers, literary journals, and relevant Web projects.

*Biographies: Zar.co.za_*. Ed. Etienne Marais. Copyright 2003. Zar.co.za. 20 Jul.
        2005, http://zar.co.za/bio.htm.
        The main purpose of the portal in which this site resides is to disseminate
positive information about South Africa, especially after apartheid. Included
among the wealth of resources that the country has to offer are its writers, whose
biographies are featured in the sections labeled "Hall of Fame" and "Special
South Africans." Each writer's page makes available biographical and bibliographical information, photos, and, where available, contact information.

Books and Writers. Ed. Petri Liukkonen. Copyright 2002. Pegasos. 20 Jul. 2005,
        http://www.kirjasto.sci.fi/calendar.htm.
        Although the creator of this site provides no autobiographical information,
this useful Web site features a wide selection of world writers, from the Roman
era (Vergil) to the contemporary world. One can search for bio-critical information on individual writers from an alphabetical list. Each dedicated author page
contains a biographical profile, excerpts from selected works, and links to related
Web resources. The site also has a calendar searchable by author's birth month.

Contemporary Africa Database. Ed. unavailable. Copyright 2001–2004. The
    Africa Centre. 20 Jul. 2005, http://africadatabase.org/.

Contemporary Africa Database (CAD) is an ambitious project developed
by one of the leading institutions in the United Kingdom specializing in the study
of Africa. It currently has two subdatabases—CAD People and CAD Institutions—
with plans for a third, *Chronology Africa*, by 2005. CAD People contains over
11,000 entries on "prominent Africans," including writers, although only under a
thousand have been developed yet. For those writers who are profiled, the biographical information is either reproduced with permission from *The Companion
to African Literature* (James Currey, 2000), edited by Douglas Killam and Ruth
Rowe, or specially commissioned by the project editors. Each profiled author's
page also offers a list of published works and Internet links.

*Contemporary Postcolonial and Postimperial Literature in English: African Post-
    colonial Literature in English.* Ed. George Landow. 25 May 2005, Brown
    U. and National U. of Singapore. 20 Jul. 2005, http://www.postcolonialweb
    .org/.

Dedicated to the study of the literatures of selected countries and regions of
the former British Empire, this excellent site offers much more than the usual
author biographies, bibliographies, and textual analyses. The project is divided
into sections, with each following a similar template of subtopics. The Africa
section currently offers essays and articles on approximately thirty authors, with
material on history, politics, geography, religion, and visual culture, all of which
are important for a fuller understanding of the texts and the contexts within which
they are produced and are to be interpreted. Two theoretical foundations critical
to the analysis and reception of these texts—postcolonial and feminist theories—
also have sections devoted to them. Articles are written by budding researchers
(university students), university professors, and critics, making the project useful
to undergraduates, graduate students, and general researchers alike. Some materials are excerpted from published print sources.

Contemporary Writers in the UK. Eds. British Council and Book Trust. Copyright
    2005. Contemporarywriters.com. 20 Jul. 2005, http://www.contemporary
    writers.com/.

This Web site, devoted to writers from the United Kingdom and the British
Commonwealth, includes approximately ten from Africa. It provides a biographical profile of each author, a list of their published works, and, where necessary, a
list of prizes and awards. A signed critical analysis is also available for some
writers, such as Nadine Gordimer and Ben Okri. The site offers two options for
searching: alphabetical quick links of author last names and a searchable database that can be accessed by an author's name, nationality, or gender, and by
genre, book title, and publisher.

DZ Lit: Littérature algérienne. Ed. Lounès Ramdani. 18 Jul. 2003. Free.fr. 20 Jul.
    2005, http://dzlit.free.fr/.

This well-developed project, devoted to Algerian writers and those who have written about the country and its peoples, serves as a portal to that country's literature. It is searchable through a variety of access points, which makes it helpful for undergraduates to find materials on the featured writers. Information is drawn primarily from published sources and is arranged by author name or publication title, with extracts from primary and secondary materials also available. The site provides bibliographies of dissertations and theses and of works on Algeria published in four European countries, dating back to the nineteenth century. There is also some introductory material to Algerian literature, such as a chronological classification of writers and excerpts from discussions about what constitutes Algerian literature.

Francophone African Poets in English Translation. Ed. Dan Reboussin. 22 Jul. 2004. U. of Florida Libraries. 20 Jul. 2005, http://web.uflib.ufl.edu/cm/ africana/poets.htm.

Although this site features only eleven francophone poets, they have been selected to represent different generations and characteristics of the literature. For each poet, the pages provide a brief biography and excerpts from poems. The main page of the site has a brief introduction to the subject, a list of more francophone African poets, and a select bibliography on African literature in general.

Guardian Unlimited: Books. 20 Jul. 2005, http://books.guardian.co.uk/.

This Web site is the online version of the British daily newspaper, *The Guardian*. The books section offers timely reviews, a list of interviews with authors, which are arranged alphabetically by last name, extracts from books, and top ten book lists. One can also search the featured books by genres.

Ile en île: Littérature orale et écrites des îliens. Ed. Thomas Spear. Copyright 2005. City U. of New York. 20 Jul. 2005, http://www.lehman.cuny.edu/ile. en.ile/.

This site brings together Web pages devoted to the francophone literature of the some Caribbean, Indian Ocean and Polynesian islands. Cited in this book are a few Indian Ocean writers. From the main project page, users can search for authors using the alphabetical list or by region. Each writer's page includes a biography, a list of works by and about them, and links to related web sites. There are also links to audio and video clips of writers reading their works and to online articles, interviews, and primary works. The site is easy to navigate and provides useful information.

Introducing South African Writers. Ed. Luis R. Mitras. Update unavailable. Oninetspeed.pt. 20 Jul.2005, http://homepage.oniduo.pt/chacmalissimo/ SAfrican/seuffefrika.html.

A simple-to-navigate site that provides a list—sometimes partial—of each featured writer's works and a select bibliography of secondary literature.

LIMAG: Littératures du Maghreb. Eds. Charles Bonn et al. Copyright 1998. U. of
    Lyon 2. 20 Jul. 2005, http://www.limag.refer.org/Default.htm.
    An extensive project on francophone literature from North Africa that
serves as both a research and an information site. Conference annoucements and
calls for papers are posted on the site. The dossiers on writers bring together on
one page a biography of each and related links to works by and about them. One
can also search the site by literary theme and genre.

The Literary Encyclopedia. Eds. Robert Clark et al. Update unavailable. The Lit-
    erary Dictionary Company. 20 Jul. 2005, http://www.litencyc.com/.
    The Literary Encyclopedia is a searchable database that combines four cate-
gories: people, works, literary topics, and books related to the topics covered
published by selected presses. An ambitious project that is still being developed,
it promises to be a great resource for research, with its glossary of literary terms,
timelines, and essays on writers. The template for each writer's page includes a
critical essay, and links to a list of works by and about the writer, and other writers from the same country.

LitNet African Library. Anne Gagiano. Update unavailable. LitNet. 20 Jul. 2005,
    http://www.litnet.co.za/africanlib/default.asp.
    This expanding site provides overviews and critical evaluation of selected
works of African literature. The parent site is devoted to South African literature
and culture, and most of the sections are written in Afrikaans.

Postcolonial African Literatures in English. Ingrid Kerkoff Copyright 2000. U. of
    Bremen. 20 Jul. 2005,
    http://www.fb10.uni-bremen.de/anglistik/kerkhoff/AfricanLit/index.htm.
    This site supports Kerkoff's university courses on African Literature. Of the
twelve writers featured in this project, the women writers appear in another of her
Web sites, *African Literature in English: Five Women Writers*, listed earlier in
this section. For a description of this site, see the annotation on the one on women
writers, as both follow the same basic organization.

Postcolonial Studies at Emory. Ed. Deepika Bahri. 13 Nov. 2002. Emory U. 20
    Jul. 2005, http://www.emory.edu/ENGLISH/Bahri/.
    Bahri's site was designed primarily to support courses on postcolonial stud-
ies at Emory. The author pages are written by students, with each typically providing a biography, a list of primary works, selected secondary literature, and
relevant off-site Web links. The site also gives the same type of information on
pertinent cultural theorists and critics, and short descriptions of related terms and
topics. The crosslinking feature within the entire project and the wide coverage of
postcolonial topics are among the significant characteristics that make this site a
very user-friendly and extremely useful research tool.

Reading Women Writers and African Literatures. Ed. Jean-Marie Volet. 20 Jul.
    2005, U. of Western Australia. 20 Jul. 2005, http://www.arts.uwa.edu.au/
    AFLIT/FEMEChomeEN.html.

With the stated objective of presenting an "overview of African women writers writing in French," this site, maintained in both English and French, contains an extensive list of writers, known and lesser known. The pages on individual writers give the usual bio–bibliographical information and links to other Web sites on them. Visitors can also access online interviews with authors, read overviews of eleven national literatures, or connect to the sister-site, Anglophone and Lusophone African Women's Writing (annotated earlier in this section) and other related Internet projects. The online journal of francophone African literature, *Mots Pluriel*, also edited by Volet, is accessible from this page.

Writers Talk: Ideas of Our Time. Ed. and update unavailable. The Roland Collection of Films and Videos on Art. 23 Sept. 2004,
    http://www.roland-collection.com/rolandcollection/literature/literature_101.
htm.

This site makes videos of conversations with writers from around the world, including seven from Africa, freely available on the Web. As an educational tool, the producers hope the videos will "inspire and bring students closer to an international body of writers." Two helpful features of the site design are the listed topics each writer discusses, and the choice of modem speeds with which to view the videos.

Frequently Cited References

Baldwin, Dean, ed. *British Short-Fiction Writers, 1945-1980.* (*Dictionary of Literary Biography,* 139). Detroit: Gale, 1994.

———— and Gregory L. Morris. *The Short Story in English: Britain and North America: An Annotated Bibliography.* Metuchen, NJ: Scarecrow Press, 1994.

Benson, Eugene and L.W. Conolly, eds. *Encyclopedia of Post-colonial Literatures in English,* 2 vols. New York: Routledge, 1994.

Berney, K. A. *Contemporary Dramatists,* 5th ed. London: St. James, 1993.

———— and N. G. Templeton. *Contemporary Women Dramatists.* London: St. James, 1994.

Brown, Susan Windisch. *Contemporary Novelists,* 6th ed. New York: St James Press, 1996.

Chevalier, Tracy, ed. *Contemporary World Writers,* 2nd ed. Detroit: St. James, 1993.

Conteh-Morgan, John. *Theatre and Drama in Francophone Africa.* Cambridge: Cambridge UP, 1994.

Contemporary Authors (eds. vary). Detroit: Gale, 1967–.

Contemporary Literary Criticism (eds. vary). Detroit: Gale, 1973–.

Cox, C. Brian, ed. *African Writers,* 2 vols. New York: Charles Scribner's Sons, 1997.

Drama Criticism, (eds. vary). Detroit: Gale, 1991–.

Draper, James P., ed. *Black Literature Criticism,* 3 vols. Detroit: Gale, 1992.

————. *World Literature Criticism: 1500 to the Present,* 6 vols. Detroit: Gale, 1992.

Ezenwa-Ohaeto. *Winging Words: Interviews with Nigerian Writers and Critics.* Ibadan, Nigeria: Kraft, 2003.

Genova, Pamela A. *Companion to Contemporary World Literature,* 2 vols. New York: Twayne, 2003.

Gikandi, Simon. *Encyclopedia of African Literature.* New York: Routledge, 2003.

Halio, Jay L. *British Novelists since 1960* (*Dictionary of Literary Biography* 14). Detroit: Gale, 1983.

Herzberger-Fofana, Pierrette. *Littérature féminine francophone d'Afrique noire.* Paris: L'Harmattan, 2000.

Hunter, Jeffrey W. and Jerry Moore. *Black Literature Criticism Supplement.* Detroit: Gale, 1999.

James, Adeola, ed. *In Their Own Words: African Women Writers Talk.* London: James Currey, 1990.

Levi, Anthony. *Guide to French Literature,* 2 vols. Chicago: St. James, 1992.

Lindfors, Bernth, ed. *Africa Talks Back: Interviews with Anglophone African Writers.* Trenton, NJ: Africa World Press, 2002.

———— and Reinhard Sander. *Twentieth-Century Caribbean and Black African Writers, First Series* (*Dictionary of Literary Biography* 117). Detroit: Gale, 1992.

————. *Twentieth-Century Caribbean and Black African Writers, Second Series* (*Dictionary of Literary Biography* 125). Detroit: Gale, 1993.

———— *Twentieth-Century Caribbean and Black African Writers, Third Series* (*Dictionary of Literary Biography* 157). Detroit: Gale, 1996.

Literature Criticism from 1400 to 1800 (eds. vary). Detroit: Gale, 1984–.

Moseley, Merrit, ed. *British Novelists since 1960, Third Series* (*Dictionary of Literary Biography* 207). Detroit: Gale, 1999.

————, ed. *British Novelists since 1960, Fourth Series* (*Dictionary of Literary Biography* 231). Detroit: Gale, 2000.

Moss, Joyce, ed. *British and Irish Literature and Its Times: The Victorian Era to the Present, (1837–)* (*World Literature and Its Times* 4). Detroit: Gale, 2001.

———— and Lorraine Valestuk, eds. *African Literature and Its Times* (*World Literature and Its Times* 2). Detroit, Gale: 2000.

Ngara, Emmanuel, ed. *New Writing from Southern Africa.* London: James Curry, 1996.

Oldsey, Bernard, ed. *British Novelists, 1930–1959,* part 1. (*Dictionary of Literary Biography* 15). Detroit: Gale, 1983.

Parekh, Pushpa Naidoo and Siga Fatima Jagne. *Postcolonial African Writers: A Bio-bibliographical Critical Sourcebook.* Westport, Conn: Greenwood Press, 1998.

Parini, Jay. *World Writers in English,* 2 vols. Detroit: Gale, 2004.

Pendergast, Sara and Tom Pendergast. *St James Guide to Children's Writers,* 5th ed. Detroit: St James Press, 1999.

Poetry Criticism: Excerpts from Criticism of the Works of the most Significant and Widely Studied Poets of world Literature, (eds. vary). Detroit: Gale, 1991.

Riggs, Thomas, ed. *Contemporary Poets,* 6th ed. New York: St. James, 1996.

————, ed. *Contemporary Poets,* 7th ed. Detroit: St. James, 2001.

Robinson, Lillian S., ed. *Modern Women Writers,* 4 vols. New York: Continuum, 1996.

Ross, Robert L., ed. *International Literature in English: Essays on the Major Writers.* New York: Garland, 1991.

Scanlon, Paul, ed. *South African Writers* (*Dictionary of Literary Biography* 225). Detroit: Gale, 2000.

Schellinger, Paul, Christopher Hudson, and Marijke Rijsberman, eds. *Encyclopedia of the Novel,* 2 vols. Chicago: Fitzroy Dearborn, 1998.

Schlager, Neil and Josh Lauer, eds. *Contemporary Novelists,* 7th ed. New York: St James Press, 2001.

Serafin, Steven R., ed. *Encyclopedia of World Literature in the 20th Century,* 3rd ed., 4 vols. Detroit: St. James Press, 1999.

Short Story Criticism, (eds. vary). Detroit: Gale, 1988–.

Twentieth-Century Literary Criticism, (eds. vary). Detroit: Gale, 1978–.

Wilkinson, Jane, ed. *Talking With African Writers: Interviews With African Poets, Playwrights and Novelists.* London: Heinemann, 1992.

Wordworks, Manitou, ed. *Modern Black Writers,* 2nd ed. Detroit: St James, 2000.

Web Sites and References for African Writers

Ferhat Abbas, 1899–1985

Web Sites

"Ferhat Abbas." *Taheriades.* Ed. and update unavailable. 22 July 2005, http://
    membres.lycos.fr/tahercom/resume.html.
    Biographical sketch with highlights of significant dates and political events. In
French.

Biographies and Criticism

Déjeux, J. "Abbas, Ferhat." Meisami and Starkey, *Encyclopedia of Arabic Literature.* 2.
Hayes, Jarrod. "Abbas, Ferhat." Gikandi, *Encyclopedia of African Literature.* [1] –2.

Lionel (Isaac) Abrahams, 1928–2004

Web Sites

Hot News. Ed. Roy Blumenthal. Update unavailable. Barefoot Press, 22 July 2005,
    http://www.pix.co.za/barefoot.press/lionela/lionela.htm.
    This site provides the text of six poems (including "Hot News"), and a brief
autobiographical profile.

"Interviews—Lionel Abrahams." *Exclusive Books. Com.* 22 July 2005, http://www
    .exclusivebooks.com/interviews/email/l_abrahams.asp?Tag=&CID=.
    Transcript of an undated interview.

"Lionel Abrahams." *The Write Stuff.* Eds. Anne Kellas and Giles Hugo. 15 Nov. 2004
    http://www. The-write-stuff.com.au. 22 July 2005, http://www.the-write-
    stuff.com.au/archives/vol-6/.
    Includes a brief biography, the text of thirteen poems from *Chaos Theory of the
Heart,* links to web sites on Abrahams, and tributes marking his death.

"Lionel Abrahams." *Contemporary Africa Database.* 22 July 2005, http://people
.africadatabase.org/people/profiles/profilesforperson15815.html.

Biographies and Criticism

Haresnape, Geoffrey. "Abrahams, Lionel." Benson and Conolly, *Encyclopedia of
Post-Colonial Literatures in English. 12–13.*

Wylie, Dan. "'Speaking Crystals:' The Poetry of Lionel Abrahams and South African
Liberalism." Eds. Eldred D. Jones and Marjorie Jones. *South & Southern
African Literature: A Review.* Trenton, NJ: Africa World Press, 2002. 101–9.
Critical analysis of Abrahams' poetry.

Dictionaries, Encyclopedias, and Handbooks

Abrahams, Lionel, and Patrick Cullinan. *Lionel Abrahams: A Reader.* Craighall: A.D.
Donker, 1988.

Peter (Henry) Abrahams, 1919–

Web Sites

"Peter Abrahams." *Contemporary Africa Database.* 22 July 2005, http://people.africa
database.org/people/profiles/profilesforperson2010.html.

Biographies and Criticism

"Abrahams, Peter." *Wordworks, Modern Black Writers. 1–5.*
Excerpts from criticism published between 1943 and 1979.

Field, Roger. *"Abrahams, Peter." Gikandi, Encyclopedia of African Literature. 4–6.*

Loy, Pamela S. "Mine Boy." Moss and Valestuk, *African Literature and Its Times
(World Literature and Its Times* 2). 269–77.

Peek, Andrew. "Peter Abrahams." Cox, *African Writers.* 1:1–14.
Provides a brief biography of Abrahams, short critical analyses of his works,
and a select bibliography of works by and about him.

"Peter Abrahams." Riley, *Contemporary Literary Criticism.* 4:1–5.
Excerpts from criticism published between 1971 and 1972.

Wade, Michael. "Peter Abrahams." Lindfors and Sander, *Twentieth-Century
Caribbean and Black African Writers, First Series* (*Dictionary of Literary
Biography* 117). 3–14.

Woeber, Catherine. "Peter Abrahams." Scanlon, *South African Writers* (*Dictionary of
Literary Biography* 225). 3–16.

Dictionaries, Encyclopedias, and Handbooks

Ensor, Robert. *The Novels of Peter Abrahams and the Rise of Nationalism in Africa.
Essen:* Verlag Die Blaue Eule, 1992.

(Albert) Chinua (lumogu) Achebe, 1930–

Web Sites

"Chinua Achebe." *Contemporary Postcolonial and Postimperial Literature in
English.* 22 July 2005, http://www.scholars.nus.edu.sg/landow/post/achebe/
achebeov.html.

"Chinua Achebe." *Books and Writers*. 22 July 2005, http://www.kirjasto.sci.fi/
    achebe.htm.

"Chinua Achebe." Ed. Jan Pridmore. 8 Oct. 2004, *Literary History.com*. 22 July 2005,
    http://www.literaryhistory.com/20thC/Achebe.htm.
    An annotated list of Achebe Web sites.

"Chinua Achebe." Ed. Cora Agatucci. 2 Apr. 2005. Central Oregon CC. 22 July 2005,
    http://www.cocc.edu/cagatucci/classes/hum211/achebe.htm.

The Achebe page of this award-winning, course-related Internet project
provides a bibliography, interviews, and a study guide to *Things Fall Apart*. Some of
the links to off-site, Achebe-related Web sites provide background information on
Nigeria and Igbo history and culture, which are useful for understanding his works

"Chinua Achebe." *Writers Talk: Ideas of Our Time*. 22 July 2005, http://www.roland-
    collection.com/rolandcollection/literature/101/W01.htm.

Ekwe Ekwe, Herbert. "Achebe, Chinua." *Literary Encyclopedia*. 22 July 2005, http://
    www.litencyc.com/php/speople.php?rec=true&UID=4996.

"Women in Achebe's World." Rose Ure Mezu. *Womanist Theory and Research*. 1995.
    U. of Georgia. 22 Jul. 2005, http://www.uga.edu/~womanist/1995/mezu.html.
    A journal article discussing the portrayal of women in Achebe's fiction.

Phillips, Caryl. "Out of Africa." *The Guardian Review* (22 Feb. 2003). 22 July 2005,
    http://books.guardian.co.uk/review/story/0,12084,900102,00.html.

Achebe discusses his interpretation of Joseph Conrad's *Heart of Darkness,* the
book that inspired the writing of *Things Fall Apart*.

Biographies and Criticism

"Achebe, Chinua." Wordworks, *Modern Black Writers*. 5–18.
    Excerpts from criticism published between 1958 and 1997.

Adeeko, Adeleke. *"Things Fall Apart."* Moss and Valestuk, *African Literature and Its
    Times* (*World Literature and Its Times* 2). 421–430.

"Chinua Achebe." Draper, *Black Literature Criticism*. 1:1–15.
    Short biography, list of major works, excerpts of criticism from1971 to 1989,
and an annotated bibliography.

"Chinua Achebe." Draper, *World Literature Criticism*. 1:1–15.
    Excerpts from criticism published between 1981 and 1988, with a short
bibliography.

"Chinua Achebe." Hunter et al., *Contemporary Literary Criticism*. 127:1–87.
    Selected criticism on Achebe from 1989 to 1997, with an annotated
bibliography.

Cornwell, Gareth. "Chinua Achebe." Parini, *World Writers in English*. 1:1–19.

Killam, G. D. "Chinua Achebe." Cox, *African Writers*. 1:15–36.
    Brief biography of Achebe, short critical analyses of his works, and a select
bibliography of works by and about him.

———— "Chinua Achebe." Lindfors and Sander, *Twentieth-Century Caribbean and
    Black African Writers, First Series* (*Dictionary of Literary Biography* 117). 15–34.

————. "Chinua Achebe: A Different Order of Reality." Ross, *International Literature in English.* 99–109.
   Frames Achebe's works within Nigerian sociopolitical history.

Nelson, Emmanuel S. "Chinua Achebe." Parekh and Jagne, *Postcolonial African Writers: A Bio-bibliographical Critical Sourcebook.* [19] –31.

"*Things Fall Apart:* Chinua Achebe." Hunter and Burns, *Contemporary Literary Criticism.* 152:1–199.
   Selected criticism on *Things Fall Apart* published between 1969 and 2000, with an annotated bibliography.

Dictionaries, Handbooks, and Encyclopedias

Bowker, Keith. Ed. *The Chinua Achebe Encyclopedia.* Westport, CT: Greenwood, 2003.

Emenyonu, Ernest M. *Emeging Perspectives on Chinua Achebe.* Trenton, NJ: Africa World Press, 2004.

Interviews

"Chinua Achebe." Jussawalla and Dasenbrock, *Interviews with Writers of the Post-Colonial World.* 64–81.

Conversations with Chinua Achebe. Ed. Bernth Lindfors. Jackson: University Press of Mississippi, 1997.
   A collection of interviews with Achebe spanning 1962 to 1995.

Catherine (Obianuju) Acholonu, 1951–

Web Sites

"Catherine Acholonu." *Contemporary Africa Database.* 22 July 2005, http://people .africadatabase.org/people/data/person11351.html.

"Catherine Obianuju Acholonu." *Contemporary Postcolonial and Postimperial Literature in English.* 22 July 2005, http://www.scholars.nus.edu.sg/landow/ post/nigeria/acholonuov.html.
   Still being developed; only active link is to a bibliography of works by and about Acholonu.

Biographies and Criticism

"Achlonu, Catherine Obianuju." *Contemporary Authors.* 180:1–2.

Remi (Aduke) Adedeji, 1937–

Web Sites

"Remi Adedeji." *Anglophone and Lusophone Women's Writing.* 22 July 2005, http:// www.ex.ac.uk/~ajsimoes/aflit/AdedejiEN.html.

Biographies and Criticism

"Adedeji, (Alu)Remi Aduke." Eds. Douglas Killam and Ruth Rowe. *The Companion to African Literatures.* Oxford: James Curry, 1999, 4.

Anne-Marie Adiaffi, 1951–1995

Web Sites

"Anne-Marie Adiaffi." *Reading Women Writers and African Literatures*. 22 July
2005, http://www.arts.uwa.edu.au/AFLIT/AdiaffiAnneMarieeng.html.

Biographies and Criticism

"Anne-Marie Adiaffi." Herzberger-Fofana, *Littérature feminine francophone
d'Afrique noire*. 459–60.
Biography, with analysis of Adiaffi's work.

Martin, Meredith. "Adiaffi, Anne-Marie." Gikandi, *Encyclopedia of African
Literature*. 10.

José Eduardo Agualusa, 1960–

Web Sites

"José Eduardo Agualusa." *Contemporary Africa Database*. 22 July 2005, http://
people.africadatabase.org/people/data/person13323.html.

"José Eduardo Agualusa." *Poesia Africana de Expressão Portuguesa*. Ed. and updatae
unavailable. 22 July 2005, http://betogomes.sites.uol.com.br/.
Accessed by selecting the country and author from the main menu, this site
offers a brief biography, with the text of two poems.

Mensah, Nana Yaa. "Voyage to Freedom." 16 June 2003. *New Statesman*. 22 July
2005, http://www.findarticles.com/cf_dls/m0FQP/4642_132/104081271/p1/
article.jhtml.
A review of the English translation of Agualusa's book *Creole* (Arcadia).

Biographies and Criticism

Gikandi, Simon. "Agualusa, José Eduardo." Gikandi, *Encyclopedia of African
Literature*. 13–14.

Leila Ahmed, 1940–

Web Sites

"Leila Ahmed." *Fresh Air Online. National Public Radio*. 22 July 2004, http://www
.npr.org/templates/story/story.php?storyId=1134224.
Biographical sketch and audioclip of a 2001 interview.

"Leila Ahmed." *VG: Voices from the Gaps*. 22 July 2005, http://voices.cla.umn.edu/
vg/Bios/entries/ahmed_leila.html.
Bio-criticsm, a bibliography of works by and about Ahmed and related links.

Biographies and Criticism

"Ahmed, Leila." *Contemporary Authors*. 140:5.

(Christina) Ama Ata Aidoo, 1942–

Web Sites

"Ama Ata Aidoo." *Books and Writers.* 22 July 2005, http://www.kirjasto.sci.fi/aidoo
.htm.

"Ama Ata Aidoo." *Anglophone and Lusophone Women's Writing.* 22 July 2005, http://
www.ex.ac.uk/~ajsimoes/aflit/AidooEN.html.

"Ama Ata Aidoo." *African Writers: Voices of Change.* 22 July 2005, http://web.uflib
.ufl.edu/cm/africana/aidoo.htm.

"Ama Ata Aidoo." *Contemporary Postimperial and Postcolonial Literature in
English.* 22 July 2005, http://www.scholars.nus.edu.sg/post/africa/ghana/aidoo/
aidoov.html.

"Ama Ata Aidoo." *African Literature in English: Five Women Writers.* 22 July 2005,
http://www.fb10.uni-bremen.de/anglistik/kerkhoff/AfrWomenWriters/Aidoo/
Aidoo.html.

Biographies and Criticism

"Aidoo, Ama Ata." Wordworks, *Modern Black Writers.* 19–26.
Excerpts from criticism published between 1965 and 1995.

"Aidoo, (Christina) Ama Ata." Robinson, *Modern Women Writers.* 1:39–46.
Excerpts from criticism published between 1965 and 1986.

"Ama Ata Aidoo." Hunter and Moore, *Black Literature Criticism Supplement.* 1–16.
Bio-critical introduction, a list of major works, excerpts from criticism on
Aidoo's works from 1982 to 1987, and an annotated bibliography.

Chew, Shirley. "Ama Ata Aidoo." Cox, *African Writers.* 1:37–48.
Brief biography of Aidoo, with short critical analyses of her works and a select
bibliography of works by and about her.

Hoeller, Hildegard. "Ama Ata Aidoo." Parekh and Jagne, *Postcolonial African
Writers: A Bio-bibliographical Critical Sourcebook.* 32–39.

Horne, Naana Banyiwa. "Ama Ata Aidoo." Lindfors and Sander, *Twentieth-Century
Caribbean and Black African Writers, First Series* (Dictionary *of Literary
Biography* 117). 34–40.

Littleton, Jacob. "Dilemma of a Ghost." Moss and Valestuk, *African Literature and
Its Times (World Literature and Its Times* 2). 87–95.

Dictionaries, Encyclopedias, and Handbooks

Azodo, Ada Uzoamaka, and Gay Wilentz, Eds. *Emerging Perspectives on Ama Ata
Aidoo.* Trenton, NJ: Africa World Press, 1999.

Odamtten, Vincent O. *The Art of Ama Ata Aidoo.* University of Florida Press, 1994.

Interviews

"Ama Ata Aidoo." James, *In Their Own Words.* 9–27.

Funso Aiyejina, 1949–

Web Sites

"Dr. Funso Ayejina." *Contemporary Africa Database.* 22 July 2005, http://people
.africadatabase.org/people/data/person15141.html.

Kundu, Vedabyhas. "The New Generation of African Writers Are No Longer Pre-
occupied with Colonialism." Meghdutam: Finest Literature on the Net. Ed. and
update unavailable. 9 Apr. 2004, http://www.meghdutam.com/authtemp.
php?name=auth11.htm&&printer=0.
Summary of an interview with Aiyejina discussing his works as part of a new
African writing.

Biographies and Criticism

"Funso Aiyejina." *Contemporary Authors.* 194:10–11.

Zaynab Alkali, 1950–

Web Sites

Bergstresser, Heinrich. "Zaynab Alkali." Eds. Annika Salomonsson et

al. 1 July 2003. *Culturebase.net.* 22 July 2005, http://www.culturebase.net/artist
.php?413.
Provides bio-critical information on Alkali.

"Zaynab Alkali." *Contemporary Africa Database.* 22 July 2005, http://people
.africadatabase.org/people/profiles/profilesforperson15825.html.

Biographies and Criticism

Alabi, Adeteyo. "Alkai, Zaynab." Benson and Conolly, *Encyclopedia of Post-colonial
Literatures in English.* 1:32.

Loflin, Christine. "Zaynab Alkali." Parekh and Jagne, *Postcolonial African Writers: A
Bio-bibliographical Critical Sourcebook.* [40] –44.

Interview

"Zaynab Alkali." James, *In Their Own Words.* 29–32.

T. M. Aluko, 1918–

Web Sites

"Timothy Mofolorunsho Aluko." *Contemporary Africa Database.* 22 July 2005,
http://people.africadatabase.org/en/person/2093.html.

Biographies and Criticism

"Aluko, T. M." Wordworks, *Modern Black Writers.* 28–30.
Excerpts from criticism published between 1960 and 1981.

Scott, Patrick. "T. M. Aluko." Lindfors and Sander, *Twentieth-Century Caribbean
and Black African Writers, First Series* (*Dictionary of Literary Biography* 117).
40–48.

Elechi (Emmanuel) Amadi, 1934–

Web Sites

"Elechi Amadi." *Books and Writers*. 22 July 2005, http://www.kirjasto.sci.fi/amadi
.htm.

Biographies and Criticism

"Elechi Amadi." Wordworks, *Modern Black Writers*. 30–34.
Excerpts from criticism published between 1966 and 1991.

Obiechina, Emmanuel. "Elechi Amadi." Lindfors and Sander, *Twentieth-Century
Caribbean and Black African Writers, First Series* (*Dictionary of Literary
Biography* 117). 49–53.

Jean Amrouche, 1907–1962

Web Sites

Chiki, Beïda. Jean Amrouche. *LIMAG : Littératures du Maghreb*. 22 July 2005, http://
www.limag.refer.org/Textes/Manuref/AMROUCHE.htm.
Excerpt from *La littérature maghrébine de langue française* edited by Charles
Bonn et al. (1996).

"Jean Amrouche." *DzLit: Littérature algérienne*. 22 July 2005, http://dzlit.free.fr/
amrouche.html.

"Jean Amrouche." Ed. Maghrebi Studies Group. Update unavailable. Middlebury C.
22 July 2005, http://goa.cet.middlebury.edu/mtoler/
algeria_writers.htm#jamrouche.
Brief biography of Amrouche.

Biographies and Criticism

Arnaud, Jacqueline. "Jean Amrouche, le précurseur." *La littérature maghrebine de
langue française*. 1:129–51.
Analyzes Amrouche's writing and politics.

Zimra, Clarissa. "Amrouche, Jean." Gikandi, *Encycolpedia of African Literature*. 21–22.

Dictionaries, Encyclopedias, and Handbooks

Chikhi, Beida. *Jean, Taos et Fadhma Amrouche: relais de la voix, châine de
l'écriture*. Paris: L'Harmattan, 1998.

Marguerite (Taos) Amrouche, 1913–1976

Web Sites

"Marguerite Taos Amrouche." *Dz Lit: Littérature algérienne*. 22 July 2005, http://
dzlit.free.fr/tamrouch.html.

"Marguerite Taos Amrouche." Ed. Maghrebi Studies Group. Update unavailable.
Middlebury C. 22 July 2005, http://goa.cet.middlebury.edu/mtoler/algeria_
writers.htm#tamrouche.
Brief biography of Amrouche.

Biographies and Criticism

Zimra, Clarissa. "Amrouche, Taos." Gikandi, *Encyclopedia of African Literature.* 22–23.

Dictionaries, Encyclopedias, and Handbooks

Brahimi, Denise. *Taos Amrouche, romancière.* Paris: J. Losfeld, 1995.

Jared Angira, 1947–

Web Sites

"Hunger." *African Letters.* 22 July 2005, http://www.bowwave.org/AfricanWriters/ Jared%20Angira.htm.

"Jared Angira." *Contemporary Africa Database.* 22 July 2005, http://people.africa database.org/people/data/person15833.html.

Biographies and Criticism

Ojwang, Dan Odhiambo. "Angira, Jared." Gikandi, *Encyclopedia of African Literature.* 23–24.

Kofi Anyidoho, 1947–

Web Sites

"Kofi Anyidoho." Ed. Nkiru Nzegwu. Cpoyright 2002. *Africa Resource Center.* 22 July 2005, http://www.africaresource.com/poe/kofi.htm. Brief biography with the text of five of Anyidoho's poems.

"Kofi Anyidoho." *Postcolonial African Literatures in English.* 22 July 2005, http:// www.fb10.uni-bremen.de/anglistik/kerkhoff/AfricanLit/Anyidoho/ Anyidoho.htm

Biographies and Criticism

"Anyidoho, Kofi." Wordworks, *Modern Black Writers.* 38–41. Excerpts from criticism published between 1979 and 1996.

King, Bruce. "Anyidoho, Kofi." Benson and Conolly, *Encyclopedia of Post-Colonial Literatures in English.* 1:66.

Gikandi, Simon. "Anyidoho, Kofi." Gikandi, *Encyclopedia of African Literature. 24.*

Mensah, A. N. "Kofi Anyidoho." Lindfors and Sander, *Twentieth-Century Caribbean and Black African Writers, Third Series* (*Dictionary of Literary Biography* 157). 3–16.

Interview

"Kofi Anyidoho." Wilkinson, *Talking With African Writers.* 6–16.

Peggy Appiah, 1921–

Web Sites

"Appiah, Peggy." *African Children's Literature.* 22 July 2005, http://web.uflib.ufledu/ cm/africana/appiah.htm. Bio-bibliographical information on Appiah.

Biographies and Criticism

"Appiah, Peggy." Ann Evory. Ed. *Contemporary Authors.* 41–44. Detroit: Gale, 1974, 28.

Mitchson, Naomi. "Appiah, Peggy." Pendergast and Pendergast, *St. James Guide to Children's Writers.* 34–35.

Armah, Ayi Kwei, 1939–

Web Sites

"Ayi Kwei Armah." *Books and Writers.* 22 July 2005 http://www.kirjasto.sci.fi/ armah.htm.

"Ayi Kwei Armah." *African Writers: Voices of Change.* 22 July 2005, http://web.uflib .ufl.edu/cm/africana/armah.htm.

Gillard, Garry. "Narrative Situation and Ideology in Five Novels of Ayi Kwei Armah." *SPAN: Journal of the South Pacific Association for Commonwealth Literature and Language Studies.* 33 (1992). 22 July 2005, http://wwwmcc .murdoch.edu.au/ReadingRoom/litserv/SPAN/33/Gillard.html.
Journal article analyzing five novels by Armah.

Biographies and Criticism

"Ayi Kwei Armah." Draper, *Black Literature Criticism.* 1:40–55.
Short biography, list of major works, excerpts from criticism from 1968 to 1989, and an annotated bibliography.

"Ayi Kwei Armah." Hunter and Cromie, *Contemporary Literary Criticism.* 136:1–74.
Criticism on Armah published between 1980 and 1998.

"Ayi Kwei Armah." Marowski and Stine, *Contemporary Literary Criticism.* 33:23–38.
Excerpts from criticism published between 1968 and 1982.

"Armah, Ayi Kwei." Wordworks, *Modern Black Writers.* 41–48.
Excerpts from criticism published between 1968 and 1997.

Bader, Rudolf. "Ayi Kwei Armah: A Vision of Past, Present, and Future." Ross, *International Literature in English.* 111–20.
Brief biography, thematic analysis of Armah's writing, with an annotated bibliography of selected critical works.

Colmer, Rosemary. "Ayi Kwei Armah." Cox, *African Writers.* 1:49–62.
Provides a biography of Armah, short analyses of his works, and a select bibliography of works by and about him.

Doshi, Neil. "Armah, Ayi Kwei." Gikandi, *Encyclopedia of African Literature.* 28–30.

Dseagu, Samuel A. "Ayi Kwei Armah." Parekh and Jagne, *Postcolonial African Writers: A Bio-bibliographical Critical Sourcebook.* [45] –51.

Littleton, Jacob. "The Beautyful Ones Are Not Yet Born." Moss and Valestuk, *African Litertaure and Its Times* (*World Litertaure and Its Times* 2). 13–22.

Ogede, Ode S. "Angled Shots and Reflections: On the Literary Essays of Ayi Kwei Armah." Genova, *Companion to Contemporary World Literature.* 1:334–40.
Discussion of Armah as essayist.

Wright, Derek. "Ayi Kwei Armah." Lindfors and Sander, *Twentieth-Century Caribbean and Black African Writers, First Series* (*Dictionary of Literary Biography* 117). 54–77.

———. "Ayi Kwei Armah." Schellinger, *Encyclopedia of the Novel*. 1:58–61.

———. "The Metaphysical and Material Worlds: Ayi Kwei Armah's Ritual Cycle." Genova, *Companion to Contemporary World Literature*. 1:430–35.
Discusses the use of the metaphor of ritual in Armah's work.

Dictionaries, Encyclopedias, and Handbooks

Ogede, Ode. *Ayi Kwei Armah, Radical Iconoclast: Pitting Imaginary Worlds Against the Actual*. Athens, OH: Ohio University Press, 2000.

Meshack Asare, 1945–

Web Sites

"Asare Meshack. Ghana (1945–). *African Children's Literature*. 22 July 2005 http://web.uflib.ufl.edu/cm/africana/asare.htm.

"Meshack Asare." *Meet the Writers*. Ed. and update unavailable. Africa Centre. 22 July 2005, http://www.africacentre.org.uk/africanvisions2002%20meet%20the%20writers.htm#Meshack%20Asare.
Bio-bibliographic information on Asare.

Biographies and Criticism

"Asare, Meshack (Yaw)." *Contemporary Authors*. 61–64:31–32.

Fawzia Assaad, 1929–

Web Site

"Fawzia Assaad." *Arab World Books*. Ed. and update unavailable. 21 Apr. 2004, http://www.arabworldbooks.com/authors/fawzia_assaad.html.
Bio-bibliography with synopses of three novels by Assaad. Also available in French

Biographies and Criticism

Ghazoul, Ferial, J. "Assaad, Fawzia." Gikandi, *Encyclopedia of African Literature*. 34.

Kofi (Nyidevi) Awoonor (George Awoonor-Williams), 1935–

Web Sites

"Kofi Awoonor (1935 –). Ghana." *African Writers: Voices of Change*. 22 July 2005, http://web.uflib.ufl.edu/cm/africana/awoonor.htm.

"Kofi Awoonor." Ed. Francis Akoto. Update unavailable. GhanaHomePage. 22 July 2005, http://www.ghanaweb.com/GhanaHomePage/ghana/PEOPLE/WRITERS/awoonor_k.html.
Bio-bibliographic information on Awoonor.

"Kofi Awoonor." *African Letters*. 22 July 2005, http://www.bowwave.org/African Writers/Kofi%20Awoonor.htm.
Text of three poems by Awoonor.

"Kofi Awoonor." *Contemprary Africa Database.* 22 July 2005, http://www.africa
   expert.org/people/data/person1921.html.

Biographies and Criticism

Anyindoho, Kofi. "Kofi Awoonor." Lindfors and Sander, *Twentieth-Century
   Caribbean and Black African Writers, First Series* (*Dictionary of Literary
   Biography* 117). 77–92.

"Awoonor, Kofi." Wordworks, *Modern Black Writers.* 51–56.
   Excerpts from criticism published between 1966 and 1996.

Billingslea-Brown, Alma Jean. "Kofi Awoonor." Parekh and Jagne, *Postcolonial
   African Writers: A Bio-bibliographical Criticial Sourcebook.* [52] –58.

Wright, Derek. "Kofi Awoonor." Cox, *African Writers.* 1:63–75.
   Provides a biography of Awoonor, short critical analyses of his works, and a
select bibliography of works by and about him.

Interviews

"Kofi Awoonor." Lindfors, *Africa Talks Back.* 10–29.

"Kofi Awoonor." Wilkinson, *Talking With African Writers.* 18–31.

Amadou Hampâté Bâ, 1901–1991

Web Sites

"Amadou Hampâté Bâ." *Awa.* Ed. Marième Aissata Jamme. 25 Aug. 2001.
   Glaine.net. 22 July 2005, http://people.glaine.net/awa/hampate/.
   Offers a bibliography of works by Bâ and a few related Web links.

"Amadou Hampâté Bâ." *Contemporary Africa Database.* 22 July 2005, http://www
   .africaexpert.org/people/data/person1929.html.

"Amadou Hampâté Bâ." Ed. unavailable. Copyright 2003. Grose Educational Media.
   22 July 2005, http://www.entrenet.com/~groedmed/litlinks.html.
   Brief biograpghy of Bâ and description of *The Fortunes of Wangrin.*

"Biographie d'Amadou Hampâté Bâ." Ed. and update unavailable. Maison des
   Sciences de L'Homme de Nantes. 22 July 2005, http://www.msh-alpes.prd.fr/
   guepin/afrique/hampate/bioba.html.
   Biography of Bâ.

Biographies and Criticism

"Bâ, (Mallam) Amadou Hampâteé." *Contemporary Authors.* 186:13–14.

Gyasi, Kwaku. "Bâ, Amadou Hampâté." Gikandi, *Encyclopedia of African
   Literature.* [43] –44.

Dictionaries, Encyclopedias, and Handbooks

Jouanny, Robert A. *Lectures de L'Oeuvre d'Hampâté Bâ.* Paris: L'Harmattan, 1992.

Mariama Bâ, 1921–1981

Web Sites

Bâ, Mariama. *The Literary Encyclopedia.* 22 July 2005, http://www.litencyc.com/
php/speople.php?rec=true&UID=5152.
Though the page is still being developed, it is very useful for its bio-critical
evaluation of Bâ as a writer.

"Mariama Bâ." *African Writers: Voices of Change.* 22 July 2005 http://web.uflib.ufl
.edu/cm/africana/ba.htm.

"Mariama Bâ." *Books and Writers.* 22 July 2005, http://www.kirjasto.sci.fi/mba.htm.

"Mariama Bâ." *Reading Women Writers and African Literatures.* 22 July 2005, http://
www.arts.uwa.edu.au/AFLIT/BaMariamaEng.html.

"Mariama Bâ." *Les Romanciers Noirs.* Ed. Cherie Maiden. Update unavailable.
Furman U. 22 July 2005, http://alpha.furman.edu/~maiden/fr42/ba/.
This page is part of a site that supports a course on African writers. It includes a
biography, links to a 1979 interview by Bâ, study questions, and background
information on Senegal.

Biographies and Criticism

Akukwe, Nwamaka B. "Mariama Bâ." Cox, *African Writers* 1:77–82.
Provides a biography, analyses of her works, and a bibliography of critical
works published between 1986 and 1992.

"Bâ, Mariama." Robinson, *Modern Women Writers.* 1: [173] –180.
Excerpts from criticism published between 1982 and 1987.

"Bâ, Mariama." Wordworks, *Modern Black Writers.* 57–61.
Excerpts of criticism published between 1982 and 1991.

Jagne, Fatima Siga. "Mariama Bâ." Parekh and Jagne, *Postcolonial African Writers:
A Bio-bibliographical Criticial Sourcebook.* [58] –74.

Loy, Pamela S. "So Long a Letter." Moss and Valestuk, *African Literature and Its
Times* (*World Literature and Its Times* 2). 377–86.

"Mariama Bâ." Hunter and Moore, *Black Literature Criticism Supplement.* 17–34.
Bio-critical introduction, list of major works, excerpts from criticism on Bâ's
works from 1988 to 1996, and an annotated bibliography.

"Mariama Bâ." Stringer, Susan. *The Senegalese Novel by Women: Through Their
Own Eyes.* New York: Peter Lang, 1996. [49] –75.
A critical analysis of Bâ's novels.

Dictionaries, Encyclopedias, and Handbooks

Azodo, Ada Uzoamaka. *Emerging Perspectives on Mariama Bâ: Postcolonialism,
Feminism, and Postmodernism.* Trenton, NJ: Africa World Press, 2003.

Hachemi Baccouche, 1917–

Web Sites

"La Dame de Carthage." Ed. Yves Chemla. 24 Feb. 2005. Homepage.mac.com.
    22 July 2005, http://homepage.mac.com/chemla/fic_doc/baccouche.html.
    Reprint of an encyclopedia entry on Baccouche's novel *La Dame de Carthage*
written by Chemla.

Biographies and Criticism

Pieprzak, Katarzyna. "Baccouche, Hachemi." Gikandi, *Encyclopedia of African
    Literature.* 46–47.

Seydou Badian, 1928–

Web Sites

"Entretien avec Seydou Badian: C'est la langue qui fond notre indentité." *Afrik.com.*
    26 Apr. 2001. L'Afrique sur Internet. 22 July 2005, http://www.afrik.com/
    article2665.html.
    Badian talks about African literature and its languages of expression in this
interview.

Biographies and Criticism

"Badian, Seydou." Wordworks, *Modern Black Writers.* 61–64.
    Excerpts from criticism published between 1968 and 1989.

Ouédraogo, Jean. "Badian, Seydou Kouyate." Gikandi, Encyclopedia of African
    Writers. 47–48.

Salwa Bakr, 1949–

Web Sites

"Salwa Bakr." *Arab World Books.* Ed and update unavailable. 22 July 2005, http://
    www.arabworldbooks.com/authors/salwa_bakr.htm.
    Provides biographical information on Bakr and a selected list of her works.

"Salwa Bakr." *Contemporary Africa Database.* 22 July 2005, http://people.africa
    database.org/people/data/person12483.html.

"Salwa Bakr——Novelist." *Arab Net.* Ed. and update unavailable. 22 July 2005, http://
    www.arab.net/egypt/et_bakr.htm.
    This site offers a brief biography and description of Bakr's *The Golden Chariot
Does Not Ascend to Heaven.*

Biographies and Criticism

Hafez, Sabry. "Bakr, Salwa." Chevalier, *Contemporary World Writers.* 43–44.

El Sadda, Hoda. "Women's Writing in Egypt: Reflecting on Salwa Bakr." Ed. Deniz.
    Kandiyoti. *Gendering the Middle East: Emerging Perspectives.* New York:
    Syracuse UP, 1996. [127] –44.
    The chapter situates Bakr's writing within the larger framework of Egyptian
women's literature.

Mikhail, Mona N. "Bakr, Salwa." Gikandi, *Encyclopedia of African Literature.* 48–49.

Biyi Bandele-Thomas, 1967–

Web Sites

"Biyi Bandele-Thomas." *Contemporary Africa Database.* 22 July 2005, http://people
.africadatabase.org/people/data/person1963.html.

"Resurrections." Ed. Ian Shuttleworth. Update unavailable. *Ian Shuttleworth.* 22 July
2005, http://www.cix.co.uk/~shutters/reviews/94004.htm.
Reprint of a review of Bandele-Thomas's play *Resurections* originally
published by Shuttleworth in *The Financial Times.*

Biographies and Criticism

"Bandele, Biyi (Biyi Bandele-Thomas)." *Contemporary Authors.* 167:32–33.

Gikandi, Simon. "Bandele-Thomas, Biyi.'" Gikandi, *Encyclopedia of African
Literature.* 50.

Interview

Diez-Tagarro, Rosa. "Interview— Biyi Bandele-Thomas Talks to Rosa Diez-
Tagarro.'" *Wasafiri.* 22 (1995):57–59.

Kesso Barry (Decoster), 1948–

Web Sites

"Kesso Barry Decoster." *Reading Women Writers and African Literatures.* 22 July
2005, http://www.arts.uwa.edu.au/AFLIT/BarryKessoEng.html.

Biographies and Criticism

d'Almeida, Irène Assiba. "Kesso Barry's *Kesso,* or Autobiograpy as a Subverted
Tale." *Research in African Literature* 28.2 (1997):66–82.
A discussion of the notion of subversion in the form and medium of *Kesso.*

"Kesso Barry." Herzberger-Fofana, *Littérature feminine francophone d'Afrique noire.*
484–485.
Brief biography and description of Barry's writing.

McNee, Lisa. "Barry, Kesso." Gikandi, *Encyclopedia of African Literature.* 50–51.

Francis Bebey, 1929–2001

Web Sites

Bebey.com. Ed. unavailable. 23 Nov. 2001. Association Francis Bebey. 22 Apr. 2004,
http://francois.granger.free.fr/bebey/html/menu.htm.
This very informative site on Bebey, part of the official Bebey site, presents
great insight into both his literary and musical achievements. In addition to a
biography, it provides links to a bibliography, discography of CDs, a separate link to
vinyl records, and the text of some of his songs. In French.

"Francis Bebey." *The African Music Encyclopedia.* Ed. Janet Planet. Update
unavailable. Africanmusic.org. 22 July 2005, http://africanmusic.org/artists/
bebey.html.

This brief biographical entry on Bebey appears in an excellent online encyclopedia devoted to African music.

"Francis Bebey." *Culture Camerounaise.* Ed and update unavailable. Ambafrance-cm.org. 22 July 2005, http://www.ambafrance-m.org/html/camero/biblio/graphie/bebey.htm.

This site, devoted to Bebey's writing, provides a webliography of his works, with brief descriptions of selected titles, and prizes won.

"Francis Bebey." *Francophone African Poets in English Translation.* 22 July 2005, http://web.uflib.efl.edu/cm/africana/bebey.htm.

Biographies and Criticism

"Bebey, Francis." Wordworks, *Modern Black Writers.* 86–88.
Excerpts from criticism published between 1976 and 1991.

Volet, Jean-Marie. "Bebey, Francis." Gikandi, *Encyclopedia of African Literature.* 32–33.

Azouz Begag, 1957–

Web Sites

"Presentation d'Azouz Begag." *ClicNet: Littérature FrancophoneVirtuel.* Eds. Brigitte Land and Carol Netter. Dec. 1998. Swarthmore C. 22 July 2005, http://www.swarthmore.edu/Humanities/clicnet/litterature/moderne/begag/presentation.html.

This Begag site is part of the content-rich, francophone literature project at Swarthmore College. In addition to a biography, there is a list of Begag's writings: novels, children's literature, and academic works. One problem with this page (and others in the project), however, is its poor navigation guide; there are no obvious hypertext links, so it is easy for one to miss the links to excerpts from Begag's books located at the bottom of the page. In addition, a page with scanned images of his handwriting can only be accessed from the "Publications de ClicNet" page.

Biographies and Criticism

Doshi, Neil. "Begag, Azouz." Gikandi, *Encyclopedia of African Literature.* 53.

Mark Behr, 1944–

Web Sites

"Mark Behr." *Introducing South African Writers.* 22 July 2005, http://homepage.oniduo.pt/chacmalissimo/SAfrican/html/mark_behr.htm.

Biographies and Criticism

"Behr, Mark." *Contemporary Authors.* 152:56–57.

Tahar Békri, 1951–

Web Sites

"L'Horizon incendié." *Al Manar: Collection "Poésie du Maghreb."* Ed. and update
    unavailable. 22 July 2005, http://almanar.ifrance.com/almanar/auteurs/L%27
    Horizon.htm.
    This site is useful for its collection of critical analyses of *L'Horizon incendié.*
Also available is a scanned image of the painting from which the title of the book is
derived and the text of an interview with Békri.

Renard, Pierette. "Tahar Békri." *Ecrits...vains?* Eds. Marie Bataille et al. Update
    unavailable. Ecrits-vains.com. 22 July 2005, http://ecrits-vains.com/projecteurs/
    bekri.htm.
    In addition to a critical analysis of Békri's writing, the site also links to excerpts
from his poems and a bibliography.

Tahar Békri. Ed. Tahar Békri. Copyright 2005. Free.com. 22 July 2005, http://tahar
    .bekri.free.fr/index.php?page=acceuil.
    The official Web site of Békri is information rich and simple to navigate. In
addition to the text of some of his poems, its list of links opens up a range of separate
bibliographies: books, articles, and translations by Békri; translations of his poems;
and secondary literature on his works. The modest length of his biography stands in
contrast to all of this. In French

"Tahar Békri." *LIMAG : Littératures du Maghreb.* 22 July 2005, http://www.limag
    .refer.org/Volumes/Bekri.htm.
    Brief biography with a list of Békri-related links. One of these is a nine-page
bibliography of secondary literature on his writing.

"Tahar Békri." *La Poètheque.* Lucy Safarty et al. Update unknown. Printemps des
    Poètes. 23 Apr. 2004, http://www.printempsdespoetes.com/le_livre/moteur
    .php?fiche_poete&cle=242&nom=Tahar%20Bekri.
    Brief biography of and a list of works by Békri.

Biographies and Criticism

Abdel-Jaouad, Hédi. "Békri, Tahar." Gikandi, *Encyclopedia of African Literature.* 53-54.

Sylvain Bemba, 1934–1995

Web Sites

"Sylvain Bemba." *Contemporary Africa Database.* 22 July 2005, http://people.africa
    database.org/people/data/person15672.html.
"Sylvain Bemba." *La Maison des Auteurs.* Ed and update unavailable. Les
    Francophonies en Limousin. 22 July 2005, http://www.lesfrancophonies.com/
    PAGES/maison/AUTEURS%202002/bemba.htm.
    Brief biography with a selected list of works by and about Bemba.

Biographies and Criticism

"Bemba, Sylvain." Wordworks, *Modern Black Writers.* 89–91.
    Excerpts from criticism published between 1984 and 1990.

Djiffack, André. "Bemba, Sylvain (Sylvain N'Tari-Bemba)." Gikandi, *Encyclopedia of African Literature.* 54.

Wylie, Hal. "Bemba, Sylvain." Serafin, *Encyclopedia of World Literature.* 1:243–44.

———. "The Dancing Masks of Sylvain Bemba." Genova, *Companion to Contemporary World Literature.* 1:329–34.
Discusses the symbolism of masks in Bemba's works.

Tahar Ben Jelloun (Tahar ben Jelloun), 1944–

Web Sites

Owen, Amy. "Tahar Ben Jelloun." *Postcolonial Studies at Emory.* 3 Feb. 2003. Emory U. 22 July 2005, http://www.emory.edu/ENGLISH/Bahri/Jelloun.html.

"Tahar Ben Jelloun." *LIMAG: Littérature du Maghreb.* 22 July 2005, http://www .limag.refer.org/Volumes/Ben%20Jelloun.htm.
Brief biography with a list of internal and off-site links.

"Tahar Ben Jelloun." *La Poètheque.* Lucy Safarty et al. Update unknown. Printemps des Poètes. 22 July 2005, http://www.printempsdespoetes.com/le_livre/moteur .php?fiche_poete&cle=79&nom=Tahar%20Ben%20Jelloun.
Brief biography, a list of works by Jelloun, and an audioclip of him reading a poem.

"Tahar Ben Jelloun." *Culture.* Ed and update unavailable. Radio Canada. 22 July 2005,http://radio-canada.ca/culture/livres/v2/200107/30/001-tahar.asp.
Includes biographical information and an audio clip of a radio conversation with Ben Jelloun. In French

Tahar Ben Jelloun: Le Site Officiel. Ed and update unavailable. Tahar Ben Jelloun.org. 22 July 2005, http://www.taharbenjelloun.org/accueil.php
This site is clean and simple to navigate. Its links point to a list of Ben Jelloun's books, some with clickable images and descriptions, interviews, current news about the author, and a travel piece written by him. Unlike many author Web sites, Ben Jelloun's biographical information is in the first person, which suggests he may be the editor of the site.

Biographies and Criticism

Erickson, John, and Faisal Azam. "The Sand Child." Moss and Valestuk, *African Literature and Its Times (World Literature and Its Times* 2). 357–66.

Mékerita Soraya. "Tahar Ben Jelloun." Parekh and Jagne, *Postcolonial African Writers: A Bio-bibliographical Criticial Sourcebook.* [241] –52.

Sellin, Eric. "Ben Jelloun, Tahar." Serafin, *Encyclopedia of World Literature in the 20th Century.* 1:254–55.

———. "The Sand Child and The Sacred Night." Schellinger, *Encyclopedia of the Novel.* 1:1158–60.

Dictionaries, Encyclopedias, and Handbooks

Elbaz, Robert. *Tahar Ben Jelloun, ou, L'inassouvissement du désir narratif.* Paris: L'Harmattan, 1996.

M'Henni, Mansour. *Tahar Ben Jelloun: Strategies d'ecriture.* Paris: L'Harmattan, 1993.

Janet (Glukman) Berliner, 1939–

Web Sites

BerlinerPhiles. Ed. unavailable. Copyright 1997-2005. BerlinerPhiles. 22 July 2005,
    http://www.janetberliner.com/index.html
    Web site of the official Berliner fan club. Includes information on her
professional business as editor/agent and links to her various works.

"Janet Berliner." *AuthorsDen.* Ed. and update unavailable. AuthorsDen.com. 22 July
    2005, http://www.authorsden.com/janetberliner.
    Brief biography with an excerpt from Berliner's *Artifacts.*

Biographies and Criticism

"Berliner, Janet." *Contemporary Authors* 163:32–35.

Mohamed Berrada, 1938–

Web Sites

El Azizi, Abdellatif. "Engagement sur tous les fronts." *Maroc Hebdo.* 497 (8–14
    February, 2002). 22 July 2005, http://www.maroc-hebdo.press.ma/MHinternet/
    Archives_497/html_497/engag.html.
    Transcript of an interview with Berrada.

"Mohamed Berrada." *Contemporary Africa Database.* 22 July 2005, http://people
    .africadatabase.org/people/data/person6324.html.

Biographies and Criticism

Abu-Haider, Farida. "Berrada, Mohamed." Serafin, *Encyclopedia of World Litertaure
    in the 20th Century* 1:265–66.

Mongo Beti (Alexandre Biyidi), (Alexandre Biyidi-Awala), (Eza Boto), 1932–2001

Web Sites

"Dossier Cameroun et Mongo Beti." *AIRCRIGE.* Ed and update unavailable.
    Wanadoo.fr. 4 May 2004, http://aircrigeweb.free.fr/parutions/paru-sommaire
    .html#MongoBet
    Of significance on this site is a conference-opening address by Beti, believed to
be the last piece he wrote before his death. Other useful resources on the Web site
include a biography, a critical appraisal of his work, and tributes honoring his life and
work.

"Dossier Mongo Beti." *Africa-Studiecentrum.* 12 Apr. 2005. U. of Leiden. 22 July
    2005, http://www.ascleiden.nl/Library/Webdossiers/MongoBeti.aspx.
    A very useful site that brings together a biography, selected bibliography of
works by and about Beti, and a list of related Internet links.

Mongo-Mboussa, Boniface. "The Publication of *Trop de Soleil Tue L'amour:
    Interview with Mongo Beti.*" *Africultures* (n.d.). 22 July 2005, http://www
    .africultures.com/anglais/articles_anglais/intdjedanoum.htm.
    Text of an interview with Beti.

Biographies and Criticism

"Beti, Mongo." Wordworks, *Modern Black Writers*. 95–101.
>Excerpts from criticism published between 1956 and 1998.

Bishop, Stephen. "Beti, Mongo." Gikandi, *Encyclopedia of African Literature*. 62–63.

Conteh-Morgan, John D. "Mongo Beti." Cox, *African Writers* 1:83–94.
>Provides a biography, with short analyses of three of Beti's novels, and a select bibliography of works by and about him published between 1953 and 1994.

Littleton, Jacob. "Mission to Kala." Moss and Valestuk, *African Literature and Its Times* (*World Literature and Its Times* 2). 279–88.

"Mongo Beti." Draper, *Black Literature Criticism*. 1:89–206.
>Short biography, list of major works, excerpts from criticism from 1963 to1981, and an annotated bibliography.

Calixthe Beyala, 1961–

Web Sites

"Calixthe Beyala." *Reading Women Writers and African Literatures*. 22 July 2005, http://www.arts.uwa.edu.au/AFLIT/BeyalaCalixtheEng.html.

Calixthe Website. Eds. Calixthe Beyala and Maguysama. Copyright 2002. Free.fr. 22 July 2005, http://calixthe.beyala.free.fr/ .
>This is Beyala's official Web site, which she herself co-edits. Three of the navigational links ("News," "Goodies," and "Press Room") are in English, yet they lead to information in French; this could be misleading to users. In addition to a short biography, the site includes a list of her works (with scanned front cover images), critical studies, interviews, and the text of the short story " Les aventures de Méri Kâ Ré l'enfant du desert."

"Calixthe Beyala." *Cameroun-Plus*. Ed and update unavailable. Cameroun-plus.com. 22 July 2005, http://www.cameroun-plus.com/s31/cb.htm.
>Residing on the site of a Cameroon portal, this Web page provides a biographical sketch, a list of published works by Beyala, and opening lines and scanned images of each.

Mongo, Boniface. "Beyala: Writing on the Edge." *Africultures* (n.d.). 22 July 2005, http://www.africultures.com/anglais/articles_anglais/02belaya.htm.
>A short article on Beyala's writing style.

Biographies and Criticism

"Calixthe Beyala: Voices of Resistance." Nikki Hitchcott, *Women Writers in Francophone Africa*. Oxford: Berg, 2000. 129–51.
>Analysis of the female voice in Beyala's novels.

Nfah-Abbenyi, Juliana Makuchi. "Calixthe Beyala." Parekh and Jagne, *Postcolonial African Writers: A Bio-bibliographical Criticial Sourcebook*. [75] –83.

Interviews

"Calixthe Beyala." Jules-Rosette, *Black Paris*. Urbana and Chicago: U. of Illinois, 1998. [201] –5.
Text of a 1990 interview.

Chanda, Tirthbankar. "L'écriture dans la peau: Entretien avec Calixthe Beyala."

Dictionaries, Encyclopedias, and Handbooks

Gallimore, Rangira Béatrice. *L'œuvre romanesque de Calixthe Beyala: le renouveau de l'écriture féminine en Afrique francophone sub-saharienne.* Paris: L'Harmattan, 1997.

Olympe Bhêly-Quénum, 1928–

Web Sites

"Olympe Bhêly-Quénum." Ed and update unavailable. Obhelyquenum.com. 22 July 2005, http://www.obhelyquenum.com/index.htm.
This seems to be the official Bhêly-Quénum site, and its stated objective is to make the author's works more widely known. The links open to a list of his writings and secondary literature in French and English.

Biographies and Criticism

"Bhêly-Quénum, Olympe." Wordworks, *Modern Black Writers.*101–4.
Excerpts from criticism published between 1961 and 1998.

Volet, Jean-Marie. "Bhêly-Quénum, Olympe." Gikandi, *Encyclopedia of African Literature.* 69–70.

Daniel Biyouala, 1953–

Web Sites

"Daniel Biyouala." *Portraits d'ecrivains.* Ed. Dieudonné Gnammankou. Update unavailable. Gnammankou.com. 22 July 2005, http://www.gnammankou.com/litterature_biyaoula.htm.
Brief biography, with excerpts from reviews of Biyouala's works.

Biographies and Criticism

Ekotto, Frieda. "Biyouala, Daniel." Gikandi, *Encyclopedia of African Literature.* 71.

Karen Blixen (Isak Dinesen), 1885–1962

Web Sites

"Karen Blixen." *Books and Writers.* 22 July 2005, http://www.kirjasto.sci.fi/blixen.htm.
Karen Blixen-Isak Dinesen Information Site. Ed. Linda Donelson. 20 July 2005. Coulsong. 22 July 2005, http://www.karenblixen.com/.
An excellent site that tries to list virtually every piece of available information related to Blixen's life and work. Apart from the expected bio-bibliographical, the resources run a wide spectrum: from her medical history to pictures of her house to recent Blixen-related events, and even factual errors published about her. Researchers will discover a wealth of links behind the main page menu and will find the easy access extremely useful.

Karen Blixen Literary Society Online. Ed. Anna Stéen. 9 Aug. 2002. Geocities.com
22 July 2005, http://www.geocities.com/Athens/Ithaca/9334/.
Created by an enthusiast and budding researcher, this site provides links to bio-bibliographical information. For ease of navigation, though, these could have been more prominently located on the page.

Wallace, Anna. "Denmark's Karen Blixen Museum." *Literary Traveler.* Copyright
1998–2004. Literarytraveler.com. 22 July 2005, http://www.literarytraveler
.com/blixen/blixen.htm.
A description of the museum and links to the African Blixen museum and Web
site.

Wolfson, Leah. "Karen Blixen/Isak Dinesen." *Postcolonial Studies at Emory.* 3 Feb.
2003. Emory U. 22 July 2005, http://www.emory.edu/ENGLISH/Bahri/Blixen
.html.

Biographies and Criticism

Weisz, Allison. "Out of Africa." *African Literature and Its Times* (*World Literature
and Its Times* 2). 317–26.

Tanella Boni, 1954–

Web Sites

"Professor Tanell Boni." *Contemporary Africa Database.* 22 July 2005, http://people
.africadatabase.org/people/data/person11371.html.

"Tanella Boni." *Reading Women Writers and African Literatures.* 22 July 2005, http://
www.arts.uwa.edu.au/AFLIT/BoniTanellaEng.html.

"Tanella Boni.(Poétesse africaine)." *L'espace vers.* Ed. Angèle Bassolé Ouédraogo.
Update unavailable. Généalogie Busiau. 22 July 2005, http://geneal.busiau
.com/poesie/texte9.htm.
Text of Boni's poem, "Labyrinthe."

"Tanella Boni." *La Poéthèque.* Lucy Safarty et al. Update unknown. Printemps des
Poètes. 22 July 2005, http://www.printempsdespoetes.com/le_livre/moteur
.php?fiche_poete&cle=397&nom=Tanella%20Boni.
Biographical sketch, a list of Boni's works, and an audioclip of her reading a
poem.

Biographies and Criticism

"City of Mud and Diamonds, City of Dis: Tanella Boni, Véronique Tadjo–a
Feminism of the Cities." Harrow, Kenneth. *Less than One and Double: A
Feminist Reading of African Women's Writing.* Portsmouth, NH: Heinemann,
2002. [277] –329.
Discusses Boni's *Une vie de crabe.*

D'Almeida, Irène Assiba. " 'Le mot juste' de Tanella Boni." *Revue des Lettres
Modernes: Histoires des Idées et de Littératures.* 1544–1588: 141–54.
Explores language and style in Boni's poetry.

Volet, Jean-Marie. "Boni, Tanella S(usane)." Serafin, *Encyclopedia of World
Literature in the 20th Century.* 1:306–7.

Interview

Herzberger-Fofana, Pierrette. "Interview de Tanella Boni (Côte-d'Ivoire)." *Littérature Féminine Francophone d'Afrique Noire.* Paris: L'Harmattan, 2000. 369–73.

Herman Charles Bosman, 1905–1951

Web Sites

Davie, Lucille. "Herman Charles Bosman, Joburg Man." *City of Johannesburg Official Site.* Update unavailable. Johannesbusrg News Agency. 22 July 2005, http://www.joburg.org.za/2004/jan/jan20_bosman.stm.
Based on Stephen Gray's book, *Bosman's Johannesburg,* this piece takes the reader to sites and happenings around the city that found their way into Bosman's writings. Also includes a photograph of his grave.

"Herman Charles Bosman." *Introducing South African Writers.* 22 July 2005, http:// homepage.oniduo.pt/chacmalissimo/SAfrican/html/ herman_charles_bosman.htm "Herman Charles Bosman." *Biographies of Special South Africans.* Ed. Etienne Marais. Update unavailable. Zar.co.za. 22 July 2005, http://zar.co.za/bosman.htm.
Provides a biography and photographs of Bosman.

Biographies and Criticism

Gikandi, Simon. "Bosman, Herman Charles." Gikandi, *Encyclopedia of African Literature.* 74–5.

Mackenzie, Craig. "Herman Charles Bosman." *South African Writers* (Dictionary of Literary Biography 225). 17–29.

Rachid Boudjedra, 1941–

Web Sites

"Rachid Boudjedra." *LIMAG: Littératures du Maghreb.* 22 July 2005, http://www .limag.refer.org/Volumes/Boudjedra.htm.

"Rachid Boudjera: 'Mon homage à L'Armée.'" *Algeria-Watch.* Ed and update unavailable. 22 July 2005, http://www.algeria-watch.de/farticle/sale_guerre/ boudjedra.htm.
Text of a Boudjera interview originally published in *Le Matin* (22 Feb. 2001).

"Rachid Boudjera." *DZ Lit: Littérature algérienne.* 22 July 2005, http://dzlit.free.fr/ fascin.html.

Biographies and Criticism

Bois, M. "Boudjera, Rachid." Meisami and Starkey, *Encyclopedia of Arabic Literature.* 1:160.

Doshi, Neil. "Boudjera, Rachid." Gikandi, *Encyclopdeia of African Literature.* 75.

Marx-Scouras, Danielle. "Boudjera, Rachid." Serafin, *Encyclopedia of World Literature in the 20th Century.* 1:316–17.

Serrano, Richard. "Translation and the Interlingual Text in the Novels of Rachid Boudjedra." Ed. Mildred Mortimer. *Maghrebian Mosaic: A Literature in Transition.* Boulder, Colo.: Lynne Rienner, 2001. 27–40.

Dictionaries, Encyclopedias, and Handbooks

Gafaiti, Hafid. *Rachid Boudjedra: une poétique de la subversion.* Paris: L'Harmattan, 1999/2000. (2 vols)

Hédi (André) Bouraoui, 1932–

Web Sites

"Hédi Bouraoui." *L'Ile: L'infocentre littéraire des écrivains.* Ed. Jean-François Gauvin. 27 Apr. 2004. Centre de documentation virtuel sur la literature québécoise. 5 May 2004, http://www.litterature.org/ile32000.asp?numero=547. Short biography

Hédi Bouraoui. Ed. Hédi Bouraoui. Update and sponsor unavailable. 22 July 2005, http://www.hedibouraoui.net/.
   This is the official Bouraoui Web site which the author himself edits. It features links to biographical information, a bibliography of primary and secondary works, and excerpts of comments and views by and about the author and his writing.

Biographies and Criticism

Graebner, Seth. "Bouraoui, Hédi." Gikandi, *Encyclopedia of African Literature.* 75–76.

Dictionaries, Encyclopedias, and Handbooks

Cotnam, Jacques. *Hédi Bouraoui : iconoclaste et chantre du transculturel.* Ottawa: Le Nordir, 1996.

Nina Bouraoui, 1967–

Web Sites

Crousiers, Armelle. "Nina Bouraoui." *LIMAG: Littératures du Maghreb.* 22 July 2005, http://www.limag.refer.org/Volumes/BouraouiNina.htm.
   List of links to works by and about Bouraoui.

"Nina Bouraoui." Ed and update unavailable. Station Hill Press. 22 July 2005, http://www.stationhill.org/bouraoui.html.
   A biography of Bouraoui from her publisher's Web site.

Biographies and Criticism

Graebner, Seth. "Bouraoui, Nina." Gikandi, *Encyclopedia of African Literature.* 76.

"Bouraoui's Ghosts: Projections of Women in the Nineties." Donna Wilkerson-Barker. *The Space of the Screen in Contemporary French and Francophone Fiction.* New York: Peter Lang, 2003. 123–61.
   A discussion of the portayal of the female body in Bouraoui's novel *La voyeuse interdite.*

Kwesi Brew (Osborne Henry), 1928–

Web Sites

"Kwesi Brew." *African Letters.* 22 July 2005, http://www.bowwave.org/African Writers/Kwesi%20Brew.htm.
   Text of three Brew poems.

Biographies and Criticism

Awuyah, Chris. "Brew, Kwesi." Benson and Conolly, Encyclopedia of Post-Colonial
Literatures in English. 1:50–51.

Odamtten, Vincent. "Brew, Kwesi Osborne Henry." Gikandi, *Ecyclopedia of African
Literature.* 77.

Breyten Breytenbach (Jan Bloom), 1939–

Web Sites

"Breyten Breytenbach." *Contemporary Africa Database.* 22 July 2005, http://www
.africaexpert.org/people/data/person2181.html.

"Breyten Breytenbach." Ed. Rosemarie Breuer. 5 May 2004. *Stellenbosch Writers.*
22 July 2005, http://www.stellenboschwriters.com/breyten.html.
Provides a biography and a list of works written and awards won by
Breytenbach.

"Breyten Breytenbach." *Dialogue Through Poetry.* Ed and update unavailable. 22 July
2005, http://www.dialoguepoetry.org/profile_breytenbach.htm.
Biographical information on Breytenbach, with an emphasis on his political
acivitism.

"Breyten Breytenbach." *Introducing South African Writers.* 22 July 2005, http://home
page.oniduo.pt/chacmalissimo/SAfrican/html/breyten_breytenbach.htm

Squire, Cleone. "Re-placing the South African Self in Breyten Breytenbach's *A
Season in Paradise.*" *Inter Action 4: Proceedings of the Fourth Postgraduate
Conference.* U. of Western Cape. 22 July 2005, http://www.uwc.ac.za/arts/
english/interaction/95cs.htm.
A reprint of a conference paper that deals with the autobiographical style in
Breytenbach's book.

Biographies and Criticism

"Breyten Breytenbach." Gunton and Stine, *Contemporary Literary Criticism* 23:83–87.
Excerpts from criticism published between 1978 and 1982.

"Breyten Breytenbach." Hunter et al., *Contemporary Literary Criticism.* 126:59–102.
Excerpts from criticism published between 1983 and 1996.

Coetzee, Carli. "Breytenbach, Breyten." Serafin, *Encyclopedia of World Literature in
the 20th Century.* 1:343.

Lafevere, André. "Breytenbach, Breyten." Chevalier, *Contemporary World Writers.*
73–75.

Parker, Grant. "Breytenbach, Breyten." Gikandi, *Encyclopedia of African Literature.*
77–79.

van Wyk, Johan. "Breyten Breytenbach." *South African Writers (Dictionary of
Literary Biography* 225). 30–41.

André Brink, 1935–

Web Sites

"André Brink." *Introducing South African Writers.* 22 July 2005, http://homepage
.oniduo.pt/chacmalissimo/SAfrican/html/andre_brink.htm.

"André Brink." *Writers Talk: Ideas of Our Time.* 18 Nov. 2003, http://www.roland-
collection.com/rolandcollection/literature/101/W8.htm.

"Audio Interview with André Brink." *Wired for Books.* Ed. David Kurz. Update
unavailable. Ohio U. 22 July 2005, http://wiredforbooks.org/andrebrink/.
An audiocast of a 1985 CBS radio interview with Brink.

"Interview–André Brink." *Exclusive Books.* Ed and update unavailable. Exclusive
Books.Com. 22 July 2005, http://www.exclusivebooks.com/interviews/ftf/andre
_brink.asp?Tag=&CID.
Transcript of an undated interview.

Biographies and Criticism

"André Brink." Schmitt et al., *Contemporary Literary Criticism.* 106:94–146.
Excerpts from criticism published between 1974 and 1996.

Ayling, Ronald. "André Brink." Cox, *African Writers* 1:95–114.
Provides a biography, with short analyses of 15 novels, a bibliography of his
works (published in Afrikaans and English), and criticism published between 1979
and 1992.

———. "André Brink." *South African Writers* (*Dictionary of Literary Biography*
225). 42–72.

Coetzee, Carli. "Brink, André P(hilippus)." Serafin, *Encyclopedia of World Literature
in the 20th Century.* 1:345–46.

Hassall, Anthony J. "André Brink: The Lives of Adamastor." Ross, *International
Literature in English.* 181–92.
Brief biography, discussion of the enduring themes in Brink's works, and an
annotated bibliography of selected critical works.

Kossew, Sue. "Brink, André Philippus." Gikandi, *Encyclopedia of African Literature.*
79–82.

Turgeon, Carolyn. "A Dry White Season." *African Literature and Its Times* (*World
Literature and Its Times* 2). 97–106.

Woods, Tim S. "André Brink." Schellinger, *Encyclopedia of the Novel.* 1:34–5.

Dennis Brutus (John Bruin), 1924–

Web Sites

"Brutus, Dennis Vincent." *The Literary Encyclopedia.* 22 July 20025, http://www
.litencyc.com/php/speople.php?rec=true&UID=621.

"En Route." *African Letters.* 22 July 2005, http://www.bowwave.org/AfricanWriters/
Dennis%20Brutus.htm.

"Dennis Brutus." *Contemporary Africa Database.* 22 July 2005, http://people.africa
database.org/people/data/person2187.html.

"Dennis Brutus." *Introducing South African Writers.* 22 July 2005, http://homepage
.oniduo.pt/chacmalissimo/SAfrican/html/dennis_brutus.htm

Biographies and Criticism

"Brutus, Dennis." Wordworks, *Modern Black Writers.* 134–40.
    Excerpts from criticism published between 1966 and 1996.

"Dennis Brutus." Draper, *Black Literature Criticism.* 1:307–20.
    Biography, list of major works, excerpts of criticism from 1966 to 1986, and a
brief annotated bibliography.

Gikandi, Simon. "Brutus, Dennis." Gikandi, *Encyclopedia of African Literature.* 82–83.

Goodwin, Ken. "Dennis Brutus." *South African Writers* (*Dictionary of Literary
    Biography* 225). 73–83.

JanMohamed, Abdul R. "Dennis Brutus." Lindfors and Sander, *Twentieth-Century
    Caribbean and Black African Writers, First Series* (*Dictionary of Literary
    Biography* 117). 98–106.

Lindfors, Bernth. "Dennis Brutus." Cox, *African Writers* 1:115–26.
    A biography, a description of the development of his poetic style, and a select
bibliography of works by and about Brutus published between 1966 and 1993.

Mcluckie, Craig W. "Dennis Vincent Frederick Brutus (John Bruin)." Parekh and
    Jagne, *Postcolonial African Writers: A Bio-bibliographical Criticial
    Sourcebook.* [84] –95.

Dictionaries, Encyclopedias, and Handbooks

McLuckie, Craig W., and Patrick J. Colbert, Eds. *Critical Perspectives on Dennis
    Brutus.* Colorado Springs, Colo.: Three Continents Press, 1995.

Ken Bugul (Marietou Mbaye), 1948–

Web Sites

"Ken Bugul." *Reading Women Writers and African Literatures.* 22 July 2005, http://
    www.arts.uwa.edu.au/AFLIT/KenBugulEng.html.

"Ken Bugul (Marietou Mbaye)." *Contemporary Africa Database.* 22 July 2005, http://
    people.africadatabase.org/people/data/person6332.html.

"Le Baobab Fou par Ken Bugul." Ed. Nicole Vaget. Update unavailable. Mt. Holyoke
    C. 22 July 2005, http://www.mtholyoke.edu/courses/nvaget/370/baobab.html.
    This Web site is part of a college course. In addition to bio-bibliographical
information, it also has links to cultural and historical resources pertinent to
understanding Bugul's life and works.

Biographies and Criticism

Higgins, Ellie. "Bugul, Ken." Serafin, *Encyclopedia of World Literature in the 20th
    Century.* 1:370.

Nyatetu-Waigwa, Wangar wa. "Bugul, Ken." Gikandi, *Encyclopedia of African
    Literature.* 83–4.

Interview

Herzberger-Fofana, Pierrette. "Ken Bugul, une forme d'écriture féminine." *Ecrivains africains et indentités culturelles.* Tübingen: Stauffenburg Verlag, 1988. 59–64.

Frederick Guy Butler, 1918–2001

Web Sites

"Frederick Guy Butler." *Contemporary Africa Database.* 22 July 2005, http://people .africadatabase.org/people/data/person15834.html.

Biographies and Criticism

Gikandi, Simon. "Butler, Guy." *Encyclopedia of African Literature.* 85–6.

Klopper, Dirk. "Guy Butler." *South African Writers (Dictionary of Literary Biography* 225). 84–104.

(Ignatius) Roy(ston) (Dunnachie) Campbell, 1901–1957

Web Sites

Pearce, Joseph. "Roy Campbell: Bombast and Fire." *CatholicAuthors.Com.* Update unavailable. Catholic Authors Press. 23 July 2005, http://www.catholicauthors .com/roy_campbell.html.
    Reprint of a bio-critical article that originally appeared in *Lay Witness.* It discusses two major influences on Campbell's writing: the Zulu language and Elizabethan dramatists.

"Roy Campbell." *Introducing South African Writers.* 23 July 2005, http://homepage .oniduo.pt/chacmalissimo/SAfrican/html/roy_campbell.htm.

"Roy Campbell." *KwaZulu-Natal Literary Map.* Eds. *Lindy Stiebel et al. Copyright 2005. The Zulu Kingdom.* 23 July 2005, http://literature.kzn.org.za/lit/5.xml.
    Provides a short biography, a chronological list of works by Campbell and the text of his poem "The Zebras."

Biographies and Criticism

Alexander, Peter F. "Roy Campbell." Scanlon, *South African Writers (Dictionary of Literary Biography* 225). 105–20.

Fletcher, John. "Roy Campbell." Cox, *African Writers.* 1:127–37.
    A biography with analyses of Campbell's major works and a select bibliography of works by and about him published between 1961 and 1989.

Gikandi, Simon. "Campbell, Roy." Gikandi, *Encyclopedia of African Literature.* [86] –7.

"(Ignatius) Roy (Dunnachie) Campbell." Hall et al., *Twentieth-Century Literary Criticism.* 5:115–28.
    Excerpts from criticism on Campbell from 1924 to 1977 with a bibliography.

Parsons, D. S. J. "Roy Campbell." Stanford, *British Poets 1914 to 1945 (Dictionary of Literary Biography* 20). 92–102.

Smith, Rowland. "Campbell, Roy." Serafin, *Encyclopedia of World Literature in the 20th Century.* 1:408.

Albert Camus, 1913–1960

Web Sites

"Albert Camus." *Books and Writers*. 22 July 2005, http://www.kirjasto.sci.fi/acamus
.htm.

"Albert Camus." *The ExistentialPrimer*. Ed. Christopher Scott Wyatt. 11 Feb. 2005.
Tameri.com. 23 July 2005, http://www.tameri.com/csw/exist/camus.shtml.
Provides significant biographical information on Camus, a bibliography and
commentaries on a number of his works, and selected quotations from them.

"Albert Camus–Biography." *Nobel E-Museum*. 13 Apr 2005. The Nobel Foundation.
23 July 2005, http://www.nobel.se/literature/laureates/1957/camus-bio.html.
Has links to Camus' presentation and banquet speeches at the 1957 award
ceremony and links to a few Camus Web sites.

Camus Studies Association. Ed. Raymond Gay-Croiser. Update unavailable. U. of
Florida. 23 July 2005, http://www.clas.ufl.edu/users/gaycros/Camus.htm.
Notable for the extensive bibliography of works on Camus, 1990 to present.

Web Camus. Ed. Georges Bénicourt. 23 Jan. 2005. Free.fr. 22 July 2005, http://web
camus.free.fr/index.html.
A wealth of information on Camus is available on this Web site, including an
online forum, links to academic societies and conferences, dissertations, and
performances of his plays. One very useful feature is the bibliographic search
capability available on this site, which makes it easy, for example, to conduct
thematic searches for books and quotes.

Wilkinson, Russell. "Solitaire et Solidaire." *Spike*. Ed. and update unavailable.
Spikemagazine.com. 7 May 2004, http://www.spikemagazine.com/0397camu
.htm.
Transcript of an interview with Camus's daughter, Catherine, discussing the
impact of the posthumous publication of her father's novel *The First Man*.

Biographies and Criticism

"Albert Camus." Hunter et al., *Contemporary Literary Criticism*. 124:1–48.
Critical essays on Camus from 1984 to 1997 with a selected bibliography.

"Albert Camus." Draper, *World Literature Criticism: 1500 to the Present*. 1:582–97.
Excerpts from criticism on Camus from 1943 to 1980.

"Albert Camus: *The Stranger*." Matuz et al., *Contemporary Literary Criticism*.
69:101–42.
Excerpts from criticism on *The Stranger* from 1962 to 1989 with a
bibliography.

Brée, Germaine. "Albert Camus." Stade, *European Writers*. 13:3049–78.
Critical analysis of Camus and his major works.

Fletcher, John. "Albert Camus." Cox, *African Writers*. 1:139–52.
A biography, a brief analysis of his works, and a select bibliography of works
by and about him published between 1962 and 1995.

Gay-Crosier, Raymond. "Albert Camus." Brosman, *French Novelists, 1930–1960* (*Dictionary of Literary Biography* 72). 110–35.

Popkin, Debra. "Camus, Albert." Serafin, *Encyclopedia of World Literature in the 20th Century.* 1:408–13.

Dictionaries, Encyclopedias, and Handbooks

Brosman, Catherine Savage. *Albert Camus.* Detroit: Gale, 2001.

Yedes, Ali. *Camus L'algerien.* Paris: L'Harmattan, 2003.

Adelaide (Smith) Casely-Hayford, 1868–1960

Web Sites

"Adelaide Casely-Hayford." *Contemporary Africa Database.* 23 July 2005, http://people.africadatabase.org/people/data/person15843.html.

"Adelaide Casely-Hayford." *Sierra Leonean Heroes.* Eds. A.K. Turay et al. Update unavailable. Sierra-Leone.org. 23 July 2005, http://www.sierra-leone.org/heroes6.html.
A biography of Casely-Hayford.

Denzer, La Ray. "Adelaide Smith Casely-Hayford." *Global Mappings: A Political Atlas of the African Diaspora.* Ed. Michael Hanchard. Copyright 2001. Northwestern U. 23 July 2005, http://diaspora.northwestern.edu/cgi-bin/WebObjects/DiasporaX.woa/wa/displayArticle?atomid=901.
A biography with a bibliography of works by and about Casely-Hayford and related links.

Biographies and Criticism

Bair, Barbara. "Pan-Africanism as Process: Adelaide Casely Hayford, Garveyism, and the Cultural Roots of Nationalism." Eds. Sidney J. Lemelle and Robin D.G. Kelley. *Imagining Home: Class, Culture, and Nationalism in the African Diaspora.* London: Verso, 1994. 121–44.
Biography, with a discussion of Casely-Hayford's pan-Africanist and feminist views.

Gikandi, Simon. "Casely-Hayford, Adelaide." Gikandi, *Encyclopedia of African Literature.* 88–89.

Gladys May Casely-Hayford (Aquah Laluah), 1904–1950

Web Sites

"Gladys May Casely-Hayford (Aquah Laluah)." *Modern American Poetry.* Ed Cary Nelson. Update unavailable. U. of Illinois Urbana Champaign. 23 July 2005, http://www.english.uiuc.edu/maps/poets/a_f/casely/casely.htm.
Links to articles on and poems by Casely-Hayford.

Biographies and Criticism

"Casely-Hayford, Gladys." *Contemporary Authors.* 152:122.

Gikandi, Simon. "Casely Hayford, Gladys May." Gikandi, *Encyclopedia of African Literature.* 89.

J(oseph) E(phraim) Casely-Hayford, 1866–1930

Web Sites

Denzer, LaRay. "Joseph Ephraim Casely-Hayford." *Global Mappings: A Political Atlas of the African Diaspora.* Ed. Michael Hanchard. Copyright 2001. Northwestern U. 23 July 2005, http://diaspora.northwestern.edu/cgi-bin/Web Objects/DiasporaX.woa/wa/displayArticle?atomid=900.
Provides a biography, a bibliography of works by and about Casely-Hayford, and related Internet links.

Biographies and Criticism

"Casely-Hayford, J(oseph) E(phraim)." *Contemporary Authors.* 152:122–24.
"J. E. Casely-Hayford." Draper, *Black Literature Criticism.* 1:343–54.
Biography, a list of major works, excerpts from criticism from 1911 to 1977, and an annotated bibliography.

"J(oseph) E(phraim) Casely-Hayford." Poupard et al., *Twentieth-Century Literary Crirticsm.* 24:130–39.
Excerpts from criticism on Casely-Hayford from 1911 to 1977 with a bibliography.

Owusu, Kofi. "Casely Hayford, Joseph E." Gikandi, *Encyclopedia of African Literature.* 89–90.

Andrée Chedid, 1920–

Web Sites

Laurentine, Renée. "Andrée Chedid et le pouvoir de l'écriture." *Ecrits...vains.* 22 July 2005, http://ecrits-vains.com/points_de_vue/renee_laurentine01.htm.
Bio-critical article on Chedid and a select bibliography of her works.

"Andrée Chedid." Ed. Judy Cochran. Update unavailable. Denison U. 12 May 2004, http://www.denison.edu/~cochran/chedid.html.
Bilingual versions of four poems by Chedid.

Biographies and Criticism

"Andrée Chedid." Michèle M. Magill and Katherine S. Stephenson. *Dit de femmes: Entretiens d'écrivaines françaises.* [27] –38.
Presents a biography, a bibliography of primary and secondary works, and an interview with Chedid.

"Andrée Chedid." Marowski et al., *Contemporary Literary Criticism.* 47:81–8.
Excerpts of criticism on Chedid from 1977 to 1987.

Ghazoul, Ferial J. "Chedid, Andrée." Gikandi, *Encyclopedia of African Literature.* 100.

Knapp, Bettina. "Chedid, Andrée." Serafin, *Encyclopedia of World Literature in the 20th Century.* 1:473–74.

Syl Cheney-Coker, 1945–

Web Sites

"Bread." *New Internationalist* 267 (May 1995). Ed. Simon Loffler. 23 July 2005,
    http://www.newint.org/issue267/bread.htm.
    Text of the poem "Bread" from Cheyney-Coker's *The Blood in the Desert's Eye*
(Heinemann).

"Syl Cheney-Coker." *Contemporary Africa Database.* 23 July 2005, http://www
    .africaexpert.org/people/data/person2227.html.

Biographies and Criticism

Bruchac, Joseph. "Cheney-Coker, Syl." Riggs, *Contemporary Poets.* 159–60.

"Cheney-Coker, Syl." Wordworks, *Modern Black Writers.* 164–66.
    Excerpts from criticism published between 1974 and 1992.

Gikandi, Simon. "Cheney-Coker, Syl." Gikandi, *Encyclopedia of African Literature.*
    100–1.

Lilleleht, Mark. "Cheney-Coker, Syl." Serafin, *Encyclopedia of World Literature in
    the 20th Century.* 1:479–80.

Steve Chimombo, 1945–

Web Sites

"Chimombo, Steve." *The Literary Encyclopedia.* 23 July 2005, http://www.litencyc
    .com/php/speople.php?rec=true&UID=861.

"Steve Chimombo." *Contemporary Africa Database.* 23 July 2005, http://people
    .africadatabase.org/people/data/person2233.html.

Biographies and Criticism

Nazombe, Anthony. "The Role of Myth in the Poetry of Steve Chimombo." Ngara,
    New Writing from Southern Africa. 93–107.
    Discusses four myths that run through Chimombo's poetry.

Vambe, M. "Chimombo, Steve." Gikandi, *Encyclopedia of African Literature.* 104–5.

Shimmer Chinodya, 1957–

Web Sites

"Ben Chirasha (Shimmer Chinodya)." *Contemporary Africa Database.* 23 July 2005,
    http://www.africaexpert.org/people/data/person2235.html.
    Review of Chinodya's novel.

Darlington, Sonja. "Can We Talk. Shimmer Chinodya." *African Studies Quarterly* 7.1
    (2003). 23 July 2005, http://web.africa.ufl.edu/asq/v7/v7i1a9.htm.

"Shimmer Chinodya." *The Literary Encyclopedia.* 23 July 2005, http://www.litencyc
    .com/php/speople.php?rec=true&UID=863.

Biographies and Criticism

Carchidi, Victoria. "Chinodya, Shimmer." Serafin, *Encyclopedia of World Literature
    in the 20th Century.* 1:492–93.

Moyana, Rosemary. "Literature & Liberation... the Second Phase: Shimmer Chinodya's *Harvest of Thorns.*" Ngara, *New Writing from Southern Africa.* 45–58. Discusses Chinodya's novel as illustrative of the new writing from post-independent Zimbabwe.

Vambe, M. "Chinodya, Shimmer." Gikandi, *Encyclopedia of African Literature.* 105.

Chinweizu, 1943–

Web Sites

"Chinweizu." *Contemporary Africa Database.* 23 July 2005, http://people.africadata base.org/people/data/person15846.html.

Biographies and Criticism

Dunton, Chris. "Chinweizu." Lindfors and Sander, *Twentieth-Century Caribbean and Black African Writers, Third Series* (*Dictionary of Literary Biography* 157). 36–48.

Gikandi, Simon. "Chinweizu." Gikandi, *Encyclopedia of African Literature.* 105.

Frank (Mkalawile) Chipasula, 1949–

Web Sites

"Dr. Frank M. Chipasula." *Contemporary Africa Database.* 23 July 2005, http://www .africaexpert.org/people/data/person2238.html.

"Frank Chipasula." *Nebraska Center for Writers.* Ed. Brent Spencer. 7 May 2004. Creighton U. 23 July 2005, http://mockingbird.creighton.edu/NCW/ chipasul.htm.
Includes a biography, bibliography, and reviews of Chipasula's works.

Biographies and Criticism

Msiska, Mpalive-Hangson. "Chipasula. Frank." Gikandi, *Encyclopedia of African Literature.* 106.

Ojaide, Tanure. "Frank (Mkalawile) Chipasula." Riggs, *Contemporary Poets.* 160–61.

Mohamed Choukri, 1935–2003

Web Sites

Bowles, Paul. "Mohamed Choukri." *Bibliomonde.* Copyright 2000-2005. Bibliomonde.com. 27 July 2005, http://www.bibliomonde.net/pages/fiche-auteur .php3?id_auteur=98.
Bio-bibliographical article in French.

"Mohamed Choukri." *LIMAG: Littératures du Maghreb.* 23 July 2005, http://www .limag.refer.org/Volumes/Choukri.htm.

"Mohamed Choukri: Madman of the Roses." *Al-Ahram Weekly* 665 (20-23 Nov. 2003). 27 July 2005, http://weekly.ahram.org.eg/2003/665/cu4.htm.
Obituary piece.

Biographies and Criticism

"Other Voices, Other Spaces." Andrea Flores Khalil. *Arab Avant-Garde: Experiments in North African Art and Literature.* Westport: Praeger, 2003. [29] –45.
    Illustrates the interplay between languages and experiences and their effect on Choukri's narratives.

Driss Chraïbi, 1926–

Web Sites

"Driss Chraïbi." *Books and Writers.* 23 July 2005, http://www.kirjasto.sci.fi/chraibi .htm.

"Driss Chraïbi." *Contemporary Africa Database.* 23 July 2005,
http://www.africaexpert.org/people/data/person6315.html.

"Flutes of Death." *LitNet.* 23 July 2005, http://www.litnet.co.za/africanlib/flutes.asp.

Biographies and Criticism

Abdel-Jaouad, Hédi. "Chraïbi, Driss." Gikandi, *Encyclopedia of African Literature.* 106–7.

Marx-Scouras, Danielle. "Chraïbi, Driss." Serafin, *Encyclopedia of World Literature in the 20th Century.* 1:495–96.

Owen, Carys. "Chraïbi, Driss." Chevalier, *Contemporary World Writers.* 118–19.

Rogers, Lynne Dumont. "Driss Chraïbi." Parekh and Jagne, *Postcolonial African Writers: A Bio-bibliographical Criticial Sourcebook.* [96] –104.

J(ohn) P(epper) Clark (Bedekeromo), 1935–

Web Sites

"John Pepper Clark." *African Letters.* 23 July 2005, http://www.bowwave.org/African Writers/John%20Pepper%20Clark.htm.
    Text of four poems.

"John Pepper Clark." *African Poetry.* 23 July 2005, http://www.aghadiuno.com/ poetry/african/jpc.html.
    Text of two poems by Pepper Clark.

"John Pepper Clark." *Contemporary Africa Database.* 23 July 2005, http://www .africaexpert.org/people/data/person3758.html.

Biographies and Criticism

Biakolo, Emevwo. "J. P. Clark-Bekederemo." Parekh and Jagne, *Postcolonial African Writers: A Bio-bibliographical Criticial Sourcebook.* [105] –10.

"Clark, John Pepper." Wordworks, *Modern Black Writers.* 171–75.
    Excerpts from criticism published between 1963 and 1992.

Gikandi, Simon. "Clark-Bedekeremo, John Pepper." Gikandi, *Encyclopedia of African Litertaure.* 116–18.

"John Pepper Clark." Draper, *Black Literature Criticism.* 1:414–29.
    Biography, list of major works, excerpts of criticism from 1964 to 1989, and a brief annotated bibliography.

"John Pepper Clark." Marowski et al., *Contemporary Literary Criticism.* 38:112–29.
Excerpts from criticism published between 1964 and 1982.

"John Pepper Clark." Trudeau, *Drama Criticism.* 5: 48–73.
Excerpts from criticism on *Song of a Goat, The Masquerade, The Rift,* and
Ozidi, from 1975 to 1988.

Okagbue, Osita. "John Pepper Clark." Cox, *African Writers.* 1:153–66.
A biography, analyses of poems and plays, and a select bibliography of works
by and about Clark published between 1969 and 1993.

Wren, Robert M. "J. P. Clark." Lindfors and Sander, *Twentieth-Century Caribbean
and Black African Writers, First Series (Dictionary of Literary Biography* 117).
112–33.

Sydney Clouts, 1926–1982

Web Sites

"Sydney Clouts." *Contemporary Africa Database.* 23 July 2005, http://people.africa
database.org/people/data/person15848.html.

Biographies and Criticism

Goddard, K. G. "Sydney Clouts." Scanlon, *South African Writers (Dictionary of
Literary Biography* 225). 121–30.

J(ohn) M(ichael) Coetzee, 1940–

Web Sites

"J. M. Coetzee." *Books.* New York Times on the Web. Copyright 1999. 23 July 2005,
http://www.nytimes.com/books/99/11/28/specials/coetzee.html.
Reviews of Coetzee's books, and articles by him originally published in the
New York Times between 1977 and 1999.

"J. M. Coetzee." *Booker McConnell Prize.* Ed. Bradley C. Shoop. Update
unavailable. U. of Tennessee at Chatanooga. 23 July 2005, http://www.utc.edu/
~engldept/booker/coetzee.htm.
A list of works by Coetzee, and a select bibliography of criticism published
between 1981 and 1994.

"J.M. Coetzee." *Introducing South African Writers.* 23 July 2005, http://homepage
.oniduo.pt/chacmalissimo/SAfrican/html/john_maxwell_coetzee.htm.

"J. M. Coetzee: An Overview." *Contemporary Postimperial and Postcolonial
Literature in English.* 13 May 2004, http://www.scholars.nus.edu.sg/post/sa/
coetzee/index.html.

Price, Jonathan. "J. M. Coetzee." *Postcolonial Studies at Emory.* May 2000. Emory
U. 23 July 2005, http://www.emory.edu/ENGLISH/Bahri/Coetzee.html.

"Reading J. M. Coetzee." Ed. unavailable. 12 Jan. 2004. U. of Buffalo Libraries.
23 July 2005, http://ublib.buffalo.edu/libraries/asl/exhibits/coetzee/index
.html#video.
An online exhibit on Coetzee with a biography and bibliography.

O'Hehir, Andrew. "Disgrace." *Salon.* 5 Nov. 1999. Salon.com. 23 July 2005, http://ww1.salon.com/books/review/1999/11/05/coetzee/.
  Review of Coetzee's Booker-winning novel, with links to other Salon articles about him.

Biographies and Criticism

Edgecombe, Rodney. "J. M. Coetzee." Ross, *International Literature in English.* 637–46.
  Biography, a discussion of the oraclelike characteristics of his novels, and an annotated bibliography of selected critical works.

Graham, Lucy Valerie. "J. M. Coetzee." Parini, *World Writers in English.* 1:81–98.

Harrison, James. "J.M. Coetzee." Cox, *African Writers* 1:167–83.
  A biography, with analyses of his works, and a select bibliography of works by and about Coetzee published between 1977 and 1994.

Kossew, Sue. "Coetzee, J.M. (John Maxwell)." Gikandi, *Encyclopedia of African Litertaure.* 118–21.

Lenta, Margaret. "Special Commisioned Entry on J. M. Coetzee." Witalec, *Contemporary Literary Criticism.* 161:205–56.
  Includes a biography of Coetzee, an overview of the themes and style in his writing, and a description of the socio-political context in which his works are produced.

Marais, Michael. "J. M. Coetzee." Lindfors and Sander, *South African Writers* (*Dictionary of Literary Biography* 225). 131–49.

Povey, John. "Coetzee, J(ohn) M." Serafin, *Encyclopedia of World Literature in the 20th Century.* 1:513–14.

Turgeon, Carolyn. "Waiting for the Barbarians." Moss and Valestuk, *African Litertaure and Its Times* (*World Literature and Its Times* 2). 443–51.

Wright, Derek. "J. M. Coetzee." Schellinger, *Encyclopedia of the Novel.* 1:227–29.

Dictionaries, Encyclopedias and Handbooks

Kossew, Sue. *Critical Essays on J. M. Coetzee.* New York: G. K. Hall, 1998.

Huggan, Graham, and Stephen Watson, Eds. *Critical Perspectives on J. M. Coetzee.* New York: Macmillan, 1996.

Bibliographies

Goddard, Kevin, and John Read. *J .M. Coetzee: A Bibliography.* Grahamstown, South Africa: National English Literary Museum, 1990.
  Lists primary and secondary materials published between 1974 and 1989.

Lindsey Collen, 1948–

Web Sites

Baird, Vanessa. "Sharp Focus on Lindsey Collen." *New Internationalist* (June 2002). 23 July 2005, http://articles.findarticles.com/p/articles/mi_m0JQP/is_2002_June/ai_88268009.
  Collen discusses her novel *Mutiny.*

Kossick, Shirley. "When the Caged Bird Sings." *Warm Africa.* Ed. Hassan El Forkani. Update unavailable. Warmafrica.com. 23 July 2005, http://www.warmafrica .com/index/geo/9/cat/3/a/a/artid/43#.
Review of *Mutiny* originally published in *Mail and Guardian* (21 Nov. 2001).

"Lindsey Collen." *Contemporary Africa Database.* 23 July 2005, http://www.africa-expert.org/people/data/person2260.html.

Biographies and Criticism

Flanagan, Joseph. "The Seduction of History: Trauma, Re-memory, and the Ethics of the Real." *Clio.* 31.4 (Summer 2002):387–402.
Critical analysis of *The Rape of Sita.*

William Conton, 1925–2003

Web Sites

"William Conton." *Contemporary Africa Database.* 23 July 2005, http://people .africadatabase.org/people/data/person15852.html.

Biographies and Criticism

Gikandi, Simon. "Conton, William." Gikandi, *Encyclopedia of African Literarature.* 127.

Palmer, Eustace. "Conton, William." Benson and Conolly, *Encyclopedia of Post-colonial Literatures in English.* 1:265–66.

Jack Cope (Robert Knox), 1913–

Web Sites

"Jack Cope." *Contemporary Africa Database.* 23 July 2005, http://people.africadata base.org/people/data/person15849.html.

Biographies and Criticism

Edmands, Ursula. "Cope, Jack." Brown, *Contemporary Novelists.* 225–27.

Felix Couchoro, 1900–1968

Web Sites

"Félix Couchoro." *Contemporary Africa Database.* 23 July 2005, http://people.africa database.org/people/data/person11460.html.

Ricard, Alain. "Felix Couchoro, 1900–1968: Pioneer of Popular Writing in West Africa?" CNRS. 23 July 2005, http://www.cean.u-bordeaux.fr/pubcean/felix .pdf.
A survey of the writing career of Couchoro.

Biographies and Criticism

Gabara, Rachel. "Couchoro, Félix." Gikandi, *Encyclopedia of African Literature.* 128.

Dictionaries, Encyclopedias, and Handbooks

Ricard, Alain. *La naissance du roman africain: Félix Couchoro (1900–1968).* Paris: Présence Africaine, 1988.

Mia Couto (Antonio EmilioLeite), 1955–

Web Sites

"Mia Couto." *Mozambican Literature in Translation.* 14 May 2004, http://homepage .oniduo.pt/chacmalissimo/Mozambique/html/mia_couto.html.

"Mia Couto (Antonio Emilio L. Couto.)." *Contemporary Africa Database.* 23 July 2005, http://www.africaexpert.org/people/data/person2270.html.

"Voices Made Night." *LitNet.* 23 July 2005, http://www.litnet.co.za/africanlib/couto. asp.

Biographies and Criticism

"Mia Couto: A Dynamic Voice of Mozambican Regeneration." Niyi Afolabi, *Golden Cage : Regeneration in Lusophone African Literature and Culture.* Trenton, N. J.: Africa World Press, 2001. 116–69.
Traces Couto's literary trajectory and analyzes his narrative style.

Banks, Jared. "Mia Couto." Parekh and Jagne, *Postcolonial African Writers: A Bio-bibliographical Criticial Sourcebook.* [111] –17.

Brookshaw, David. "Mia Couto." Cox, *African Writers.* 1:185–95.
A biography of Couto, with analyses of his works, and a select bibliography of works by and about him published between 1983 and 1995.

Rothwell, Phillip. "Couto, Mia (Antonio Emilio Leite)." Gikandi, *Encyclopedia of African Literature.* 128–29.

Jeni Couzyn, 1942–

Web Sites

"Jeni Couzyn." *Firelizard.* Ed and update unavailable. 23 July 2005, http://www.fire lizard.co.uk/jeni/jenic.htm.
Biographical information, with excerpts from critical reactions to Couzyn's poetry.

Biographies and Criticism

Hobsbaum, Philip. "Jeni Couzyn." Parini, *World Writers in English.* 1:99–117.

José Craveirinha, 1922–2003

Web Sites

"José Craveirinha." *Contemporary Africa Database.* 23 July 2005, http://people .africadatabase.org/people/data/person2272.html.

"José Craveirinha." *The Journal of African Travel-Writing 2* (Mar. 1997). 23 July 2005, http://www.unc.edu/~ottotwo/craveirinha.html.
English translation of a Craveirinha poem, "A Spring of Bullets."

"José Craveirinha." *Mozambican Literature in Translation.* 23 July 2005, http://home
   page.oniduo.pt/chacmalissimo/Mozambique/html/jose_craveirinha.html

da Silva, Calane. "The Word's Voice: Flame of National Identity." 8 Feb. 2003.
   African Review of Books. 23 July 2005, http://www.africanreviewofbooks.com/
   Newsitems/calanetrib.html.

   A tribute marking Craveirinha's death, this article analyzes the poetics of his
writing. The page also features links to extracts (in English and Portuguese) from
some of his poems.

Biographies and Criticism

Rothwell, Phillip. "Craveirinha, José João." Gikandi, *Encyclopedia of African
   Literature.* 129.

Jeremy Cronin, 1949–

Web Sites

"Jeremy Cronin." *Contemporary Africa Database.* 23 July 2005, http://people.africa
   database.org/people/data/person11655.html.

Sheehan, Helena. "Interview with Jeremy Cronin." Update unavailable. Dublin City
   U. 23 July 2005, http://www.comms.dcu.ie/sheehanh/za/cronin02.htm.
   Transcript of a 2002 interview with Cronin. Includes a link to Sheehan's
previous interview with him and to some related Web sites.

Biographies and Criticism

Macaskill, Brian. "Jeremy Cronin." Riggs, *Contemporary Poets.* 7th ed. 220–22.

———. "Inside Out: Jeremy Cronin's Lyrical Politics." Eds. Derek Attridge and
   Rosemary Jolly. *Writing South Africa: Literature, Apartheid, and Democracy
   1970–1995.* New York: Cambridge University Press, 1998. 187–203.
   Analysis of Cronin's poetry.

Bernard Binlin Dadié, 1916–

Web Sites

"Bernard Binlin Dadié." *Contemporary Africa Database.* 23 July 2005, http://people
   .africadatabase.org/people/data/person2288.html.

"Bernard Binlin Dadié." *Francophone African Poets in English Translation.* 23 July
   2005, http://web.uflib.ufl.edu/cm/africana/dadie.htm.

Case, David Allen. "Bernard Binlin Dadié's Observations." *The Journal of African
   Travel-Writing* 1 (Sept. 1996). 23 July 2005, http://www.unc.edu/~ottotwo/
   dadie.html.
   Review of Dadié's books *An African in Paris* and *One Way: Bernard Dadié
Observes America.*

Biographies and Criticism

"Bernard Dadié: *Béatrice du Congo; Iles de Tempête.*" Conteh-Morgan, *Theatre and
   Drama in Francophone Africa.* 123–51.

"Dadié, Bernard Binlin." Wordworks, *Modern Black Writers.* 201–3.
   Excerpts from criticism published between 1956 and 1998.

Nyatetu-Waigwa, Wangar wa. "Dadié, Bernard." Gikandi, *Encyclopedia of African Literature.* [131] –34.

Popkin, Debra. "Dadié, Bernard Binlin." Serafin, *Encyclopedia of World Literature in the 20th Century.* 1:566–67.

Dictionaries, Encyclopedias, and Handbooks

Edebiri, Unionwam. *Bernard Dadié: Hommages et Etudes.* Ivry-sur-Seine: Nouvelles du Sud, 1992.

Vincileoni Nicole. *Comprendre l'œuvre de Bernard B. Dadié.* Issy les Moulineaux: Les classiques africains, 1986.

Interview

"Bernard Binlin Dadié." Jules-Rosette, *Black Paris.* Urbana and Chicago: U. of Illinois, 1998. [140] –146.
Text of a 1992 interview.

Tsitsi Dangarembga, 1958(9)–

Web Sites

Bhana, Hershini. "The Condition of the Native: Autodestruction in Dangarembga's *Nervous Conditions.*" *Alternation: International Journal for the Study of Southern African Literature and Languages.* 6:1 (1999). 24 July 2005, http://singh.reshma.tripod.com/alternation/alternation6_1/08BHANA.htm.
A critical analysis of Dangarembga's novel.

Grady, Rebecca. "Tsitsi Dangarembga." *Postcolonial Studies at Emory.* 13 Jan. 2001. Emory U. 23 July 2005, http://www.emory.edu/ENGLISH/Bahri/Dangar.html.

"Tsitsi Dangarembga." *African Authors.* Ed. Cora Agatucci. 26 Aug. 2004. Central Oregon CC. 23 July 2005, http://www.cocc.edu/cagatucci/classes/hum211/dangarembga.htm.
A content-rich site on Dangarembga that contains a biography and a list of interviews, a study guide for students, and a comprehensive bibliography. It also points to off-site links relevant to understanding Zimbabwean culture and Dangarembga's works.

"Tsitsi Dangarembga." *Books and Writers.* 23 July 2005, http://www.kirjasto.sci.fi/tsitsi.htm.

"Tsitsi Dangarembga." *Anglophone and Lusophone African Women's Writing.* 23 July 2005, http://www.ex.ac.uk/~ajsimoes/aflit/DangarembgaEN.html.

"Tsitsi Dangarembga." *Contemporary Postimperial and Postcolonial Literature in English.* 23 July 2005, http://www.scholars.nus.edu.sg/post/zimbabwe/td/dangarembgaov.html.

Biographies and Criticism

Chennells, Anthony. "Authorizing Women, Women's Authoring: Tsitsi Dangarembga's *Nervous Conditions.*" Ngara, *New Writing from Southern Africa.* 59–75.
Discusses *Nervous Conditions* within the context of women writing about the female condition in Africa.

Coundouriotis, Eleni. "Tsitsi Dangarembga." Parekh and Jagne, *Postcolonial African Writers: A Bio-bibliographical Criticial Sourcebook*. [118] –22.

"Dangarembga, Tsisti." Wordworks, *Modern Black Writers*. 208–10.
Excerpts from criticism published between 1995 and 1997.

Khader, Jamil. "Nervous Conditions." Moss and Valestuk, *African Literature and Its Times* (*World Literature and Its Times* 2). 297–307.

Dictionaries, Encyclopedias, and Handbooks

Willey, Ann Elizabeth, and Jeannette Trieber, Eds. *Negotiating the Postcolonial: Emerging Perspectives on Tsitsi Dangarembga*. Trenton, N. J.: Africa World Press, 2002.

Interviews

George, Rosemary Marangoly and Helen Scott. "An Interview with Tsitsi Dangarembga." *Novel* (Spring 1993). 309–19.
Text of a 1991 interview.

"Tsitsi Dangarembga." Wilkinson, *Talking With African Writers*. 188–98.
Text of a 1989 interview.

Achmat Dangor, 1948–

Web Sites

"Achmat Dangor." *Bold Type*. 2.12 (Mar. 1999). Random House. 23 July 2005, http://www.randomhouse.com/boldtype/0399/dangor/index.html.
Text of an interview with Dangor and an excerpt from *Kafka's Curse*.

Breysse, Serge. "Interviews with South African Writers (Mike Nicol - Achmat Dangor - Bridget Pitt - Pamel Jooste - Peter Horn)." *Alizés*. 21. U. of Réunion. 23 July 2005, http://www2.univ-reunion.fr/~ageof/text/74c21e88-337.html#_ftnref3.
Text of a 2001 interview.

Gbadamosi, Gabriel. "Clouds over the Rainbow Nation." *Guardian: Reviews*. 13 Dec. 2003. Guardian Unlimited. 23 July 2005, http://books.guardian.co.uk/review/story/0,12084,1104673,00.html.
Review of *Bitter Fruit*.

Jeffries, Stuart. "Legacy of Abuse." *Guardian: Books*. 14 Jan. 2004. Guardian Unlimited. 23 July 2005, http://books.guardian.co.uk/departments/generalfiction/story/0,6000,1122596,00.html.
Dangor discusses family events fictionalized in *Bitter Fruit*.

Biographies and Criticism

Mackenzie, Craig. "Dangor, Achmat." Benson and Conolly, *Encyclopedia of Postcolonial Literatures in English*. 1:329–30.

Samuelson, Meg. "Dangor, Achmat." Gikandi, *Encyclopedia of African Literature*. 135.

Joe (Coleman) de Graft, 1924–

Web Sites

"Joe de Graft." *Contemporary Africa Database.* 23 July 2005, http://www. africa
expert.org/people/data/person3904.html.

Biographies and Criticism

Agovi, Kofi Ermeleh. "Joe de Graft." Lindfors and Sander, *Twentieth-Century
Caribbean and Black African Writers, First Series* (*Dictionary of Literary
Biography* 117). 134–41.

Interview

Joe de Graft. Lindfors, *Africa Talks Back.* [69] –88.

Annette Mbaye d'Erneville, 1926–

Web Sites

"Annette Mbaye d'Erneville." *Reading Women Writers and African Literatures.*
23 July 2005, http://www.arts.uwa.edu.au/AFLIT/
MbayedErnevilleAnnetteEng.html.

"Annette Mbaye d'Erneville." *Francophone African Poets in English Translation.*
23 July 2005, http://web.uflib.ufl.edu/cm/africana/mbaye.htm.

Biographies and Criticism

Martin, Meredith. "Mbaye d'Erneville, Annette." Gikandi, *Encyclopedia of African
Literature.* 322.

Ananda Devi (A. Nirsimloo-Anenden), 1957–

Web Sites

"Ananda Devi." *Contemporary Africa Database.* 23 July 2005, http://people.africa
database.org/people/data/person16905.html.

"Ananda Devi." *Indes réunionnaises.*" Ed. Philippe Pratx. Update unavailable.
Indereunion.net. 23 July 2005, http://www.indereunion.net/actu/ananda/
intervad.htm.
Includes the text of an undated interview, a list of her novels, and short
descriptions of four of them.

Sultan, Patrick. "Ananda Devi." *Littérature îlienne.* Ed. Thomas Spear. 9 Nov. 2003.
Lehman, CUNY. 23 July 2005, http://www.lehman.cuny.edu/ile.en.ile/paroles/
devi.html.
Biography, bibliography of works by and about Devi, and links to Web sites
about her.

Sultan, Patrick. "L'enfermement, la rupture, l'envoi : Lecture de *Pagli* d'Ananda
Devi." *Orées.* 2.1 (Autumn 2001–Winter 2002). Concordia U. 23 July 2005,
http://orees.concordia.ca/numero2/essai/
Lecture%20de%20PAGLI%20corrig.html.
A critical analysis of *Pagli.*

Biographies and Criticism

Lionnet, Françoise. "Evading the Subject: Narration and the City in Ananda Devi's *Rue La Poudrière. L'Esprit Createur.* 33.2 (Summer 1993): 9–22.
A critical analysis of Devi's novel.

Herbert Isaac Ernest Dhlomo, 1903–1956

Web Sites

"Herbert Dhlomo." *A Dictionary of South African Writers.* 23 July 2005, http://home page.oniduo.pt/chacmalissimo/SAfrican/html/herbert_dhlomo.htm.

Biographies and Criticsm

Couzens, Tim. "H. I. E. Dhlomo." Lindfors and Sander, *Twentieth-Century Caribbean and Black African Writers, Third Series* (*Dictionary of Literary Biography* 157). 79–84.

———. "Dhlomo, Herbert Isaac Ernest." Benson and Conolly, *Encyclopedia of Post-colonial Literatures in English.* 1:361–62.

Haresnape, Geoffrey. "H. I. E. Dhlomo." Scanlon, *South African Writers* (*Dictionary of Literary Biography* 225). 150–56.

Peterson, Bhekiziziwe. "Dhlomo, Herbert Isaac Ernest." Gikandi, *Encylopedia of African Literature.* 138–39.

Dictionaries, Encyclopedias, and Handbooks

Couzens, Tim. *The New African: A Study of the Life and Work of H. I. E. Dhlomo.* Johannesburg: Ravan, 1985.

Nafissatou (Niang) Diallo, 1941–1982

Web Sites

"Nafissatou Niang Diallo." *Reading Women Writers and African Literatures.* 23 July 2005, http://www.arts.uwa.edu.au/AFLIT/DialloNafissatouEng.html.

"Nafissatou Diallo." *Contemporary Africa Database.* 23 July 2005, http://www .africaexpert.org/people/data/person3893.html.

Biographies and Criticism

"Diallo, Nafissatou Niang." Wordworks, *Modern Black Writers.* 227–30.
Excerpts from criticsm published between 1982 and 1997.

McNee, Lisa. "Nafissatou Diallo." Parekh and Jagne, *Postcolonial African Writers: A Bio-bibliographical Criticial Sourcebook.* [123] –28.

"Nafissatou Diallo." Stringer, Susan. *The Senegalese Novel by Women: Through Their Own Eyes.* New York: Peter Lang, 1999. 19–47.
Critical overview of Diallo's works.

Mohammed Dib, 1920–2003

Web Sites

"Mohammed Dib." *Books and Writers.* 23 July 2005, http://www.kirjasto.sci.fi/dib .htm.

"Mohammed Dib." *Contemporary Africa Database.* 23 July 2005, http://www.africa expert.org/people/data/person12187.html.

Yemloul, Aziz. "Mohammed Dib." *DZ Lit: Littérature algérienne.* 23 July 2005, http://dzlit.free.fr/dib.html.

Biographies and Criticism

Bonn, Charles (trans. John Fletcher). "Mohammed Dib." Cox, *African Writers.* 1:199–207.

Brief biography, analyses of Dib's works, and select bibliography of works by and about him published between 1970 and 1994.

Hayes, Jarrod. "Dib, Mohammed." Gikandi, *Encyclopedia of African Literature.* 144–45.

Joseph Diescho, 1955–

Web Sites

"Professor Joseph Diescho." *Contemporary Africa Database.* 23 July 2005, http://people.africadatabase.org/people/data/person11469.html.

Biographies and Criticism

Ba, Ousmane. "Diescho, Joseph." Gikandi, *Encyclopedia of African Literature.* 146.

Modikwe Dikobe, 1913–

Web Sites

"Modikwe Dikobe (Marks Rammitloa). *Contemporary Africa Database.* 23 July 2005, http://people.africadatabase.org/en/profile/2351.html.

Biographies and Criticism

Couzens, Tim. "Dikobe, Modikwe." Benson and Conolly, *Encyclopedia of Postcolonial Literatures in English,* 1:361–2.

Birago (Ismael) Diop, 1906–1989

Web Sites

Birago Diop. Ed. Patrice Birago Neveu. 24 June 2005. Tiscali.fr. 23 July 2005, http://neveu01.chez.tiscali.fr/.

This is an excellent site for researching Diop's writing and his contribution to the francophone African literary and cultural movements. Apart from being easy to navigate, the site offers links to an interesting array of multimedia materials; a bibliography of Diop's works, including descriptions of and extracts from them, and of critical studies; a photo album with scanned documents, such as his passport and some personal letters; and video and audio clips of interviews and lectures.

"Birago Diop." *Books and Writers.* 23 July 2005, http://www.kirjasto.sci.fi/bdiop .htm.

Biographies and Criticism

Cap, Biruta. "Diop, Birago." *Columbia Dictionary of Modern European Literature.*
  Eds. Jean-Albert Bédé and William B. Edgerton. New York: Columbia
  University Press, 1980. 205.

"Diop, Birago." Wordworks, *Modern Black Writers.* 230–32.
  Excerpts from criticism published between 1948 and 1976.

Drame, Kandioura. "Diop, Birago." Gikandi, *Encyclopedia of African Literature.*
  146–47.

Boubacar Boris Diop, 1946–

Web Site

"Boubacar Boris Diop, Écrivain et Journaliste Sénégalais." Ed. Jean-Luc Fontaine.
  Update unavailable. 23 July 2005, http://perso.club-internet.fr/jlucf/boubaca
  .htm.
  Transcript of a brief interview anda bio-bibliographical sketch.

Biographies and Criticism

Drame, Kandioura. "Diop, Boubacar Boris." Gikandi, *Encyclopedia of African
  Literature.* 147.

David Mandessi Diop, 1927–1960

Web Sites

"David Diop." *Francophone African Poets in English Translation.* 23 July 2005,
  http://web.uflib.ufl.edu/cm/africana/diop.htm.

"David Diop." *Books and Writers.* 23 July 2005, http://www.kirjasto.sci.fi/diop.htm.

Biographies and Criticism

"Diop, David." Wordworks, *Modern Black Writers.* 232–34.
  Excerpts from criticism published between 1956 and 1991.

Drame, Kandioura. "Diop, David Mandessi." Gikandi, *Encyclopedia of African
  Literature.* 147–48.

Ogede, Ode S. "David Mandessi Diop." Parekh and Jagne, *Postcolonial African
  Writers: A Bio-bibliographical Criticial Sourcebook.* [129] –34.

Mbella Sonne Dipoko, 1936–

Web Sites

"Mbella Sonne Dipoko" *Contemporary Africa Database.* 23 July 2005, http://people
  .africadatabase.org/people/data/person2367.html.

Biographies and Criticism

Bishop, Stephen. "Dipoko, Mbella Sonne. Gikandi, *Encyclopedia of African
  Literature.* 148.

"Dipoko, Mbella Sonne." *Contemporary Authors.* 152:167.

Tahar Djaout, 1954–1993

De Zoysa, Dana. "Vision of God." *January Magazine* (Mar. 2002). 23 July 2005 http://
www.januarymagazine.com/fiction/lastsummerreason.html.
    Critical review of the English translation (2001) of Djaout's book, *The Last
Summer of Reason.*

"Tahar Djaout." *LIMAG: Littératures du maghreb.* 23 July 2005, http://www.limag
.refer.org/Volumes/Djaout.htm.

Biographies and Criticism

Abu-Haidar, F. "Djaout, Tahar." Meisami and Starkey, *Encyclopedia of Arabic
Literature.* 1:196–97.

Hayes, Jarrod. "Djaout, Tahar." Gikandi, *Encyclopedia of African Literature.* 148–49.

Assia Djebar (Fatima-Zohra Imalyène), 1936–

Web Sites

"Assia Djeba." *Books and Authors.* 23 July 2005, http://www.kirjasto.sci.fi/djebar
.htm.

"Assia Djebar." *Contemporary Africa Database.* 23 July 2005, http://www.africa
expert.org/people/data/person12476.html.

Barnhardt, Jennifer. "Assia Djebar." *Postcolonial Studies at Emory.* 17 Aug. 1998.
Emory U. 23 July 2005, http://www.emory.edu/ENGLISH/Bahri/Djebar.html.

Braziel, Jana Evans. "Assia Djebar, *Fantasia, An Algerian Cavalcade.*" *ACLANet.* Ed.
Sarah Lawall. Update unavailable. U. of Massachussetts at Amherst. 23 July
2005, http://www.umass.edu/complit/aclanet/Djebar.html.
    This page on Djebbar resides in a faculty Web project aimed at sharing syllabi
and course materials on world literatures. It provides a bibliography of books and film
scripts by Djebar, critical works on *Fantasia,* and questions for teaching the novel.
Students will find the latter useful for a critical reading and understanding of the
novel.

"Fantasia: An Algerian Cavalcade." *LitNet.* 23 July 2005, http://www.litnet.co.za/
africanlib/fantasia.asp.

Biographies and Criticism

Accad, Evelyne. "Assia Djebar's Contribution to Arab Women's Literature:
Rebellion, Maturity, Vision." Genova, *Companion to Contemporary World
Literature.* 1:154–67.

Mortimer, Mildred. "Fantasia." Moss and Valestuk, *African Literature and Its Times*
(*World Literature and Its Times* 2). 163–72.

Vogl, Mary B. "Assia Djebar." Parekh and Jagne, *Postcolonial African Writers: A
Bio-bibliographical Criticial Sourcebook.* [135] –43.

Zimra, Clarissa. "Djebar, Assia." Gikandi, *Encyclopedia of African Literature.* 149–52.

Dictionaries, Encyclopedias, and Handbooks

Chikhi, Beïda. *Les romans d'Assia Djebar.* Alger: Office des publications
universitaires, 1990.

Amu Djoleto (Solomon Alexander), 1929–

Web Sites

"Amu Djoleto." *Contemporary Africa Database.* 23 July 2005, http://people.africa
    database.org/en/person/2375.html.

Biographies and Criticism

Awuyah, Chris Kwame. "Djoleto, Amu." Benson and Conolly, *Encyclopedia of Post-
    colonial Literatures in English.* 1:365.

Owusu, Kofi. "Djoleto, Amu." Gikandi, *Encyclopedia of African Literature.*153.

Emmanuel Boundzeki Dongala, 1941–

Web Sites

"Across the Cosmos." *Q and A: A Magazine of Art and Culture.* 1.1 (Aug. 2001).
    Qmag.org. 23 July 2005, http://www.qmag.org/qaart01.html.
    Transcript of an undated interview.

"Emmanuel Dongala." *Contemporary Africa Database.* 23 July 2005, http://www
    .africaexpert.org/people/data/person6335.html.

"Emmanuel Dongala." New York State Writers Institute. Ed and update unavailable.
    State U. of New York at Albany. 23 July 2005, http://www.albany.edu/writers-inst/
    dongalaemmanuel.html.
    Biographical information on Dongala and a link to a related article in *Writers
Online.*

Shlaim, Avi. *Fresh Air Online.* 12 Apr. 2001. National Public Radio. 23 July 2005,
    http://www.npr.org/templates/story/story.php?storyId=1121385.
    Audio clip of an interview with Dongala.

Valdes, Marcela. "A World Atop the Ruins." *Books.* 22 (May 9, 2001).
    Citypages.com. 23 July 2005, http://www.citypages.com/databank/22/1066/
    article9544.asp.
    Reviews of *The Fire of Origins* and *Little Boys Come from the Stars.*

Biographies and Criticism

Lesick-Xiao, Anne E. "Emmanuel Boundzeki Dongala." Parekh and Jagne,
    Postcolonial African Writers: A Bio-bibliographical Criticial Sourcebook.
    [144] –47.

Martin, Meredith. "Dongala, Emmanuel." Gikandi, *Encyclopedia of African
    Literature.* 154.

Menan du Plessis, 1952–

Web Sites

"Menan du Plessis." *Anglophone and Lusophone African Women's Writing.* 23 July
    2005, http://www.ex.ac.uk/~ajsimoes/aflit/duPlessisEN.html.

"Menan du Plessis." *Contemporary Africa Database.* 23 July 2005, http://people
    .africadatabase.org/en/person/15864.html.

Biographies and Crtiticism

Pearson, Elaine M. "du Plessis, Menan." Gikandi, *Encyclopedia of African Literature.* 155.

R(aymond) Sarif Easmon, 1913–1997

Web Site

"Dr. R. Sarif Easmon." *Contemporary Africa Database.* 23 July 2005, http://www .africaexpert.org/people/data/person3907.html.

Biographies and Criticism

Bruschac, Joseph. "Easmon, R(aymond) Sarif." Berney, *Contemporary Dramatists.*160.

Gikandi, Simon. "Easmon, Raymond Sarif." Gikandi, *Encyclopedia of African Literature.* [158] .

Palmer, Eustace. "Easmon, Raymond Sarif." Benson and Conolly, *Encyclopedia of Post-colonial Literatures in English.* 1:429.

Gaston-Paul Effa, 1965–

Web Sites

"Gaston-Paul Effa." *Contemporary Africa Database.* 23 July 2005, http://people .africadatabase.org/people/data/person6337.html.

"Gaston-Paul Effa." *Frontiers: A Franco-British Writers' Festival about Identity.* Ed and update unavailable. British Council. 23 July 2005, http://www.aerta.saffas .com/frontieres/effa1.html
Bio-bibliographical profile of Effa.

Lorca, Alexie. "Questions à… Gaston-Paul Effa." *Lire.* (Feb. 2000). 23July 2005, http://www.lire.fr/entretien.asp?idC=36053&idR=201&idTC=4&idG=. Transcript of an interview.

Biographies and Criticism

Ekotto, Frieda. "Effa, Gaston-Paul." Gikandi, *Encyclopedia of African Literature.* 168–69.

Kossi Efoui, 1962–

Web Sites

"Kossi Efoui." *Contemporary Africa Database.* 23 July 2005. http://people.africa database.org/people/data/person6338.html.

Tervonen, Taina. "Entretien avec Kossi Efoui." *Africultures.* 12 (Sept. 1998). 23 July 2005, http://www.africultures.com/index.asp?menu=revue_affiche_article&no =555. Transcript of a 1998 interview.

Biographies and Criticism

Ekotto, Frieda, "Efoui, Kossi." Gikandi, *Encyclopedia of African Literature.* 169.

Christiane Akoua Tchotcho Ekué, 1954–

Web Sites

"Christiane Akoua Ekué." Reading Women Writers and African Literatures. 23 July
    2005, http://www.arts.uwa.edu.au/AFLIT/EkueAkouaEng.html.

Biographies and Criticsim

Ambroise Téko-Agbo and Simon Amegbleame. *Les femmes dans le processus*
    littéraire au Togo. New York: Peter Lang, 1999. 85–105.
    Discussion of the voyage motif in Ekué's novel.

Cyprian (Odiatu Duaka) Ekwensi, 1921–

Web Sites

"Cyprian Ekwensi." *Contemporary Africa Database.* 23 uly 2005, http://people
    .africadatabase.org/people/data/person2429.html.

Larson, Charles. "Cyprian Ekwensi." *Bellagio Publishing Newsletter.* 29 (Dec. 2001).
    23 May 2004, http://apm.brookes.ac.uk/sulaiman/bellagio/newsletter29/larson
    .htm.
    Presents an overview of Ekwensi's writing and his responses to a questionnaire
by Larson on the question of being an African writer.

Biographies and Criticism

Cosentino, Donald. "Jagua Nana." Moss and Valestuk, *African Literature and Its*
    Times (*World Literature and Its Times* 2). 215–24.

"Cyprian Ekwensi." Draper, *Black Literature Criticism.* 1:643–60.
    Biography, list of major works, excerpts from criticism from 1964 to 1986, and
an annotated bibliography.

"Ekwensi, Cyprian." Wordworks, *Modern Black Writers.* 247–49.
    Excerpts from criticism published between 1954 and 1971.

Emenyonu, Ernest N. "Cyprian Ekwensi." Lindfors and Sander, *Twentieth-Century*
    Caribbean and Black African Writers, First Series (*Dictionary of Literary*
    Biography 117). 149–59.

———. "Cyprian Ekwensi." Schellinger, *Encyclopedia of the Novel.* 1:349–51.

Okwonko Chidi. "Cyprian Ekwensi." Cox, *African Writers.* 1:223–34.
    A biography, analyses of Ekwensi's works, and a select bibliography of works
by and about him published between 1961 and 1992.

Schmidt, Nancy J. "Ekwensi, Cyprian (Odiatu Duaka)." Pendergast and Pendergast,
    St James Guide to Children's Writers. 346–47.

Interviews

"Cyprian Ekwensi." Lindfors, *Africa Talks Back.* [113] –127.

Grandqvist, Raoul. "Interview with Cyprian Ekwensi." *Kunapipi.* 4:1 (1982): 124–29.
    Text of a 1981 interview.

Buchi (Florence Onye) Emecheta, 1944–

Web Sites

"Buchi Emecheta." *African Writers: Voices of Change.* 23 July 2005, http://web.uflib
.ufl.edu/cm/africana/emecheta.htm.

"Buchi Emecheta." *Anglophone and Lusophone Women's Writing.* 23 July 2005,
http://www.ex.ac.uk/~ajsimoes/aflit/EmechetaEN.html.

"Buchi Emecheta." *Contemporary Africa Database.* 24 July 2005, http://www.africa
expert.org/people/profiles/profilesforperson2442.html.

"Buchi Emecheta." *Contemporary Postcolonial and Postimperial Literature in
English: African Postcolonial Literature in English.* 24 July 2005, http://www
.scholars.nus.edu.sg/post/nigeria/emecheta/emechetaov.html.

"Buchi Emecheta." *Postcolonial African Literatures in English.* 24 July 2005, http://
www.fb10.uni-bremen.de/anglistik/kerkhoff/AfricanLit/Emecheta/
Emecheta.htm.

"Buchi Emecheta." *Women Writers.*Ed. and update unavailable. BBC World Service.
24 July 2005, http://www.bbc.co.uk/worldservice/arts/features/womenwriters/
emechetta_life.shtml.
A quick guide to Emecheta and her works. Includes a biographical sketch, brief
description of her style and the themes of her novels, and links to online interviews.

"Buchi Emecheta." *Writers Talk: Ideas of Our Time.* 24 July 2005, http://www
.roland-collection.com/rolandcollection/literature/101/W100.htm.

"Buchi Emecheta." Ed. Ed Vavra. Update unavailable. Pennsylvania C. of
Technology. 24 July 2005, http://nweb.pct.edu/homepage/staff/evavra/SDM/
W10/Emecheta _Bib.htm.
A bibliography of primary works and critical studies from 1982 to 2002.

Williams, Benecia L. "Buchi Emecheta." *Postcolonial Studies at Emory.* 17 Aug.
1998. Emory U. 24 July 2005, http://www.emory.edu/ENGLISH/Bahri/Emech.
html.

Biographies and Criticism

"Buchi Ememcheta." Draper, *Black Literature Criticism.* 1:707–18.
Biography, list of major works, excerpts of criticism from 1982 to 1988, and an
annotated bibliography.

Eko, Ebele O. "Emecheta, Buchi." Benson and Conolly, *Encyclopedia of Post-
Colonial Literatures in English. 1:439–40.*

"Emecheta, Buchi." Robinson, *Modern Women Writers.* 1:792–803.
Excerpts from criticism published between 1976 and 1991.

"Emecheta, Buchi." Wordworks, *Modern Black Writers.* 255–60.
Excerpts from criticism published between 1980 and 1995.

Franey, Laura. "The Joys of Motherhood." Moss and Valestuk, *African Literature and
Its Times* (*World Literature and Its Times* 2). 225–35.

Petersen, Kirsten Holt. "Buchi Emecheta." Linfors and Sander, *Twentieth-Century Caribbean and Black African Writers, First Series* (*Dictionary of Literary Biography* 117). 159–65.

———. "Buchi Emecheta: Unorthodox Fictions about Women." Ross, *International Literature in English.* 283–92.
Analysis of Emecheta's novels.

Smith, Christopher. "Buchi Emecheta." Cox, *African Writers.* 1:235–47.
A biography, analyses of Emecheta's works, and a select bibliography of works by and about her published between 1972 and 1994.

Umeh, Marie. "Buchi Emecheta." Parekh and Jagne, *Postcolonial African Writers: A Bio-bibliographical Criticial Sourcebook.* [148] –63.

Dictionaries, Encyclopedias, and Handbooks

Fishburn, Katherine. *Reading Buchi Emecheta: Cross-Cultural Conversations.* Westport, Conn: Greenwood Press, 1995.

Umeh, Marie. Ed. *Emerging Perspectives on Buchi Emecheta.* Lawrenceville, NJ: Africa World Press, 1996.

Interviews

"Buchi Emecheta." James, *In Their Own Words.* 35–45.

"Buchi Emecheta." Jussawala and Dasenbrock, *Interviews with Writers of the Post-Colonial World.* 83–99.

Oulaudah Equiano, 1745–1797

Web Sites

"Oulaudah Equiano, or, Gustavus Vassa, The African." *Slavery, Emancipation, and Abolition.* Ed. Brycchan Carey. 26 Dec. 2004. Brycchancaey.com. 24 July 2005. http://www.brycchancarey.com/equiano/.
A comprehensive site on Equiano that provides a plethora of multiformat resources that would enhance the understanding of his work and its contexts. Going beyond the critical biography, the site leads researchers to the following: extracts from Equiano's book, arranged according to its narrative structure; images of a map tracing his travels and a 1798 newspaper advertisement for the book; a list of related links; an extensive bibliography that lists multiple editions and translations of the book; and critical analyses from the nineteenth century to date.

"Olaudah Equiano." *Africans in America: The Terrible Transformation.* WBGH and PBS Online. 24 July 2005, http://www.pbs.org/wgbh/aia/part1/1p276.html.
This page is part of a larger Web project that complemented the 1998 television series of the same title. The focus is not so much on Equiano's book as on the bigger issue of slavery in Africa and the Americas. Included on this site are interviews with academics who have researched Equiano's origins in Nigeria or the impact of slave raids on African societies.

"Olaudah Equiano (Gustavus Vassa)." Ed. Donna M. Campbell. 3 Oct. 2003. Gonzaga U. 24 July 2005, http://guweb2.gonzaga.edu/faculty/campbell/enl310/equiano.htm.

A simply arranged site listing links to other Equiano Web projects, study guides, and definitions and examples of slave narratives.

"Olaudah Equiano. The Interesting Narrative of the Life of Olaudah Equiano, or, Gustavus Vassa, the African." *Hanover Historical Texts Project.* Ed. Frank Luttmer. Mar. 2001. Hanover C. 24 July 2005, http://history.hanover.edu/texts/equiano/equiano_contents.html.
Electronic text of the autobiography, with brief chapter synopses.

Biographies and Criticism

Gikandi, Simon. "Equiano, Olaudah." Gikandi, *Encyclopedia of African Literature.* 173–74.

Littleton, Jacob. "Equiano's Travels: The Interesting Narrative of the Life of Olaudah Equiano or Gustavus Vassa the African." Moss and Valestuk, *African Literature and Its Times* (*World Litertaure and Its Times* 2). 141–50.

"Olaudah Equiano." Draper, *Black Literature Criticism.* 2:719–39.
Biography, excerpts of criticism from 1789 to 1985, and an annotated bibliography.

"Olaudah Equiano." Person, *Literature Criticism from 1400 to 1800.* 16:58–102.
Excerpts of criticsm from 1789 to 1988 and an annotated bibliography.

O'Neale, Sondra. "Olaudah Equiano (Gustavus Vassa)." Elliott, *American Writers of the Early Republic* (*Dictionary of Literary Biography* 37): 153–158.

Samuels, Wilfred D. "Olaudah Equiano (Gustavus Vassa)." Harris, *Afro-American Writers Before the Harlem Renaissance* (*Dictionary of Literary Biography* 50). 123–29.

Ahmed Essop, 1931–

Web Sites

"Ahmed Essop." *Contemporary Africa Database.* 24 July 2005, http://people.africa database.org/people/data/person15866.html.

Chetty, Rajender. "A Community Bard: Interview with Ahmed Essop." *Alternation: International Journal for the Study of Southern African Literatures and Languages.* 6:1 (1999). 23 July 2005, http://singh.reshma.tripod.com/alternation/alternation6_1/23rajen.htm.
Transcript of a 1999 interview with Essop.

Biographies and Criticism

Smith, Rowland. "Ahmed Essop." Scanlon, *South African Writers* (*Dictionary of Literary Biography* 225). 157–63.

———. "Essop, Ahmed." Benson and Conolly, *Encyclopedia of Post-Colonial Literatures in English.* 1:460–61.

Ravenscroft, Arthur. " Essop, Ahmed." Schlager and Lauer, *Contemporary Novelists.* 299–300.

Daniel Olorunfemi Fagunwa, 1903–1963

Web Sites

"Daniel Olurunfemi Fagunwa." *Contemporary Africa Database.* 25 July 2005, http://
people.africadatabase.org/people/data/person13077.html.

Biographies and Criticism

George, Olakunle. "Fagunwa, Daniel Olorunfemi." Gikandi, *Encyclopedia of African
Literature.* [181] –83.

Aminata Sow Fall, 1941–

Web Sites

"Aminata Sow Fall." *Reading Women Writers and African Literatures.* 25 July 2005,
http://www.arts.uwa.edu.au/AFLIT/SowFallAminataEng.html.

"Aminata Sow Fall." *Contemporary Africa Database.* 25 July 2005, http://people
.africadatabase.org/people/data/person3549.html.

Biographies and Criticsm

"Aminata Sow Fall." Susan Stringer, *The Senegalese Novel by Women: Through Their
Own Eyes.* New York: Peter Lang, 1996. [77] –111.
An overview of Fall's writing.

Gadjigo, Samba. "Social Vision in Aminata Sow Fall's Literary Work." Genova,
Companion to Contemporary World Literature. 1:372–77.

———. "Fall, Aminata Sow." Chevalier, *Contemporary World Writers.* 175–76.

McNee, Lisa. "Sow Fall, Aminata." Gikandi, *Encyclopedia of African Literature.*
518–19.

"Sow Fall, Aminata." Robinson, *Modern Women Writers.* 4:224–33.
Excerpts from criticism published between 1982 and 1991.

"Sow Fall, Aminata." Wordworks, *Modern Black Writers.* 687–89.
Excerpts from criticism published between 1984 and 1989.

Thomas, Dominic. "Aminata Sow Fall." Parekh and Jagne, *Postcolonial African
Writers: A Bio-bibliographical Criticial Sourcebook.* [171] –74.

Interview

Herzberger-Fofana, Pierrette. "Aminata Sow Fall, regard critique sur la société
sénégalaise." *Ecrivains africains et identités culturelles.* Tübungen:
Stauffenburg Verlag, 1989. 103–107.

Nuruddin Farah, 1945–

Web Sites

Donaldson, Andrew. "Secrets of a Gypsy Scribe." *Sunday Times.* 15 Aug. 1999.
25 July 2005, http://www.suntimes.co.za/1999/08/15/insight/in01.htm.
A bio-bibliographical article.

"Nuruddin Farah." *Books and Writers.* 23 July 2005, http://www.kirjasto.sci.fi/farah
.htm.

"Nuruddin Farah." *Contemporary Africa Database.* 25 July 2005, http://www.africa
    expert.org/people/data/person2472.html.

"Nuruddin Farah." *International Writers Series.* Ed. John Gregory Brown. Update
    unavailable. Sweet Briar C. 23 July 2005, http://worldwriters.english.sbc.edu/
    farah.html.
    Contains a brief biography, extracts from reviews of his books, and links to Web
resources on Farah and Somalia.

"Nuruddin Farah Archive." *Nomad Net.* Ed. and update unavailable. 23 July 2005,
    http://www.netnomad.com/nuruddinfarah.html.
    Although the links on this site are few, they lead to significant interviews by
Farah and reviews of some of his novels.

"Sweet and Sour Milk." *LitNet.* 23 July 2005, http://www.litnet.co.za/africanlib/farah
    .asp.

Waberi, Abdourahman A. "Women in Movement in Nuruddin Farah's Writing."
    Africultures. 35. 25 May 2004, http://www.africultures.com/anglais/articles_
    anglais/35wabe.htm.
    This article provides a perspective on the view of Farah as a "feminist" writer.

Biographies and Criticism

Azam, Faisal. "Sweet and Sour Milk." Moss and Valestuk, *African Literature and Its
    Times* (*World Literature and Its Times* 2). 409–20.

Bardolph, Jacqueline. "Brothers and Sisters in Nuruddin Farah's Two Trilogies."
    Genova, *Companion to Contemporary World Literature.* 1:377–83.
    A study of sibling groups in Farah's trilogies to explore his socio-political
vision.

———. "Nuruddin Farah." Lindfors and Sander, *Twentieth-Century Caribbean and
    Black African Writers, Second Series* (*Dictionary of Literary Biography* 125).
    35–40.

Chari, Hema. "Nuruddin Farah." Parekh and Jagne, *Postcolonial African Writers: A
    Bio-bibliographical Criticial Sourcebook.* [175] –80.

Colmer, Rosemary. "Nuruddin Farah: Territories of Pain." Ross, *International
    Literature in English.*131–42.
    Biography, a discussion of Farah's works as socio-political critiques, and an
annotated bibliography of selected criticism.

"Farah, Nuruddin." Wordworks, *Modern Black Writers.* 261–65.
    Excerpts from criticism published between 1984 and 1997.

McDowell, Robert. "Nuruddin Farah." Cox, *African Writers.* 1:249–62.
    A biography, with analyses of Farah's works, and a select bibliography of works
by and about him published between 1965 and 1991.

Ntalindwa, Raymond. "Farah, Nuruddin." Gikandi, *Encyclopedia of African
    Literature.* 185–88.

"Nuruddin Farah." Draper, *Black Literature Criticism.* 2:757–70.
    Biography, list of major works, excerpts of criticism from 1981 to 1989, and an
annotated bibliography.

"Nuruddin Farah." Hunter et al., *Contemporary Literary Criticism.* 137:79–133.
　　Excerpts from criticism published between 1986 and 1998.

Dictionaries, Encyclopedias, and Handbooks

Wright, Derek. *Emerging Perspectives on Nuruddin Farah.* Trenton, NJ: Africa
　　World Press, 2004.

——. *The Novels of Nuruddin Farah.* Bayreuth, Germany: Bayreuth U, 1994.

Interview

"Nuruddin Farah." Jusswalla and Dasenbrock, *Interviews with Writers of the Post-
　　Colonial World.* 43–62.

Aicha (Aminata Laila) Fofana , 1957–2003

Web Sites

"Aicha Fofana." *Reading Women Writers and African Literatures.* 25 July 2005, http://
　　www.arts.uwa.edu.au/AFLIT/FofanaAicha.Eng.html.

Biographies and Criticism

"Aïcha Fofana." Herzberger-Fofana, *Littérature feminine francophone d'Afrique
　　noire.* 490.
　　Brief biography and description of Fofana's work.

Lynn Freed, 1945–

Web Sites

Franklin, Erica. "Persephone and Demeter Revisted." *The Yale Review of Books*
　　(Summer 2002). 23 July 2005, http://www.yalereviewofbooks.com/archive/
　　summer02/review08.shtml.htm.
　　A review of Freed's *House of Women.*

"Interviews: Lynn Freed." *Exclusive Books.Com.* Ed. and update unavailable. 23 July
　　2005, http://www.exclusivebooks.com/interviews/ftf/lynn_freed.asp?Tag=&
　　CID=.
　　Transcript of an interview with Freed after the publication of *The Mirror.*

LynnFreed.com. Ed. Lynn Freed. Copyright 2005. 23 July 2005, http://www
　　.lynnfreed.com/.
　　The official Web site of Freed provides links to excerpts from critical reviews of
her books, a list of essays and articles by her, and interviews with her.

Biographies and Criticism

"Freed, Lynn." *Contemporary Authors.* 108:165.

(Harold) Athol Fugard, 1932–

Web Sites

"Athol Fugard." *Contemporary Africa Database.* 23 July 2005, http://www.africa
　　expert.org/people/data/person2506.html.

"Athol Fugard." *Introducing South African Writers.* 23 July 2005, http://homepage
.oniduo.pt/chacmalissimo/SAfrican/html/athol_fugard.htm.

Athol Fugard. Ed. Iain Fisher. Update unavailable. Iainfisher.com. 23 July 2005,
http://www.iainfisher.com/fugard.html.
A comprehensive site on Fugard with a wide array of extensive research
material. For example, behind the "Much more" heading lies links to film versions of
his plays, information on stage actors who have performed in his plays, books and
articles written by and about Fugard, and a glossary of South Africa–specific words.
A note-worthy feature of this Web site is its search capability.

"Conversation on line with South African Dramatist Athol Fugard." Ed. unavailable.
29 Sept. 2000. Indiana U. 23 July 2005, http://www.homepages.indiana.edu/
092900/text/conversations.html.
Audio stream of a conversation with Fugard.

McDonald, Marianne. "A Gift for His Seventieth Birthday: Athol Fugard's *Sorrows
and Rejoicings.*" *TheatreForum* 21 (Summer/Fall 2002). 23 July 2005, http://
www-theatre.ucsd.edu/TF/fugard.html.
Review of Fugard's play *Sorrows and Rejoicings* with performance photos.

Biographies and Criticism

"Athol Fugard." Bryfonski and Harris, *Contemporary Literary Criticism.* 14:189–92.
Excerpts from criticism published between 1973 and 1978.

"Athol Fugard." Draper et al., *Contemporary Literary Criticism.* 80:59–89.
Excerpts from criticism published between 1984 and 1993 with an annotated
bibliography.

"Athol Fugard." Marowski et al., *Contemporary Literary Criticism.* 40:195–204.
Excerpts from criticism published between 1980 and 1986.

"Athol Fugard." Trudeau, *Drama Criticism.* 3:220–64.
Excerpts from criticism published between 1964 and 1987.

Collins, Michael J. "The Sabotage of Love: Athol Fugard's Recent Plays." Genova,
Companion to Contemporary World Literature. 1:390–93.
Reviews *A Lesson from Aloes* and *Master Harold . . . and the Boys.*

Hauptfleisch, Temple. "Athol Fugard: The Image, The Word, and The 'Carnal
Reality.'" Ross, *International Literature in English.* 607–20.
Examines the elements of "image" and "word" in Fugard's writing.

Littleton, Jacob. "Valley Song." Moss and Valestuk, *African Literature and Its Times*
(*World Liertaure and Its Times* 2). 431–41.

Nel, Jo E. "Athol Fugard." Parekh and Jagne, *Postcolonial African Writers: A Bio-
bibliographical Criticial Sourcebook.* [181] –86.

Ukaegbu, Victor I. "Athol Fugard." Cox, *African Writers.* 1:263–75.
A biography, analyses of theme and style in Fugard's works, and a select
bibliography of works by and about him published between 1966 and 1996.

Walder, Dennis. "Athol Fugard." Scanlon, *South African Writers* (*Dictionary of
Literary Biography* 225). 164–83.

Dictionaries, Encyclopedias, and Handbooks

Gray, Stephen. Ed. *File on Fugard.* London: Methuen, 1991.
    Provides a brief chronology, synopses and excerpts of criticsm on Fugard's
stage and television plays, feature films, and nondramatic works, with excerpts of his
views on his writing and a select bibliography of primary and secondary works.

Sheila Fugard, 1932–

Web Sites

"Sheila Fugard." *Luxlapis.* Ed and update unavailable. 23 July 2005, http://members
    .tripod.com/luxlapis/fugard.html
    Provides a biography of Fugard, the text of six poems, and the electronic edition
of *Lady of Realization.*

"Sheila Meiring Fugard." *Contemporary Africa Database.* 23 July 2005, http://people
    .africadatabase.org/people/data/person15868.html.

Biographies and Criticism

"Fugard, Sheila." *Contemporary Authors.* 125:138–39.

"Sheila Fugard." Marowski and Matuz, *Contemporary Literary Criticism.* 48:108–13.
    Excerpts from criticism published between 1972 and 1986.

Tsegaye Kawessa Gabre-Medhin (Tseggayé Gebre-Medhin), 1936–

Web Sites

Ayele, Negussay. "Poet Laureate Tsegaye Gabre-Medhin of Ethiopia: A Short Walk
    Through His Literary Park." *MediaEthiopia.* Ed. and update unavailable.
    MediaEthiopia.com. 23 July 2005, http://www.ethiopians.com/tsegaye/.
    Bio-critical article on Gabre-Medhin.

Belcher, Wendy. "Ethiopia's Poet Laureate Tsegaye Gabre-Medhin." *Ethiopian
    Review* (Sept–Oct. 1998). 23 July 2005, http://ethiopianreview.homestead.com/
    Interview_TsegayeGMSep98.html.
    Transcript of a 1998 interview.

Biographies and Criticism

Molvaer, Reudulf. "Tseggayé Gebre-Medhin." Gikandi, *Encyclopedia of African
    Literature.* 537.

Plastow, Jane. "Gebre-Medhin, Tsegaye." Dennis Kennedy, *Encyclopedia of Theatre
    and Performance.* 1. Oxford: Oxford UP, 504–5.

———. 'Tsegaye Gabre-Medhin and Ethiopian Reformist Theatre." Biodun Jeyifo,
    Modern African Drama. New York: W.W. Norton, 2002. 578–81.
    An analysis of Gabre-Medhin's work and his contribution to the new drama of
Ethiopia.

Nadine Gordimer, 1923–

Web Sites

"Biography of Nadine Gordimer." *UNDP in South Africa.* 11 May 2004. United
    Nations Development Program. 23 July 2005, http://www.undp.org.za/docs/
    misc/gordimerbio.html.
    In addition to bio-biliographic information, the site also lists literary awards
won and films produced by Gordimer.

Garner, Dwight. "Nadine Gordimer." *Salon.* (Mar. 1998). 23 July 2005, http://archive
    .salon.com/books/int/1998/03/cov_si_09int.html.
    Gordimer discusses post-apartheid South Africa and her novel *The House Gun*
in this interview.

"Nadine Gordimer." *Anglophone and Lusophone African Women's Writing.* 23 July
    2005, http://www.ex.ac.uk/~ajsimoes/aflit/FEMECalireEN.html#gordimer.

"Nadine Gordimer." *Books and Writers.* 23 July 2005, http://www.kirjasto.sci.fi/
    gordimer.htm.

"Nadine Gordimer." *Contemporary Africa Database.* 23 July 2005, http://people
    .africadatabase.org/people/data/person2550.html.

"Nadine Gordimer." *Contemporary Postcolonial and Postimperial Literature in
    English.* 23 July 2005, http://www.scholars.nus.edu.sg/post/sa/gordimer/
    gordimerov.html.

"Nadine Gordimer." *Nobel e-Museum.* 20 May 2005. The Nobel Foundation. 23 July
    2005, http://www.nobel.se/literature/laureates/1991/gordimer-bio.html.
    Includes a biography, the text of Gordimer's Nobel lecture and banquet speech,
and a scanned image of her award.

"Nadine Gordimer." *Writers Talk: Ideas of Our Time.* 23 July 2005, http://www
    .roland-collection.com/rolandcollection/literature/101/W62.htm.

"The Pickup by Nadine Gordimer." *Discusson Guides from The Great Books
    Foundation.* Ed and update unavailable. PenguinPutnam.com. 23 July 2005,
    http://www.penguinputnam.com/static/rguides/us/pickup.html.

Plot summary of *The Pickup,* discussion questions, and a brief biography of
    Gordimer.

"Tribute to Nadine Gordimer." Ed. and update unavailable. 23 July 2005, http://home
    page.oninet.pt/027mft/.
    An enthusiast's site, still under construction, but useful for its chronological
bibliography of works by and about Gordimer.

Biographies and Criticism

Eckstein, Barbara J. "Nadine Gordimer: Nobel Laureate in Literature, 1991." Genova,
    Companion to Contemporary World Literature. 1:393–397.
    Tribute commemorating Gordimer's Nobel Prize.

"Gordimer, Nadine." Robinson, *Modern Women Writers.* 2: 194–202.
    Excerpts from criticism published between 1953 and 1991.

Loflin, Christine. "Nadine Gordimer." Fallon et al., *A Reader's Companion to the Short Story in English*. 182–89.
    Overview and analyses of Gordimer's short stories and a select bibliography of primary and secondary works.

Marsh-Lockett, Carol P. "Nadine Gordimer." Parekh and Jagne, *Postcolonial African Writers: A Bio-bibliographical Criticial Sourcebook*. [187] –200.

"Nadine Gordimer." Harris et al., *Short Story Criticism*. 17:150–96.
    Excerpts from criticism published between 1952 and 1993 and an annotated bibliography.

"Nadine Gordimer." Hunter et al., *Contemporary Literary Criticism*. 123:111–63.
    Excerpts from criticism published between 1965 and 1996 and an annotated bibliography.

Newman, Judith. "Special Commissioned Entry on Nadine Gordimer." Witalec, *Contemporary Literary Criticism*. 161:334–83.
    Traces Gordimer's trajectory as a writer, in addition to an analysis of her style and a description of the cultural context in which her works are produced.

———. "Special Commissioned Essay on *The Lying Days* by Nadine Gordimer." Witalec, *Contemporary Literary Criticism*. 160. 84–123.
    Critical analysis of Gordimer's first published novel.

Rudikoff, Sonya. "Nadine Gordimer." Cox, *African Writers*. 1:277–90.
    Bio-critical information on Gordimer and a select bibliography of works by and about her published between 1953 and 1995.

Smith, Rowland. "Nadine Gordimer." Scanlon, *South African Writers* (*Dictionary of Literary Biography* 225). 184–204.

———. "Nadine Gordimer: Truth, Irony, and Commitment." Ross, *International Literature in English*. 171–80.
    Biography, a discussion of Gordimer's commitment to writing about the injustices of apartheid, and a short annotated bibliography of critical works.

Turgeon, Carolyn. "Burgher's Daughter." Moss and Valestuk, *African Literature and Its Times* (*World Literature and Its Times* 2). 23–34.

Bibliographies

Driver, Dorothy, Ann Dry, Craig Mackenzie, and John Read. *Nadine Gordimer: A Bibliography of Primary and Secondary Sources, 1937–1992*. London: Hans Zell, 1994.
    A comprehensive bibliography of about 3,000 works by and about Gordimer.

Green Robert J. "Nadine Gordimer: A Bibliography of Works and Criticism. *Bulletin of Bibliography*. 42:1 (1985): 5–11.
    Lists primary and secondary sources published between 1949 and 1983.

Interviews

Bazin, Nancy Topping, and Marilyn Dallman Seymour. *Conversations with Nadine Gordimer*. Jackson: University Press of Mississippi, 1990.
    A collection of 34 interviews from 1958 to 1989, with a bio-bibliographical chronology.

Abdulrazak Gurnah, 1948–

Web Sites

"Abdulrazak Gurnah." *Contemporary Africa Database.* 23 July 2005, http://www
.africaexpert.org/people/data/person13628.html.

"Abdulrazak Gurnah." *Contemporary Writers.* Ed. and update unavailable. British
Council. 23 July 2005, http://www.contemporarywriters.com/authors/?p=auth
46&state=index%3Dg.
Brief biography, with a list of Gurnah's books and literary prizes.

Erouart-Siad, Patrick. "By the Sea." *Boston Review* (Summer 2001). 23 July 2005,
http://bostonreview.mit.edu/BR26.3/erouartsiad.html.
Review of Gurnah's novel.

Biographies and Criticism

"Gurnah, Abdulrazak (S)." *Contemporary Authors.* 179:269–70.

Mesher, David. "Gurnah, Abdulrazak." Serafin, *Encyclopedia of World Literature in
the 20th Century.* 2:322.

Ojwang, Dan Odhiambo. "Gurnah, Abdulrazak." Gikandi, *Encyclopedia of African
Literature.* 212.

Mafika (Pascal) Gwala, 1946–

Web Sites

"Mafika Pascal Gwala." *Contemporary Africa Database.* 23 July 2005, http://people
.africadatabase.org/people/data/person15890.html.

Biographies and Criticism

Bayer, Jogamaya. "Mafika Gwala." Parekh and Jagne, *Postcolonial African Writers:
A Bio-bibliographical Criticial Sourcebook.* [201] –5.

Mzamane, Mbulolo Vizikhungo. "Gwala, Mafika Pascal." Benson and Conolly,
Encyclopedia of Post-colonial Literatures in English. 1:618–19.

Ngwenya, Thengani H. "Gwala, Mafika Pascal." Gikandi, *Encyclopedia of African
Literature.* 212–13.

Flore Hazoumé, 1959–

Web Sites

"Flore Hazoumé." *Reading Women Writers and African Literatures.* 23 July 2005.
http://www.arts.uwa.edu.au/AFLIT/HazoumeFlore.Eng.html.

Biographies and Criticism

Coundouriotis, Eleni. "Hazoumé, Flore." Gikandi, *Encyclopedia of African
Literature.* 218.

Bessie Head, 1937–1986

Web Sites

"Bessie Head." *African Literature in English: Five Women Writers.* Ed Ingrid Kerkhoff. Update unavailable. Universitat Bremen. 23 July 2005, http://www .fb10.uni-bremen.de/anglistik/kerkhoff/AfrWomenWriters/Head/Head.html.

"Bessie Head." *African Writers: Voices of Change.* 23 July 2005, http://web.uflib.ufl .edu/cm/africana/head.htm.

"Bessie Head." *Anglophone and Lusophone African Women's Writing.* 23 July 2005, http://www.ex.ac.uk/~ajsimoes/aflit/HeadEN.html.

"Bessie Head. *Contemporary Africa Database.* 23 July 2005, http://people .africadatabase.org/people/data/person2600.html.

"Bessie Head." *Introducing South African Writers.* 23 July 2005, http://homepage .oniduo.pt/chacmalissimo/SAfrican/html/bessie_head.htm.

Bissell, Kate. "Bessie Head." *Postcolonial Studies at Emory.* 23 July 2005, http:// www.emory.edu/ENGLISH/Bahri/Head.html.

Biographies and Criticism

"Bessie Head." Draper, *Black Literature Criticism.* 2:995–1003.
    Biography, list of major works, excerpts of criticism from 1976 to 1986, and an annotated bibliography.

"Bessie Head." Matuz et al., *Contemporary Literary Criticism.* 67:91–112.
    Excerpts from criticism published between 1981 and 1991,with an annotated bibliography.

"Bessie Head." Stine et al., *Contemporary Literary Criticism.* 25:232–39.
    Excerpts from criticism published between 1969 and 1982.

"Bessie Head." Witalec, *Short Story Criticism.* 52:186–249.
    Criticism on Head's short stories from 1983 to 1998, with a short bibliography.

"Head, Bessie." Robinson, *Modern Women Writers.* 2:293–301.
    Excerpts from criticsm published between 1976 and 1991.

"Head, Bessie." Wordworks, *Modern Black Criticism.* 312–20.
    Excerpts from criticism published between 1981 and 1996.

Ibrahim, Huma. "Head, Bessie." Gikandi, *Encyclopedia of African Literature.* 219–20.

Katrak, Ketu H. "Bessie Head." Parini, *World Writers in English.* 1:157–76.

Little, Greta D. "Bessie Head." Lindfors and Sander, *Twentieth-Century Caribbean and Black African Writers, First Series* (*Dictionary of Literary Biography* 117). 186–93.

MacKenzie, Craig. "Bessie Head." Scanlon, *South African Writers* (*Dictionary of Literary Biography* 225). 205–12.

———. "Bessie Head: Alienation, Breakdown, and Renewal." Ross, *International Literature in English.* 557–69.
    Thematic study of Head's novels, with an annotated bibliography.

Osagie, Iyunolu. "When Rain Coulds Gather." Moss and Valestuk, *African Litertaure and Its Times* (*World Literature and Its Times* 2). 481–91.

Peek, Andrew. "Bessie Head." Cox, *African Writers*. 1:303–20.

A biography, with analyses of Head's works, and a select bibliography of works by and about her published between 1970 and 1992.

Savory, Elaine. "Bessie Head." Parekh and Jagne, *Postcolonial African Writers: A Bio-bibliographical Criticial Sourcebook.* [206] –20.

Dictionaries, Encyclopedias, and Handbooks

Sample, Maxine. Ed. *Critical Essays on Bessie Head.* Westport, Conn: Greenwood, 2003.

Bibliographies

Gardner, Susan and Patricia E. Scott. *Bessie Head: A Bibliography.* Grahamstown, South Africa: National English Literary Museum, 1986.

Luis Bernardo Honwana, 1942–

Web Sites

"Luis Bernardo Honwana." *Contemporary Africa Database.* 23 July 2005, http://people.africadatabase.org/people/data/person2611.html.

Biographies and Criticism

"Luis Bernardo Honwana and the Allegory of Mozambican Regeneration." Niyi Afolabi, *Golden Cage; Regeneration in Lusophone African Literature and Culture.* Trenton, New Jersey: Africa World Press. [34] –[76] .

Uses two short story collections by Honwana to illustrate the of anti-Portuguese colonialist nature of his writing.

Rothwell, Phillip. "Honwana, Luís Bernardo." Gikandi, *Encyclopedia of African Literature.* 226.

Christopher (David Tully) Hope, 1944–

Web Sites

"Christopher Hope." *Contemporary Africa Database.* 23 July 2005, http://people .africadatabase.org/en/person/15891.html.

"Christopher Hope." *Contemporary Writers.* 23 July 2005, http://www.contemporary writers.com/authors/?p=auth50.

"Christopher Hope." *Writers Talk: Ideas of Our Time.* 23July 2005, http://www .roland-collection.com/rolandcollection/literature/101/W96.htm.

Biographies and Criticism

"Christopher (David Tully) Hope." Marowski et al., *Contemporary Literary Criticism.* 52: 207–17.

Excerpts from criticism published between 1974 and 1988.

Grant, Damian. "Christopher Hope." Cox, *African Writers.* 1:331–43.

Biography, analyses of Hope's works, and a select bibliography of works by and about him published between 1980 and 1995.

Smith, Rowland. "Christopher Hope." Scanlon, *South African Writers (Dictionary of Literary Biography* 225). 213–20.

Chenjerai Hove, 1956–

Web Sites

"Chenjerai Hove." *Contemporary Africa Database.* 23 July 2005, http://people. africadatabase.org/people/data/person2618.html.

"Chenjerai Hove." *Contemporary Postcolonial and Postcolonial Literature in English.* 23 July 2005, http://www.scholars.nus.edu.sg/post/zimbabwe/hove/ hoveov.html.

"Chenjerai Hove." *Postcolonial African Literatures in English.* 23 July 2005, http:// www.fb10.uni-bremen.de/anglistik/kerkhoff/AfricanLit/Hove/Hove.htm.

"Chenjerai Hove." *Zimbabwe — Poetry International Web.* Ed. and update unavailable. Poetry International Web. 25 July 2005, http://zimbabwe.poetry international.org/cwolk/view/17257.

Biographies and Criticism

Vambe, M. "Hove, Chenjerai." Gikandi, *Encyclopedia of African Literature.* 228.

Zhuwarara, R. "Gender and Liberation: Chenjerai' Hove's *Bones.*" Ngara, *New Writing from Southern Africa.* 29–44
Analysis of *Bones.*

Ebrahim Hussein, 1943–

Web Sites

"Ebrahim Hussein." *Contemporary Africa Database.* 23 July 2005, http://people .africadatabase.org/people/data/person15704.html.

Fiebach, Joachim. "Ebrahim Hussein's Dramaturgy: A Swahili Multiculturalist's Journey in Drama and Theater." *Research in African Literatures.* 28:4 (Winter 1997). 19–37. 23 July 2005, http://www.fb10.uni-bremen.de/anglistik/kerkhoff/ AfricanLit/AfricanTheatre.htm.
Reproduces article on Hussein's use of multiple dramatic forms to portray his multicultural experiences.

Biographies and Criticism

Mbele, Joseph. "Hussein, Ebrahim." Gikandi, *Encyclopedia of African Literature.* 230–31.

Mulokozi, M. M. "Hussein Ebrahim." Benson and Conolly, *Encyclopedia of Post-colonial Literatures in English.* 1:706.

(Vincent) Chukwuemeka Ike, 1931–

Web Sites

"Chukwuemeka Ike." *Contemporary Africa Database.* 23 July 2005, http://www
.africaexpert.org/people/data/person3908.html.

Biographies and Criticism

Ezenwa-Ohaeto. "Chukuemeka Ike." Lindfors and Sander, *Twentieth-Century
Caribbeana and Black African Writers* (*Dictionary of Literary Biography* 157).
96–104.

Gikandi, Simon. "Ike, Chukwuemeka." Gikandi, *Encyclopedia of African Literature.*
236.

Okafor, Chinyere Grace. "Vincent Chukwuemeka Ike." Parekh and Jagne,
Postcolonial African Writers: A Bio-bibliographical Critical Sourcebook.
[221]–27.

Interviews

"Chuckwuemeka Ike." Ezenwa-Ohaeto, *Winging Words: Interviews with Nigerian
Writers and Critics.* 83–92.

Dictionaries, Encyclopedias, and Handbooks

Ugbabe, Kanchana. *Chukwuemeka Ike: A Critical Reader.* Oxford: Malthouse, 2001.
Includes a useful bibliography of works by and about Ike.

Monique Ilboudo, n.d.

Web Sites

"Monique Ilboudo." *Contemporary Africa Database.* 23 July 2005, http://people
.africadatabase.org/people/data/person16103.html.

"Monique Ilboudo." *Reading Women Writers and African Literatures.* 23 July 2005,
http://www.arts.uwa.edu.au/AFLIT/IlboudoMoniqueEN.html.

Biographies and Criticism

Ekotto, Frieda. "Ilboudo, Monique." Gikandi, *Encyclopedia of African Literature.* 237.

King, Adele. "Le mal de peau." *World Literature Today.* 76:1 (Winter 2002). 120.
Review of *Le Mal de Peau.*

Francis Davies Imbuga, 1947–

Web Sites

"Francis Imbuga." *Contemporary Africa Database.* 23 July 2005, http://people.africa
database.org/people/data/person11795.html.

Biographies and Criticism

Kurtz, J. Roger. "Francis Imbuga." Parekh and Jagne, *Postcolonial African Writers: A
Bio-bibliographical Critical Sourcebook.* [228]–33.

Muli, James M.. "Francis D. Imbuga." Lindfors and Sander, *Twentieth-Century
Caribbean and Black African Writers, Third Series* (*Dictionary of Literary
Biography* 157). 105–12.

Outa, George Odera. "Imbuga, Francis Davies." Gikandi, *Encyclopedia of African Literature.* 237–38.

Moses Isegawa, 1963

Web Sites

Ball, Magdalena. "Interview with Moses Isegawa." *The Compulsive Reader.* (30 May 2002). Ed. Magdalena Ball. 23 July 2005, http://www.compulsivereader.com/html/modules.php?op=modload&name=News&file=article&sid=90.

"Moses Isegawa." *Contemporary Africa Database.* 23 July 2005, http://people .africadatabase.org/people/data/person13078.html.

Tepper, Anderson. "Abyssinian Chronicles by Moses Isegawa." *Salon.com* (27 June 2000). 16 Apr. 2004, http://dir.salon.com/books/review/2000/06/27/isegawa/index.html.
Review of *Abyssinia Chronicles.*

Biographies and Criticism

Hawley, John C. "Moses Isegawa's Abyssinian Chronicles as the Bildungsroman of Despair: AIDS and the Irrelevance of Reconciliation." Eds. Bruce Bennett et al. *Resistance and Reconciliation: Writing in the Commonwealth.* Canberra, Australia: Association for Commonwealth Literature and Language Studies, 2003. 187–200.
Examines the socio-historical aspect of Isegawa's novel.

Festus Iyayi, 1947–

Web Sites

"Festus Iyayi." *Contemporary Africa Database.* 23 July 2005, http://people .africadatabase.org/people/data/person11794.html.

Biographies and Criticism

Gikandi, Simon. "Iyayi, Festus." Gikandi, *Encyclopedia of African Literature.* 246.

"Iyayi, Festus." Wordworks, *Modern Black Writers.* 345–49.
Excerpts from criticism published between 1984 and 1998.

Maduakor, Obi. "Festus Iyayi." Cox, *African Writers.* 1:367–75.
Biography, analyses of two novels, and a select bibliography of works by and about him published between 1979 and 1992.

Okafor, Chinyere Grace. "Festus Ikhuoria Ojeaga Iyayi." Parekh and Jagne, *Postcolonial African Writers: A Bio-bibliographical Criticial Sourcebook.* [234]–40.

Omowoyela, Oyekan. "Festus Iyayi." Lindfors and Sander, *Twentieth-Century Caribbean and Black African Writers, Third Series* (*Dictionary of Literary Biography* 157). 113–122.

Edmond Jabès, 1912–1991

Web Site

"Edmond Jabès: A Poet from Egypt." *Bassatine News.* 1:10 (Dec. 1998). 25 July
   2005, http://www.geocities.com/RainForest/Vines/5855/jabes.htm.
   Two short biographical articles on Jabés, in French and English.

Biographies and Criticism

Ghazoul, Ferial J. "Jabès, Edmond." Gikandi, *Encyclopedia of African Literature.*
   248–49.

Bibliographies

Stoddard, Roger E. *Edmond Jabès in Bibliography: "du blanc des mots et du noir des
   signes": a record of the printed books.* Paris: Lettres Moderne Minard, 2001.
   A list of works, including reprints, by and about Jabès, from 1930 to 1999.

Interviews

Jabès, Edmond. *From the Desert to the Book: Edmond Jabès Dialogues with Martin
   Cohen* (trans. Pierre Joris). Barrytown, N. Y. : Station Hill, 1990.
   Jabès discusses his life, writing, and the Jewish dispersal in this collection of
interviews.

Dan(iel) Jacobson, 1929–

Web Sites

"Dan Jacobson." *Introducing South African Writers.* 25 July 2005, http://homepage
   .oniduo.pt/chacmalissimo/SAfrican/html/dan_jacobson.htm.

"Dan Jacobson." Contemporary Writers. Ed. and update unavailable. British Council.
   25 July 2005, http://www.contemporarywriters.com/authors/?p=auth232 &state
   =index%3Dj.
   Biography and a list of Jacobson's books and literary awards.

"Professor Dan Jacobson." *Contemporary Africa Database.* 25 July 2005, http://
   people.africadatabase.org/en/person/15924.html.

Biographies and Criticism

Fisher, Anne. "Dan Jacobson." Halio, *British Novelists since 1960* (*Dictionary of
   Literary Biography* 14). 427–33.

Gossage, Anne Fisher. "Dan Jacobson." Moseley, *British Novelists since 1960, Third
   Series* (*Dictionary of Literary Biography* 207). 149–55.

"Jacobson, Dan." Bryfonski and Harris, *Contemporary Literary Criticism.* 14:289–91.
   Excerpts from criticism published between 1955 and 1979.

"Jacobson, Dan." Riley, *Contemporary Literary Criticism.* 4:253–56.
   Excerpts from criticism published between 1968 and 1974.

Mosdell, Jenny. "Jacobson, Dan." Gikandi, *Encyclopedia of African Literature.* 250.

Roberts, Sheila. "Dan Jacobson." Cox, *African Writers.* 1:377–89.
   Biography, analyses of Jacobson's works, and a select bibliography of works by
and about him published between 1955 and 1993.

————. "Dan Jacobson." Scanlon, *South African Writers* (*Dictionary of Literary Biography* 225). 221–234.

Sousa Jamba, 1966–

Web Sites

"Sousa Jamba." *Contemporary Africa Database.* 27 Aug. 2004, http://people.africa database.org/people/data/person12791.html.

Biographies and Criticism

"Jamba, Sousa." *Contemporary Authors.* 134:265.

Paulin Joachim, 1931–

Web Sites

"Paulin Joachim." *Contemporary Africa Database.* 25 July 2005, http://www.africa expert.org/people/data/person2650.html.

"Paulin Joachim." *Francophone African Poets in English Translation.* 25 July 2005, http://web.uflib.ufl.edu/cm/africana/joachim.htm.
Includes excerpts from two poems by Joachim.

Biographies and Criticism

Manheim, James. "Paulin Joachim." Ashiya N. Henderson. Ed. Contemporary Black Biography. 34. Farmington Hill, Mich.: Gale, 2002. 80–82.

Lemuel A. Johnson, 1941–2002

Web Sites

Fuller, Lincoln. "Lemuel A. Johnson.." *Gefame* 1.1 (2004). U. of Michigan. 25 July 2005, http://www.hti.umich.edu/cgi/t/text/text-idx?c=gefame;cc=gefame;q1= dlps;rgn=main;view=text;idno=4761563.0001.101.
Biographical profile of Johnson.

"Professor Lemuel Johnson." *Contemporary Africa Database.* 25 July 2005, http:// people.africadatabase.org/people/data/person15296.html.

Biographies and Criticism

"Johnson, Lemuel." Gikankdi, *Encyclopedia of African Literature.* 251.

Elsa Joubert, 1922–

Web Sites

"Elsa Joubert." *Anglophone and Lusophone African Women's Writing.* 25 July 2005, http://www.ex.ac.uk/~ajsimoes/aflit/JoubertEN.html.

"Elsa Joubert." *Introducing South African Writers.* 25 July 2005, http://home page.oniduo.pt/chacmalissimo/SAfrican/html/elsa_joubert.htm.

"Elsa Joubert." *The Stellenbosch Writers.* Ed. Rosemarie Breuer. 6 June 2004. Stellenboschwriters.com. 25 July 2005, http://www.stellenboschwriters.com/ jouberte.html.

Lists works written and awards won by Joubert.

Biographies and Criticism

Jansen, Ena. "Joubert, Elsa." Gikandi, *Encyclopedia of African Literature.* 251–52.

"Joubert, Elsa." Robinson, *Modern Women Writers.* 2:476–81.
Excerpts from criticism published between 1979 and 1990.

Aminata Maïga Ka, 1940–

Web Sites

"Aminata Maiga Ka." *Contemporary Africa Database.* 25 July 2005, http://people
.africadatabase.org/en/person/15928.html.

"Rohkayatou Aminata Maiga Ka." *Reading Women Writers and African Literatures.*
25 July 2005, http://www.arts.uwa.edu.au/AFLIT/MaigaKaAminataEng.html.

Biographies and Criticism

"Aminata Maïga Ka." Stringer, *The Senegalese Novel by Women: Through Their Own
Eyes.* 120–122.
Brief descriptions of Ka's novels.

McNee, Lisa. "Maïga Kâ, Aminata." Gikandi, *Encyclopedia of African Literature.* 309.

Aubrey Kachingwe, 1926–

Web Sites

"Aubrey Kachingwe." *Contemporary Africa Database.* 25 July 2005, http://people
.africadatabase.org/people/data/person15929.html.

Biographies and Criticism

Msiska, Mpalive-Hangson. "Kachingwe, Aubrey." Gikandi, *Encyclopedia of African
Literature.* [252].

Alexis Kagame, 1912–1981

"Abbe Alexis Kagame." *Contemporary Africa Database.* 25 July 2005, http://people
.africadatabase.org/people/data/person2672.html.

Brockman, Nobert. "Kagame, Alexis." *Dictionary of African Christian Biography.*
Eds. Jonathan Bonk and Michèle Sigg. May 2004. Overseas Ministry Study
Center. 25 July 2005, http://www.gospelcom.net/dacb/stories/rwanda/
kagame_alexis.html.
Biography reproduced from *An African Biographical Dictionary* (1994).

Biographies and Criticism

Nzabatsinda, Anthére. "Kagame, Alexis (Abbé)." Gikandi, *Encyclopedia of African
Literature.* [253]–54.

Kama Sywor Kamanda, 1952–

Web Sites

"Kama Kamanda." *Congonline.* Ed. and update unavailable. 25 July 2005, http://
www.congonline.com/Culture/Litterature/KamaKaman.htm.
Biographical sketch, with a list of Kamanda's books and literary prizes. In
French

Kama Sywor Kamanda. Ed. Kama Kamanda. Update unavailable. Webplaza.lu.
25 July 2005, http://webplaza.pt.lu/kamanda/.
This official site of the author is graphics-intensive, with scanned images of
book covers, including translations, photos of the author, and links to audio clips. The
bilingual (English-French) headings on most pages are a useful feature of the site.

"Kama Sywor Kamanda." *Contemporary Africa Database.* 25 July 2005, http://www
.africaexpert.org/people/data/person6344.html.

Biographies and Criticism

Evenson, Brian. "Les Contes des Crepuscules." *World Literature Today.* 75.3/4
(Summer 2001):116.
Reviews Kamanda's collection of tales.

Dictionaries, Encyclopedias, and Handbooks

De Coninck, Marie-Claire. *Kama Kamanda au pays du conte.* Paris: L'Harmattan,
1993.

Sartin, Pierrette. *Kama Kamanda, poete de l'exil.* Paris, L'Harmattan, 1994.

Cheikh Hamidou Kane, 1928–

Web Sites

"Ambiguous Adventure by Cheikh Hamidou Kane." *The Complete Review.* Ed. and
update unavailable. 25 July 2005, http://www.complete-review.com/reviews/
senegal/kanech.htm.
Review of *Ambiguous Adventure* and links to author-related sites.

Gagiano, Anne. "Ambiguous Adventure." *LitNet: African Library.* 25 July 2005,
http://www.litnet.co.za/africanlib/kane.asp.
Overview of Kane's novel.

Johnson, Timothée. "A L'ecoute de Monsieur Cheikh Hamidou Kane, Ecrivain
sénégalais." *Togo-Contact Magazine.* 5 (Apr. 1997.) 25 July 2005, http://www
.tg.refer.org/togo_ct/med/journal/journal5/inter.htm.
Text of an interview with Kane.

Biographies and Criticism

Gikandi, Simon. "Kane, Cheikh Hamidou." Gikandi, *Encyclopedia of African
Literature.* 256.

"Kane, Cheikh Hamidou." Wordworks, *Modern Black Writers.* 369–70.
Excerpts from criticism published between 1961 and 1981.

Interview

Herzberger-Fofana, Pierrette. "Cheikh Hamidou Kane, 'L'aventure ambigüe."
    Ecrivains africains et identités culturelles. Tübungen: Stauffenburg Verlag,
    1989. 77–83.

Farida Karodia, 1942–

Web Sites

Fanchin, Gérard. "Writing in South Africa after the End of Apartheid. Literary
    Discourse and Transition: Farida Karodia's *Other Secrets.*" *Alizés.* 21 (Dec.
    2001). U. of Réunion. 25 July 2005, http://www2.univ-reunion.fr/~ageof/text/
    74c21e88-328.html.
    Analysis of *Other Secrets* and a list of Karodia's works.

"Farida Karodia." *Anglophone and Lusophone African Women's Writing.* 25 July
    2005, http://www.ex.ac.uk/~ajsimoes/aflit/KarodiaEN.html.

"Farida Karodia" *Contemporary Africa Database.* 25 July 2005, http://www
    .africaexpert.org/people/data/person2698.html.

Biographies and Criticism

Ibrahim, Huma. "Karodia, Farida." Gikandi, *Encyclopedia of African Literature.* 258.

"Karodia, Farida." *Contemporary Authors.* 168:162–63.

Yacine Kateb (Kateb Yacine), 1929–1989

Web Sites

"Kateb Yacine." *Books and Writers.* 25 July 2005, http://www.kirjasto.sci.fi/kateb
    .htm.

"Kateb Yacine." *Contemporary Africa Database.* 25 July 2005, http://www.africa
    expert.org/people/data/person13274.html.

"Kateb Yacine." *LIMAG: Littératures du Maghreb.* 25 July 2005, http://www.limag
    .refer.org/Volumes/Kateb.htm.

"Kateb Yacine." *Theatre-contemporain.* Ed. Laurent Froment. Update unavailable.
    25 July 2005, http://www.theatre-contemporain.net/auteurs/yacine/default.asp.
    Brief biography and a list of Yacine's publications, in French.

Biographies and Criticism

Bonn, Charles (trans. John Fletcher). "Kateb Yacine." Cox, *African Writers.* 1:391–400.
    Biography, analyses of Yacine's works, and select bibliography of works by and
    about him published between 1956 and 1993.

Hayes, Jarrod. "Kateb, Yacine." Gikandi, *Encyclopedia of African Literature.* 259–60.

Serrano, Richard. "Nedjma." Moss and Valestuk, *African Literature and Its Times_
    (World Literature and Its Times* 2). 289–96.

Dictionaries, Encyclopedias, and Handbooks

Arnaud, Jacqueline. *La littérature maghrébin de langue française* 2: *Le cas de Kateb
    Yacine.* [Paris]: Publisud, 1986.

Sahli, Kamal. *The Politics and Aesthetics of Kateb Yacine: From Fracophone Literature to Popular Theatre in Algeria and Outside.* Lewiston, N. Y.: Peter Lang, 1999.

Legson Didimu Kayira, 1940–

Web Sites

"Legson Kayira." *Contemporary Africa Database.* 25 July 2005, http://www.africa expert.org/people/data/person3910.html.

Biographies and Criticism

"Kayira, Legson (Didimu)." Metzger et al, *Black Writers.* Detroit: Gale, 1989. 316–17.

Roscoe, Adrian. "Kayira, Legson." Benson and Conolly, *Encyclopedia of Post-colonial Literatures in English.* 1:759.

Msiska, Mpalive-Hangson. "Kayira, Legson." Gikandi, *Encyclopedia of African Literature.* 261.

Anne Kellas, 1951–

Web Sites

"Anne Kellas." *Poetpage.* Ed. and update unavailable. Women Tasmania. 25 July 2005, http://www.women.tas.gov.au/poetry/kellas/kellas.html.
Text of a poem and link to Kellas' biography.

"Anne Kellas." *The Write Stuff: Showcase of Tasmanian Poetry.* Eds. Anne Kellas and Giles Hugo. 15 June 2004. 25 July 2005, http://www.the-write-stuff.com.au/ archives/vol-3/index.html.
Links to many Kellas poems and reviews of her work.

"Three Poems by Anne Kellas." *Eclectica.* 6.4 (Oct./Nov. 2002). 25 July 2005 http:// www.eclectica.org/v6n4/kellas.html.
Text of "Parable and a Rose Tree," "Your Planet Moon," and "From the City of Alice."

Keorapetse William Kgositsile, 1938–

Web Sites

"Keorapetse Kgositsile." *Introducing South African Writers.* 25 July 2005, http:// homepage.oniduo.pt/chacmalissimo/SAfrican/html/keorapetse_kgositsile.htm.

"Keorapetse Kgositsile." *South Africa: Poetry International Web.* Ed. and update unavailable. Poetry International Web. 25 July 2005, http://southafrica. poetryinternational.org/cwolk/view/21495.
Biography, with links to poems and articles.

"Keorapetse William (Willie) Kgositsile." *Contemporary Africa Database.* 25 July 2005, http://people.africadatabase.org/people/data/person2723.html.

Robertson, Heather. "A Poet for the People." *Sunday Times.* 19 May 2002. Sundaytimes.co.za. 25 July 2005, http://www.suntimes.co.za/2002/05/19/ lifestyle/life04.asp.
Discusses Kgositsile's views on poetry and his experiences in exile.

Biographies and Criticism

Gikandi, Simon. "Kgositsile, William Keorapetse." Gikandi, *Encyclopedia of African Literature*. 264.

"Kgositsile, Keorapetse (William)." Malinowski, *Black Writers*. Detroit: Gale, 1994. 346–47.

Mohamed Khair-Eddine, 1941–1995

Web Sites

Bijdiguen, Loubna. "Mohammed Khair-Eddine's *Legend and Life of Agoun'chich*." 12 May 2001. *Contemporary Postcolonial and Postimperial Literature in English*. 18 June 2004, http://www.postcolonialweb.org/landow/post/poldiscourse/casablanca/bijdiguen2.html.
Analysis of the use of oral tradition in Khaïr-Eddine's novel.

"Mohammed Khair-Eddine." *Bibliomonde*. Ed. and update unavailable. Bibliomonde.com. 25 July 2005, http://www.bibliomonde.com/pages/fiche-auteur.php3?id_auteur=92.
Brief biography and bibliography, in French.

Kusserow, Mourad. "Mohammed Khair-Eddine: An Intimate Look at Berber Culture." Dialogue with the Islamic World. 5 Oct. 2004. Quantara.de. 25 July 2005, http://www.qantara.de/webcom/show_article.php/_c-564/_nr-28/_p-1/i.html.
A discussion of the author and his writing.

Biographies and Criticism

Abdel-Jaouad, Hédi. "Khaïr-Eddine, Mohammed." Gikandi, *Encyclopedia of African Literature*. 265.

Rogers, Lynne Dumont. "Mohammed Khaïr-Eddine." Parekh and Jagne, *Postcolonial African Writers: A Bio-bibliographical Criticial Sourcebook*. [253]–36.

Ungulani Khosa, 1957–

Web Sites

"Ungulani ba ka Khosa." *Mozambican Literature in Translation*. Ed. Luis R. Mitras. Update unavailable. 25 July 2005, http://homepage.oniduo.pt/chacmalissimo/Mozambique/html/ungulani_ba_ka_khosa.html.
Biographical sketch and a short list of references.

"Ungulani ba ka Khosa." *MaderaZinco* (Aug. 2002). 18 June 2004, http://www.maderazinco.tropical.co.mz/entrevista/ungula.htm.
Transcript of an interview, in Portuguese.

Biographies and Criticism

"Ungulani Ba Ka Khosa: A Rebellious Voice of Mozambican Regeneration." Niyi Afolabi, *Golden Cage: Regeneration in Lusophone African Literature and Culture*. Trenton, N. J.: Africa World Press, 2001. [169]–225.
Uses two works by Ba Ka Khosa to critically analyze his narrative style and evaluate his contribution to contemporary Mozambican literature.

Banks, Jared. "Ungulani Ba Ka Khosa." Parekh and Jagne, *Postcolonial African Writers: A Bio-bibliographical Criticial Sourcebook*. [257] –61.

Leonard Kibera, 1942–1983

Web Sites

"Leonard Kibera." *Contemporary Africa Database*. 25 July 2005, http://people .africadatabase.org/people/data/person15931.html.

Biographies and Criticism

Gikandi, Simon. "Kibera, Leonard." Gikandi, *Encyclopedia of African Literature*. 268.

Gititi, Gitahi. "Kibera, Leonard N." Benson and Conolly, *Encyclopedia of Post-colonial Literatures in English*. 1:769–70.

Barbara Kimenye, 1930 (1939; 1940)–

Web Sites

"Barbara Kimenye." *Contemporary Africa Database*. 25 July 2005, http://people .africadatabase.org/people/data/person15933.html.

"Kimenye, Barbara. *African Children's Literature*. 25 July 2005, http://web.uflib.ufl .edu/cm/africana/kimenye.htm.

Biographies and Criticism

Bardolph, J. "Kimenye, Barbara." Benson and Conolly, *Encyclopedia of Post-colonial Literatures in English*. 1:771.

"Kimenye, Barbara. *Contemporary Authors*. 101:256.

Ahmadou Kourouma, 1923–2003

Web Sites

"Ahmadou Kourouma." *Contemporary Africa Database*. 25 July 2005, http://www .africaexpert.org/people/data/person2788.html.

"Ahmadou Kourouma." *The Complete Review*. Ed. and update unavailable. 25 July 2005, http://www.complete-review.com/authors/kourouma.htm. Includes reviews of Kourouma's works and related Web links.

Daoust, Philip. "Things Fall Apart." *Guardian Books*. 15 Mar. 2003. Guardian Unlimited. 25 July 2005, http://books.guardian.co.uk/reviews/generalfiction/ 0%2C6121%2C914413%2C00.html. Review of *Waiting for the Wild Beasts to Vote* (trans. Frank Wynne).

Lefort, René and Mauro Rosi. "Ahmadu Kourouma: An African Novelist's Inside Story." *The Courier*. (Mar. 1999). UNESCO. 25 July 2005, http://www.unesco .org/courier/1999_03/uk/dires/txt1.htm. Transcript of an interview.

Biographies and Criticism

"Kourouma, Ahmadou." Wordworks, *Modern Black Writers*. 389–94. Excerpts from criticism published between 1976 and 1992.

Ouédraogo, Jean. "Kourouma, Ahmadou." Gikandi, *Encyclopedia of African Literature*. 270–71.

Interview

Gray, Stephen. "Ahmadou Kourouma." *Research in African Literatures*. 32.1 (2001): [122] –123.
  Transcript of a 2000 interview.

Mazisi (Raymond) (KaMdabuli) Kunene, 1930–

Web Sites

"Mazisi Kunene." *Contemporary Africa Database*. 25 July 2005, http://www.africa expert.org/people/data/person3911.html.

Ndaba, Sandile C. "Visionary Commitment in Mazisi Kunene's *Ancestors and the Sacred Mountain.*" *Alternation: International Journal for the Study of Southern African Literature and Languages*. 6.1 (1999). 25 July 2005, http://singh .reshma.tripod.com/alternation/alternation6_1/05SNDABA.htm.
  Thematic study of Kunene's work.

"The Ancestors and The Sacred Mountain." *LitNet*. 25 July 2005, http://www.litnet .co.za/africanlib/kunene.asp.

Biographies and Criticsm

"Kunene, Mazisi." Wordworks, *Modern Black Writers*. 394–99.
  Excerpts from criticism published between 1971 and 1996.

Masilela, Ntongela. "Kunene, Mazisi." Gikandi, *Encyclopedia of African Literature*. 273.

Mathabela, Francis. "Mazisi Kunene." Lindfors and Sander, *Twentieth-Century Caribbean and Black African Writers, First Series* (*Dictionary of Literary Biography* 117). 204–11.

"Mazisi Kunene." Giroux et al., *Contemporary Literary Criticism*. 85. Detroit: Gale, 1995. 159–88.
  Excerpts from criticism on Kunene from 1975 to1987, with a brief
bibliography.

Interview

"Mazisi Kunene." Wilkinson, *Talking With African Writers*. 136–45.
  Text of a 1986 interview.

Ellen Kate Kuzwayo, 1914–

Web Sites

"Ellen Kuzwayo." *Anglophone and Lusophone Women's Writing*. 25 July 2005, http:// www.ex.ac.uk/~ajsimoes/aflit/KuzwayoEN.html.

"Ellen Kuzwayo." *Contemporary Africa Database*. 25 July 2005, http://people.africa database.org/people/data/person15927.html.

"Ellen Kuzwayo." *Writers Talk: Ideas of Our Time*. 25 July 2005, http://www.roland-collection.com/rolandcollection/literature/101/W23.htm.

Biographies and Criticism

Aegerter, Lindsay Pentolfe. "Ellen Kuzwayo." Parekh and Jagne, *Postcolonial African Writers: A Bio-bibliographical Criticial Sourcebook.* [265]–67.

Daymond, M. J. "Kuzwayo, Ellen Kate." Benson and Conolly, *Encyclopedia of Postcolonial Literatures in English.* 1:790.

Ibrahim, Huma. "Kuzwayo, Ellen." Gikandi, *Encyclopedia of African Literature.* 273–74.

Interview

"Ellen Kuzwayo." James, *In Their Own Words.* 53–7.
    Text of a 1985 interview.

Koffi Kwahulé, 1956–

Web Sites

Gardner, Lyn. "Bintou." *Guardian Arts.* 31 July 2002. Guardian Unlimited. 25 July 2005, http://www.guardian.co.uk/arts/critic/review/0,1169,766870,00.html. Synopsis and review of a London production of Kwahulé's play.

"Koffi Kwahulé." *Contemporary Africa Database.* 25 July 2005, http://people.africa database.org/people/data/person6346.html.

Biographies and Criticism

King, Adele. "Village fou ou Les deconnards." *World Literature Today.* 75.2 (Spring 2001): 308.
    Review of Kwahule's play.

Goretti Kyomuhendo, 1965–

Web Sites

Kyomuhendo, Goretti. "I Watch You My Sister." *African Women's Voices.* Ed. and update unavailable. Women's WORLD. 25 July 2005, http://www.wworld.org/programs/regions/africa/goretti_kyomuhendo.htm.
    Text of a short story by Kyomuhendo

Matsamura, Evelyn Kiapi. "The Power of the Pen." *International Press Service News Agency: Arts Weekly/Books-Uganda.* 25 Jan. 2003. Ipsnews.net. 21 June 2004, http://www.ipsnews.net/interna.asp?idnews=15294.
    Article tracing the development of Kyomuhendo's writing.

Biographies and Criticsm

Nazareth, Peter. "Secrets No More." *World Literature Today.* 74.2 (Spring 2000):351.
    Review of *Secrets No More.*

Interview

Gray, Stephen. "Goretti Kyomuhendo." *Research in African Literatures.* 32.1 (2001):123–25.
    Transcript of a 2000 interview.

(Justin) Alex(ander) La Guma, 1925–1985

Web Sites

"Alex La Guma." *African Writers: Voices of Change.* 25 July 2005, http://web.uflib
    .ufl.edu/cm/africana/laguma.htm.

"Alex La Guma." *Contemporary Africa Database.* 25 July 2005, http://people.africa
    database.org/en/person/3912.html.

"Alex la Guma." *Introducing South African Writers.* 25 July 2005, http://homepage
    .oniduo.pt/chacmalissimo/SAfrican/html/alex_la_guma.htm.

Biographies and Criticism

Abrahams, Cecil A. "Alex La Guma." Lindfors and Sander, *Twentieth-Century
    Caribbean and Black African Writers, First Series* (*Dictionary of Literary
    Biography* 117). 211–27.

———. "Alex La Guma: Defiance and Resistance." Ross, *International Literature in
    English.* 193–204.
    Biocriticism, with a short annotated bibliography.

Barrat, Harold. "Alex La Guma." Parekh and Jagne, *Postcolonial African Writers: A
    Bio-bibliographical Criticial Sourcebook.* [268]–74.

Booker, M. Keith. "Alex La Guma." Schellinger, *Encyclopedia of the Novel.* 3:685–86.

Colmer, Rosemary. "Alex La Guma." Cox, *African Writers.* 1:401—11.
    Biography, with analyses of La Guma's works, and a select bibliography of
wotks by and about him published between 1962 and 1991.

Filed, Roger. "La Guma, Alex." Gikandi, *Encyclopedia of African Literature.* [275] –78.

Jung, Jeff. "A Walk in the Night." Moss and Valestuk, *African Literature and Its
    Times* (*World Literature and Its Times* 2). 453–60.

"La Guma, Alex." Wordworks, *Modern Black Writers.* 404–7.
    Excerpts from criticism published between 1980 and 1992.

"La Guma, (Justin) Alex(ander)." Gunton, *Contemporary Literary Criticism.* 19:272–77.
    Excerpts from criticism published between 1965 and 1980.

Scanlon, Paul A. "Alex La Guma." Scanlon, *South African Writers* (*Dictionary of
    Literary Biography* 225). 235–46.

van der Vlies, Andrew. "Alex La Guma." Parini, *World Writers in English.* 1: 249–67.

Dictionaries, Encyclopedias, and Handbooks

Balutansky, Kathleen M. *The Novels of Alex La Guma: Representation of a Political
    Conflict.* Washington DC: Three Continents Press, 1990.

Duro Ladipo, 1931–1978

"Duro Ladipo." *Contemporary Africa Database.* 25 July 2005, http://people.africa
    database.org/people/data/person15906.html.

"Duro Ladipo (late)." *Nigeria-Arts.Net.* Eds. Andrew Frankel et al. Update
    unavailable. Rakumi Arts International. 25 July 2005, http://www.nigeria-arts
    .net/Performance/Theatre/Duro_Ladipo/.
    Brief biography.

Biographies and Criticism

Adéeko, Adéléké. "Ladipo, Duro." Gikandi, *Encyclopedia of African Literature.* 278.

Killam G. D. "Ladipo, Duro." Benson and Conolly, *Encyclopedia of Post-colonial Literatures in English.* 1:822.

Kojo B(ernard) Laing, 1946–

Web Sites

"B. Kojo Laing." *Contemporary Africa Database.* 25 July 2005, http://people.africa database.org/en/person/11552.html.

Biographies and Criticism

Dakubu, M. E. Kropp. "Kojo Laing." Lindfors and Sander, *Twentieth-Century Caribbean and Black African Writers, Third Series* (*Dictionary of Literary Biography* 157). 140–49.

"Laing, Kojo." Wordworks, *Modern Black Writers.* 407–11.
Excerpts from criticism published between 1993 and 1997.

Osei-Nyame, Kwadwo. "Laing, Bernard Kojo." Gikandi, *Encyclopedia of African Literature.* 279–80.

Interview

Maja-Pearce, Adewale. "Interview with Kojo Laing." *Wasafiri.* 6/7 (1987):27–9.

Barnabé Laye, 1941–

Web Sites

"Barnabé Laye." *Le Bénin Littéraire: 1980–1999.* Ed. Simon Bouisset. Update unavailable. Campus numérique francophone de Cotonou. 25 July 2005, http:// www.er.uqam.ca/nobel/r16130/auteur/laleye/index.htm.
Biographical sketch, with a list of Laye's publications.

"Barnabé Laye." *Le site de Dieudonne Gnammankou.* Ed. Dieudonne Gnammankou. Update unavailable. Gnammankou.com. 25 July 2005, http://www .gnammankou.com/litterature_laye.htm.
Biographical sketch, with a short description of his works.

Biographies and Criticism

Gabara, Rachel. "Laye, Bernabé." Gikandi, *Encyclopedia of African Literature.* 283.

Camara Laye (Laye Camara), 1928–1980

Web Sites

"Camara Laye." *Books and Writers.* 25 July 2005, http://www.kirjasto.sci.fi/laye.htm.

"Camara Laye." *Contemporary Africa Database.* 25 July 2005, http://www.africa expert.org/people/data/person2832.html.

Biographies and Criticism

Badders, Anne-Lancaster. "The Dark Child." Moss and Valestuk, *African Literature and Its Times* (*World Literature and Its Times* 2). 67–75.

"Camara Laye." Draper, *Black Literature Criticism.* 2:1251–60.
 Biography, list of major works, excerpts of criticism from 1967 to 1980, and an annotated bibliography.

"Camara Laye." Marowski et al., *Contemporary Literary Criticism.* 38:284–92.
 Excerpts from criticism on Laye from 1980 to 1984.

"Camara Laye." Wordworks, *Modern Black Writers.* 147–51.
 Excerpts from criticism published between 1954 and 1994.

Conteh-Morgan, John D. "Camara Laye."Cox, *African Writers.* 1:413–25.
 Biography, with analyses of Laye's major works, and a select bibliography of primary texts and criticism published between 1953 and 1994.

Evenson, Brian and David Beus. "Camara Laye." Parekh and Jagne, *Postcolonial African Writers: A Bio-bibliographical Criticial Sourcebook.* [275]–81.

King, Adele. "Radiance of the King." Schellinger, *Encyclopedia of the Novel.* 3:1070–71.

Dictionaries, Encyclopedias, and Handbooks

Azodo, Ada Uzoamaka. *L'Imaginaire dans les romans de Camara Laye.* New York: Peter Lang, 1993.

Doris May Lessing (Jane Somers), 1919–

Web Sites

"Audio Interviews: Doris Lessing." *Bookshelf.* 14 Jan. 1987. BBC Four. 25 July 2005, http://www.bbc.co.uk/bbcfour/audiointerviews/profilepages/lessingd1.shtml.
 Audioclips of Lessing discussing her writing and their reception.

"Doris Lessing." *Contemporary Writers.* 25 July 2005, http://www.contemporary writers.com/authors/?p=auth60&state=index%3Dl.
 Biography, with a bibliography and a list of Lessing's literary awards.

Doris Lessing: A Retrospective. Ed. Jan Hanford. Update unavailable. Redmood.com. 25 July 2005, http://lessing.redmood.com/.
 A user-friendly site that offers extensive information on Lessing's works, variously arranged by genre, publisher, edition, and publication year. Also includes audio and video clips of interviews and readings, a biography, and a bibliography of primary and secondary works covering 1948 to 2002.

"Doris (May) Lessing." *Books and Writers.* 25 July 2005, http://www.kirjasto.sci.fi/dlessing.htm.

"Featured Author: Doris Lessing." *New York Times on the Web.* Ed and update unavailable. Nytimes.com. 25 July 2005, http://www.nytimes.com/books/99/01/10/specials/lessing.html.
 Links to full text reviews of and articles by and about Lessing published in the New York Times between 1950 and 1999. Also includes audio clips of conversations with her and readings by her.

Garner, Dwight. "A Notorious Life." *Salon.* 11 Nov. 1997. Salon.com. 25 July 2005, http://www.salon.com/books/feature/1997/11/cov_si_11lessing.html.

Transcript of an interview.

Mercer, Trudy. "The Convictions of a Promise: Doris Lessing's *Memoirs of a Survivor.*" *Trudy Mercer's Eclectic Edition.* 10 Oct. 2002. Drizzle.com. 25 July 2005, http://www.drizzle.com/~tmercer/write/lessing/memoirs-survivor1.shtml. Critical analysis of Lessing's novel.

Biographies and Criticism

Barnes, Fiona R. "Doris Lessing." Baldwin, *British Short-Fiction Writers, 1954–1980* (*Dictionary of Literary Biography* 139). 159–72.

"Doris Lessing." Riley et al., *Contemporary Literary Criticism.* 94:250–96.
Excerpts from criticism on Lessing from 1988 to 1995 and an annotated bibliography.

"Doris (May) Lessing." Harris et al., *Short Story Criticism.* 6:184–221.
Excerpts from criticism on Lessing from 1952 to 1989 and an annotated bibliography.

"Lessing, Doris." Robinson, *Modern Women Writers.* 2:700–21.
Excerpts from criticism published between 1950 and 1991.

Marchino, Lois A. "Doris Lessing: Maps of New Worlds." Ross, *International Literature in English.* 393–403.
Biocriticism, with an annotated bibliography.

Renée, Diane. Moss, *British and Irish Literature and Its Times: The Victorian Era to the Present, 1837 –.* (*World Literature and Its Times* 4). 141–50.

Oehling, Rick. Doris Lessing." Fallon et al., *A Reader's Companion to the Short Story in English.* [241] –51.
Overview of critical studies, an analysis of Lessing's short stories, and a selected bibliography of primary and secondary works.

Sage, Lorna. "Doris Lessing." Cox, *African Writers.* 1:427–49.
Biography, with analyses of Lessing's writings, and a select bibliography of works by and about her published between 1950 and 1996.

Schlueter, Paul. "Doris Lessing." Oldsey, *British Novelists, 1930–1959, Part 1* (*Dictionary of Literary Biography* 15). 274–97.

Sizemore, Christine W. "Doris Lessing." Parekh and Jagne, *Postcolonial African Writers: A Bio-bibliographical Criticial Sourcebook.* [283] –95.

Valestuk, Lorraine. "African Laughter: Four Visits to Zimbabwe." Moss and Valestuk, *African Literature and Its Times* (*World Literature and Its Times* 2). 1–11.

Journals

Doris Lessing Studies (formerly *Doris Lessing Newsletter* 1976–2001). Baltimore County, MD: Doris Lessing Soc., 2001–

Bibliographies

Baldwin, Dean R., and Gregory L. Morris. "Doris Lessing." *The Short Story in English: Britain and North America: An Annotated Bibliography.* 209–11.

Descriptions of eight biographical and critical studies on Lessing published between 1965 and 1990.

Seligman, Dee. Doris Lessing: An Annotated Bibliography of Criticism. Westport: Greenwood, 1981.

Muthoni Likimani, 1926? 1940?–

Web Sites

"Muthoni Likimani." *Contemporary Africa Database*. 25 July 2005, http://people .africadatabase.org/en/person/15913.html.

Biographies and Criticism

Beahan, Maxine. "Muthoni Likimani." Parekh and Jagne, *Postcolonial African Writers: A Bio-bibliographical Critical Sourcebook.* [298]–99.

Outa, Georege Odera. "Likimani, Muthoni." Gikandi, *Encyclopedia of African Literature.* 287–88.

Interview

"Muthoni Likimani." James, *In Their Own Words.* 59–62.
    Text of a 1986 interview.

Werewere Liking, 1950–

Web Sites

"Werewere Liking." *Contemporary Africa Database.* 25 July 2005, http://people .africadatabase.org/en/person/6348.html.

"Werewere Liking: An Overview." *Contemporary Postcolonial and Postimperial Literature in English.* 25 July 2005, http://www.scholars.nus.edu.sg/landow/ post/africa/cameroon/liking/.

"Werewere Liking Gnepo." *Reading Women Writers and African Literatures.* 25 July 2005, http://www.arts.uwa.edu.au/AFLIT/WerewereLiking.html.

Biographies and Criticism

"Werewere Liking: *La Puissance d'Um.*" Conteh-Morgan, *Theatre and Drama in Francophone Africa.* 211–20.
    Biographical overview and analysis of *La Puissance d'Um.*

Ekotto, Frieda. "Liking, Werewere." Gikandi, *Encyclopedia of African Literature.* 288–89.

"Liking, Werewere." Wordworks, *Modern Black Writers.* 418–22.
    Excerpts from criticism published between 1984 and 1996.

Volet, Jean-Marie. "Werewere Liking." Serafin, *Encyclopedia of African Literature.* 3: 483–84.

Interview

Mielly, Michelle. "The Aesthetics of Necessity: An Interview with Werewere Liking." *World Literature Today* (Jul–Sept. 2003). [52] –56.

Douglas (James) Livingstone, 1932–1996

Web Sites

"Douglas Livingstone." *Contemporary Africa Database.* 25 July 2005, http://people
.africadatabase.org/people/profiles/profilesforperson15915.html.

"Douglas Livingstone." *Introducing South African Writers.* 25 July 2005, http://home
page.oniduo.pt/chacmalissimo/SAfrican/html/douglas_livingstone.htm.

Biographies and Criticism

Chapman, Michael. "Livinstone, Douglas James." Benson and Conolly, *Encyclopedia
of Post-colonial Literatures in English.* 1:913–16.

Haresnape, Geoffrey. "Douglas Livingstone." Scanlon, *South African Writers*
(*Dictionary of Literary Biography* 225). 247–56.

Taban lo Liyong, 1939–

Web Sites

Raditlhalo, Sam. "Interview: Taban lo Liyong." *Chimurenga.* (Dec. 2002). 25 July
2005, http://www.ru.ac.za/institutes/isea/newcoin/docs/97/i97june.htm.
Reprint of a 1997 interview.

"Taban lo Liyong." *Contemporary Africa Database.* 25 July 2005, http://people.africa
database.org/en/person/2843.html.

"Taban lo Liyong." *Postcolonial African Literatures in English.* 25 July 2005, http://
www.fb10.uni-bremen.de/anglistik/kerkhoff/AfricanLit/Taban.htm.

Biographies and Criticism

Bardolph, J. "Liyong, Taban Lo." Benson and Conolly, *Encyclopedia of Post-colonial
Literatures in English.* 1:916.

Nazareth, Peter. "Taban lo Liyong." Lindfors and Sander, *Twentieth-Century
Caribbean and Black African Writers, Second Series* (*Dictionary of Literary
Biography* 125). 327–31.

"Taban lo Liyong." Wordworks, *Modern Black Writers.* 709–14.
Excerpts from criticism published between 1970 and 1997.

Henri (Marie-Joesph) Lopes, 1937–

Web Sites

Brown, Peter. "L'Enfant chez Henri Lopes: 'Il n'y a pas d'orphelin en Afrique.'"
Mots Pluriels. 22 (Sept. 2002). 25 July 2005, http://www.arts.uwa.edu.au/
MotsPluriels/MP2202pb.html.
Explores the trope of the child in Lopès's writing.

"Henri Lopès." *Contemporary Africa Database.* 25 July 2005, http://people.africa
database.org/en/person/2848.html.

Le Lys et le Flamboyant. Mots Pluriels 7 (1998). 25 July 2005, http://www.arts.uwa
.edu.au/MotsPluriels/MP798jvindex.html.

Though the site may be annoying to navigate because of the many frames, it is useful for the summary of and critical article on Lopès' novel. Also includes an interview with him and a few links to relevant Web sites.

"Tribaliks." *LitNet.* 25 July 2005, http://www.litnet.co.za/africanlib/09tribaliks.asp.

Biographies and Criticism

Kemedjio, Cilas. "Lopes, Henri." Gikandi, *Encyclopedia of African Literature.* 299.

"Lopes, Henri." Wordworks, *Modern Black Writers.* 422–25.
    Excerpts from criticism published between 1978 and 1998.

Alain Mabanckou, 1966–

Web Sites

Herzberger-Fofana, Pierette. "A L'écoute de Alain Mabanckou." *Mots Pluriels.* 12 (Dec. 1999). 25 July 2005, http://www.arts.uwa.edu.au/MotsPluriels/MP1299 mabanckou.html.
    Transcript of an interview.

Biographies and Criticism

Ekotto, Frieda. "Mabanckou, Alain." Gikandi, *Encyclopedia of African Literature.* [302] –3.

Marjorie Oludhe Macgoye, 1928–

Web Sites

McGonicle, Thomas. "Independence Day." *Village Voice Literary Supplement* (Mar. 2001). 25 July 2005, http://www.villagevoice.com/vls/173/mcgonigle.shtml.
    Review of U. S. editions of *Coming to Birth* and *The Present Moment.*

Biographies and Criticism

Ojwang, Dan Odhiambo. "Macgoye (Oludhe-Macgoye), Marjorie Oludhe." Gikandi, *Encyclopedia of African Literature.* 303–04.

"Oludhe-Macgoye, Marjorie." *Contemporary Authors.* 133:301–2.

Yulisa Amadu (Pat) Maddy, 1936–

Web Sites

"Yulisa Amadu Maddy." *Contemporary Africa Database.* 25 July 2005, http://www .africaexpert.org/people/data/person14016.html.

Biographies and Criticism

Dunton, Chris. "Maddy, Yulisa Amadu." Benson and Conolly, *Encyclopedia of Post-colonial Litertaures in English.* 2:950–51

Gikandi, Simon. "Maddy, Yulisa Amadu (Pat)." Gikandi, *Encyclopedia of African Literature.* 304–5.

King, Bruce. "Maddy, Yulisa Amadu." Berney, *Contemporary Dramatists.* 408–10.

Sindiwe Magona, 1943–

Web Sites

Hewett, Heather. "Out of South Africa's Pain." *The Christian Science Monitor* (7 Oct. 1999). 25 July 2005, http://csmonitor.com/cgi-bin/durableRedirect.pl?/durable/1999/10/07/p20s1.htm.
Provides background information and the context that engendered Magona's writing of *Mother to Mother.*

"Sindiwe Magona." *African Literature in English: Five Women Writers.* 25 July 2005, http://www.fb10.uni-bremen.de/anglistik/kerkhoff/AfrWomenWriters/Magona/Magona.html.

"Sindiwe Magona." *Anglophone and Lusophone African Women's Writing.* 25 July 2005, http://www.ex.ac.uk/~ajsimoes/aflit/MagonaEN.html.

"Sindiwe Magona." *Contemporary Africa Database.* 25 July 2005, http://people.africadatabase.org/people/data/person12880.html.

Biographies and Criticism

"Magona, Sindiwe." *Contemporary Authors.* 170:275–6.

Samuelson, Meg. "Magona, Sindiwe." Gikandi, *Encyclopedia of African Literature.* 305.

Dictionaries, Handbooks, and Encyclopedias

Koyana, Siphokazi. Ed. *Sindiwe Magona: The First Decade.* Scottsville, South Africa: U. of KwaZulu-Natal Press, 2004.
Critical essays on Magona's works and transcripts of four interviews

Interviews

Atwell, David and Barbara Harlow. "Interview with Sindiwe Magona." *Modern Fiction Studies.* 46.1 (Spring 2000): 282–295.
Transcript of a 1999 interview.

Naguib Mahfouz (Najib Mafuz), 1911–

Web Sites

"Naguib Mahfouz." *Arab Gateway.* Ed. Brian Whitaker. 14 July 2003. Al-bab.com. 25 July 2005, http://www.al-bab.com/arab/literature/mahfouz.htm.
A cleanly arranged site that offers links to biographies of Mahfouz, a list of English translations of his works, and criticism on his writing.

"Naguib Mahfouz." *Books and Writers.* 25 July 2005, http://www.kirjasto.sci.fi/mahfouz.htm.

"Naguib Mahfouz: Biased to Grassroots." *Information on Egypt.* Ed. and update unavailable. Egyptian State Information Service. 29 June 2004, http://www.sis.gov.eg/egyptinf/culture/html/nmahfouz.htm.
Provides bio-critical information on Mahfuz and his works.

"Naguib Mahfouz." *World Literature Website.* Ed. Fidel Fajardo-Acosta. 8 Nov. 2003 unavailable. Fajardo-acosta.com. 29 June 2004, http://fajardo-acosta.com/worldlit/mahfouz/.

Developed by a Creighton University professor, this basic site provides a biographical chronology, synopses of Mahfouz's main works, and some historical and cultural contexts to them.

"Naguib Mahfouz at 90." *Al-Ahram Weekly Online* (13–19 Dec. 2001). 29 June 2004, http://weekly.ahram.org.eg/2001/564/special.htm.
    The collection of eight full text articles about Mahfouz and his works listed on this sites provide great insights into his views on writing, politics, theatre, and cinema. Also includes excerpts from four of his works.

"Naguib Mahfouz–Biography." *Nobel e-Museum.* 12 Apr. 2005. The Nobel Foundation. 25 July 2005, http://www.nobel.se/literature/laureates/1988/mahfouz-bio.html.
    Biography and links to the full text of the prize announcement, the presentation speech, Mahfouz's Nobel Lecture, and an article about him.

Proyect, Louis. "Naguib Mahfouz, 'Midaq Alley.'" *Swans* (14 Apr. 2003). 25 July 2005, http://www.swans.com/library/art9/lproy02.html.
    Review of *Midaq Alley.*

Rose, Mark. "Early Pharoanic Tales of Naguib Mahfouz." *Archaeology* (28 Jan. 2003). 29 June 2004, http://www.archaeology.org/online/features/mahfouz/.
    Review of *Voices from the Other World* and internal links to an interview with Mahfouz's friend and translator, Robert Stock.

Said, Edward. "Naguib Mahfouz and the Cruelty of Memory." *CounterPunch* (16 Dec. 2001). 25 July 2005, http://www.counterpunch.org/mahfouz.html.
    A critical analysis of Mahfouz and his writing.

Biographies and Criticism

Allen, Roger. "Mahfuz, Najib (Naguib Mahfouz)." Gikandi, *Encyclopedia of African Literature.* 306–9.

———. "Najib Mahfuz." Cox, *African Writers.* 2: 451–65.
    Biography, analyses of Mahfuz's works, and a select bibliography of works by and about him published between 1932 and 1996.

———. "Najib Mahfuz: Nobel Laureate in Literature, 1988." Genova, *Companion to Contemporary World Literature.* 1:177–82.
    Tribute to Mahfuz after winning the Nobel Prize.

DeYoung, Terri. "Midaqq Alley." Moss and Valestuk, *African Literature and Its Times* (*World Literature and Its Times* 2). 259–68.

Hutchins, William M. "Mahfuz, Nagib." Chevalier, *Contemporary World Writers.* 337–39.

"Naguib Mahfouz." Hunter et al., *Contemporary Literary Criticism.* 153:229–375.
    Criticism on Mahfouz published between 1989 and 2001.

Dictionaries, Handbooks, and Encyclopedias

El-Enany, Rasheed. *Naguib Mahfouz: The Pursuit of Meaning.* New York: Routledge, 1993.

Menahem, Wilson. *Najib Mahfuz; The Novelist-Philosopher of Cairo.* New York: St. Martin's, 1998.

Moosa, Matti. *The Early Novels of Naguib Mahfouz: Images of Modern Egypt.* Gainesville, Fla.: U. of Florida, 2003.

Interviews

Salamawy, Mohamed. *Naguib Mafouz at Sidi Gaber: Reflections of a Nobel Laureate, 1994–2001.* Cairo: American U. in Cairo, 2001.

David G. Maillu, 1939–

Web Sites

"David Maillu." *Contemporary Africa Database.* 25 July 2005, http://people.africa database.org/people/data/person11629.html.

Biographies and Criticism

Indangasi, Henry. "David G. Maillu." Lindfors and Sander, *Twentieth-Century Caribbean and Black African Writers, Third Series* (*Dictionary of Literary Biography* 157). 150–58.

"Maillu, David." Wordworks, *Modern Black Writers.* 435–39.
    Excerpts from criticism published between 1979 and 1998.

Outa, George Odera. "Maillu, David." Gikandi, *Encyclopedia of African Literature.* 309–10.

Interviews

"David Maillu." Lindfors, *Africa Talks Back.* [155] –66.

Edmond Amran El Maleh, 1917–

"Edmond Amran El Maleh." *Contemporary Africa Database.* 25 July 2005, http:// people.africadatabase.org/people/data/person6328.html.

Biographies and Criticism

Graebner, Seth. "El Maleh, Edmond Amran." Gikandi, *Encyclopedia of African Literature.* 311–12.

Scharfman, Ronnie. "The Other's Other: The Moroccan-Jewish Trajectory of Edmond Amran El Maleh." *Yale French Studies.* 82.1 (1993):135 –45.

Moloud Mammeri, 1917–1989(88?)

Web Sites

"Mouloud Mammeri." *DZ Lit: Littérature algérienne.* 25 July 2005, http://dzlit.free .fr/mammeri.html.
    Extracts from articles about, and interviews with, Mammeri.

"Mouloud Mammeri." *LIMAG: Littératures du Maghreb.* 25 July 2005, http://www .limag.refer.org/Volumes/Mammeri.htm.

"Mouloud Mammeri."Ed. unavailable. *Kabyle.com.* 24 July 2005. Kabyle.com.
    25 July 2005, http://www.kabyle.com/rubrique.php?id_rubrique=509.
    A list of links to articles on Mammeri, in French.

"Mouloud Mammeri: A Novelist's Vocation." Ed. Chris Kutscher. Update
   unavailable. ChrisKutscher.com. 25 July 2005, http://www.chris-kutschera.
   com/A/Mouloud%20Mammeri.htm.
   Article, originally published in *The Middle East* (Feb. 1984), about Mammeri's
views on Kabyle rights in Algeria and a discussion of his work *La Traversée*.

Biographies and Criticism

Graebner, Seth. "Mammeri, Mouloud." Gikandi, *Encyclopdeia of African Literature*.
   312–14.

Sellin, Eric. "Moloud Mammeri Returns to the Mountains." Genova, *Companion to
   Contemporary World Literature*. 1:176–77.
   Text of an obituary.

Matsemala Manaka, 1956–1998

Web Sites

Barron, Chris. "Matsemela Manaka: Visual Artist, Musician and Dramatist." *Sunday
   Times*. 2 Aug. 1998. Suntimes.co.za. 25 July 2005, http://www.suntimes.co.za/
   1998/08/02/insight/in11.htm.
   Obituary that highlights the impact of Manaka's other creative talents on his
playwriting.

"Matsemela Manaka." *Contemporary Africa Database*. 25 July 2005, http://people
   .africadatabase.org/en/person/11718.html.

Biographies and Criticism

Davis, Geoffrey V. "Matsemela Manaka." Lindfors and Sander, *Twentieth-Century
   Caribbean and Black African Writers, Third Series* (*Dictionary of Literary
   Biography* 157). 159–69.

(John Alfred Clement) Jack Mapanje, 1944–

Web Sites

"Jack Mapanje." *African Poetry*. 25 July 2005, http://www.aghadiuno.com/poetry/
   african/jack.html.
   Reproduces "The Sweet Brew at Chitakale" and "When This Carnival Finally
Closes."

"Jack Mapanje." *Contemporary Africa Database*. 25 July 2005, http://people.africa
   database.org/people/data/person2932.html.

"Jack Mapanje." *My Century*. Ed. and update unavailable. BBC World Service.
   25 July 2005, http://www.bbc.co.uk/worldservice/people/features/mycentury/
   wk32.shtml.
   Mapanje discusses his incarceration and its impact on his writing. Includes an
audio clip.

"Mapanje, Jack." *Literary Encyclopedia*. 25 July 2005, http://www.litencyc.com/php/
   speople.php?rec=true&UID=2927.

Biographies and Criticism

"Mapanje, Jack." Wordworks, *Modern Black Writers*. 443–47.
  Excerpts from criticism published between 1980 and 1996.

Gibbs, James. "Jack Mapanje." Lindfors and Sander, *Twentieth-Century Caribbean and Black African Writers, Third Series* (*Dictionary of Literary Biography* 157). 170–80.

Gikandi, Simon. "Mapanje, Jack." Gikandi, *Encyclopedia of African Literature*. 315.

Hobsbaum, Philip. "Jack Mapanje." Parini, *World Writers in English*. 1:289–306.
  Critical analysis, with a selected bibliography of works by and about Mapanje.

Roscoe, Adrian. "Mapanje, Jack." Benson and Conolly, *Encyclopedia of Post-colonial Literatures in English*. 2:982–83.

J. Nozipo Maraire, 1966–

Web Sites

"Nozipo Maraire." *Anglophone and Lusophone African Women's Writing*. 25 July 2005, http://www.ex.ac.uk/~ajsimoes/aflit/MaraireEN.html.

Shufro, Cathy. "The Many Worlds of Nozipo Maraire." *Yale Medicine* (Summer 1999). 25 July 2005, http://info.med.yale.edu/external/pubs/ym_su99/nozipo/nozipo.html.
  Biographical article.

Whol, Melissa. "J. Nozipo Maraire." *Postcolonial Studies at Emory*. 25 July 2005, http://www.emory.edu/ENGLISH/Bahri/Maraire.html.

Biographies and Criticism

"Maraire, J. Nozipo." *Contemporary Authors*. 179:323–24.

Dambudzo Marechera, 1952–1987

Web Sites

"Dambudzo Marechera." *African Writers: Voices of Change*. 25 July 2005, http://web.uflib.ufl.edu/cm/africana/marecher.htm.

"Dambudzo Marechera." *Books and Writers*. 25 July 2005, http://www.kirjasto.sci.fi/marec.htm.

"Dambudzo Marechera." *Contemporary Africa Database*. 25 July 2005, http://people.africadatabase.org/people/data/person2937.html.

"Dambudzo Marechera." *Zimbabwe: Poetry International Web*. Ed. and update unavailable. *Poetry International Web*. 25 July 2005, http://zimbabwe.poetryinternational.org/cwolk/view/17261.
  Biography, with the text of eleven Marechra poems and a short bibliography.

"The House of Hunger." *LitNet*. 25 July 2005, http://www.litnet.co.za/africanlib/hunger.asp.

Taitz, Laurice. "The Black Outsider." *Sunday Times*. 29 June 1999. Suntimes.co.za. 25 July 2005, http://www.suntimes.co.za/1999/06/27/lifestyle/life01.htm.
  Examines the life experiences that molded Marechera's writing.

Biographies and Criticism

Evenson, Brian. "Dambudzo Marechera." Parekh and Jagne, *Postcolonial African Writers: A Bio-bibliographical Critical Sourcebook.* [300] –04.

Gunner, Liz. "Marechera, Dambudzo." Benson and Conolly, *Encyclopedia of Post-colonial Literatures in English.* 2:983.

"Marechera, Dambudzo." Wordworks, *Modern Black Writers.* 451–56.
Excerpts from criticism published between 1981 and 1996.

Tinkler, Alan. "Marechera, Dambudzo." Serafin, *Encyclopedia of World Literature in the 20th Century.* 3:204.

Vambe, M. "Marechera, Dambudzo Charles." Gikandi, *Encyclopedia of African Literature.* 316–18.

Veit-Wild, Flora. "Dambudzo Marechera." Lindfors and Sander, *Twentieth-Century Caribbean and Black African Writers, Third Series* (*Dictionary of Literary Biography* 157). 181–91.

Dictionaries, Encyclopedias, and Handbooks

Chennelles, Anthony, and Flora Veit-Wild, Eds. *Emerging Perspectives on Dambudzo Marechera.* Tenton, NJ: Africa World Press, 1999.

Veit-Wild, Flora. *Dambudzo Marechera: A Source Book on his Life and Work.* New York: Hans Zell, 1992.

Interviews

Petersen, Kirsten Holst. *An Articulate Anger: Dambudzo Marechera.* Sydney, Australia: Dangaroo Press, 1988. 11–38.

Leila Marouane, 1960–

Web Sites

Cheniki, Ahmed. "L'écriture au bout de désir: Entretien avec la romancière Leïla Marouane." *Pour!* Ed and update unknown. Pourinfo.ouvation.org. 25 July 2005, http://pourinfo.ouvaton.org/culture/litterature/livleilamarouane.htm.
Reproduces the transcript of an interview originally published in *Le Quotidien d'Oran* (18 Nov. 2001).

Lëila Marouane." *DZ Lit: Littérature algérienne* 25 July 2005, http://dzlit.free.fr/marouane.html.

Biographies and Criticism

Ireland, Susan. "The Abductor." *World Literature Today.* 75.3/4 (Summer 2001):113.
Review of Marouane's novel in translation.

(Umaruiddin) Don Mattera, 1935–

Web Sites

Davie, Lucie. "Don Mattera: A Poet of Compassion." *Joburg*. 15 Oct. 2002.
Johannesburg News Agency. 25 July 2005, http://www.johannesburg.gov.za/
people/don_mattera.stm.
Biographical article, with text of a Mattera poem and related links on South
African literature.

"Don Mattera." *Contemporary Africa Database*. 25 July 2005, http://people.africa
database.org/people/data/person11740.html.

"Don Mattera." *Southern Africa Environment Project*. Ed. unknown. 19 June 2003.
Saep.org. 25 July 2005, http://www.saep.org/Sinethemba/Poetry/studied/
Mattera/Mattera.htm.
Text of four poems.

Biographies and Criticism

De Kock, Leon. "Mattera, Don." Benson and Conolly, *Encyclopedia of Post-colonial
Literatures in English*. 2:1001–2.

Edouard Maunick, 1931–

Web Sites

"Edouard Maunick." *Contemporary Africa Database*. 25 July 2005, http://people
.africadatabase.org/people/data/person2968.html.

Biographies and Criticism

Martin, Meredith. "Maunick, Edouard J." Gikandi, *Encyclopedia of African
Literature*. 321–2.

Interview

Gray, Stephen. "Interview with Edouard J. Maunick." *Research in African
Literatures*. 29.2 (Summer 1998):193–7.

Mzwakhe Mbuli, 1959–

Web Sites

"Mzwakhe." Ed and update unavailable. *Free Mzwakhe*. 24 Jan. 2004, http://www
.mzwakhe.org/.
In addition to news about his arrest and the campaign for his release, the site
also has the text of some of his poems, articles about his poetry and music, and audio
clips of Mbuli reading his poetry.

"Mzwakhe Mbuli." *The African Music Encyclopedia*. Ed. Janet Planet. Update
unavailable. Africanmusic.org. 25 July 25, 2005, http://africanmusic.org/artists/
mbuli.html.
Brief biography of Mbuli.

Biographies and Criticism

Brown, Duncan. "South African Oral Performance Poetry of the 1980s: Mwzakhe Mbuli and Alfred Qabula." Ngara, *New Writing from Southern Africa.* 120–48. Bio-critical analysis of Mbuli and his writing.

Zakes (Zanemvula Kizito Gatyeni) Mda, 1948–

Web Sites

Hawley, John. "Village Scandal, Mountain Spirits." *America: The National Catholic Weekly.* 191.1 (July 5 2004). Americamagazine.org. 25 July 2005, http://www.americamagazine.org/BookReview.cfm?articleTypeID=31&textID=3659&issueID=489.
Reviews of *The Madonna of Excelsior* and *She Plays with the Darkness.*

Isaacson, Maureen. "The Free State Madonnas Prevail in Mda's New Novel." *The Connection.* Ed. and update unavailable. Wbur.org. 25 July 2005, http://www.theconnection.org/features/zakesarticle.asp.
Discusson of Mda's writing, political views, and his novel *The Madonna of Excelsior.*

"Zakes Mda." *Contemporary Africa Database.* 25 July 2005, http://people.africadatabase.org/people/data/person3818.html.

"Zakes Mda." *Introducing South African Writers.* 25 July 2005, http://homepage.oniduo.pt/chacmalissimo/SAfrican/html/zakes_mda.htm.

Biographies and Criticism

Dunton, Chris. "Mda, Zakes." Benson and Conolly, *Encyclopedia of Post-colonial Literatures in English.* 2:1006–7.

Peterson, Bhekiziziwe. "Mda, Zakes." Gikandi, *Encyclopedia of African Literature.* 323–4.

———. "Zakes Mda." Scanlon, *South African Writers* (*Dictionary of Literary Biography* 225). 257–69.

Albert Memmi, 1920–

Web Sites

"Albert Memmi." *Contemporary Africa Database.* 25 July 2005, http://people.africadatabase.org/people/data/person11550.html.

"Albert Memmi." *LIMAG: Littératures du Maghreb.* 25 July 2005, http://www.limag.refer.org/Volumes/Memmi.htm.

White, Helaena. "Albert Memmi." *Postcolonial Studies at Emory.* 25 July 2005. http://www.emory.edu/ENGLISH/Bahri/Memmi.html.

Biographies and Criticism

Clancy-Smith, Julia. "The Pillar of Salt." Moss and Valestuk, *African Literature and Its Times* (*World Literature and Its Times* 2). 337–46.

Dugas, Guy (trans. John Fletcher). "Albert Memmi." Cox, *African Writers.* 2:467–77.

Biography, with analyses of Memmi's works, and a select bibliography of works by and about him published between 1953 and 1995.

Abdul-Jaouard, Hédi. "Memmi, Albert." Serafin, *Encyclopedia of World Literature in the 20th Century.* 3:248–49.

T(h)eresa Ekwutosi Meniru, 1931–

Web Sites

"Meniru, Theresa." *African Children's Literature.* 25 July 2005, http://web.uflib.ufl.
edu/cm/africana/meniru.htm.

"Theresa Ekwutosi Meniru." *Contemporary Africa Database.* 25 July 2005, http://
people.africadatabase.org/people/data/person15954.html.

Biographies and Criticism

"Meniru, Teresa." By Alethea K. Helbig and Agnes Regan Perkins. *Dictionary of Children's Fiction from Australia, Canada, India, New Zealand, and Selected African Countries.* Westport, Conn.: Greenwood Press, 1992.
Contains a brief biography (252) and a desciption of Meniru's novel *Unoma* (406–7).

Ruth Miller, 1919–1969

Web Sites

"Ruth Miller." *Contemporary Africa Database.* 25 July 2005, http://people.africa
database.org/people/data/person15919.html.

Biographies and Criticism

Metelerkamp, Joan. "Miller, Ruth." Benson and Conolly, *Encyclopedia of Post-colonial Literatures in English.* 2:1025–6.

Sarah Gertrude Millin, 1888–1968

Web Sites

"Sarah Gertrude Millin." *Introducing South African Writers.* 25 July 2005, http://
homepage.oniduo.pt/chacmalissimo/SAfrican/html/sarah_gertrude_millin.htm.

Biographies and Criticism

Green, Michael. "Sarah Gertrude Millin." Scanlon, *South African Writers* (*Dictionary of Literary Biography* 225). 270–82.

———. "Millin, Sarah Gertrude." Benson and Conolly, *Encyclopedia of Post-colonial Literatures in English.* 2:1026–27.

Marquard, Jean. "Millin, Sarah Gertrude." Serafin, *Encyclopedia of World Literature in the Twentieth Century.* 3:267–68.

"Millin, Sarah Gertrude." Robinson, *Moden Women Writers.* 3:188–95.
Excerpts from criticism published between 1925 and 1984.

Rachid Mimouni, 1945–1995

Web Sites

Kutschera, Chris. "Rachid Mimouni: A Case Study of Dictatorship."
ChrisKutschera.com. 12 July 2004, http://www.chris-kutschera.com/%20A/
Rachid%20Mimouni.htm.
Reprint of a February 1992 article originally published in *The Middle East*
magazine.

"Rachid Mimouni." *DZ Lit: littérature algérienne.* 25 July 2005, http://dzlit.free.fr/
tombeza.html.

"Rachid Mimouni." *LIMAG: Littératures du Maghreb.* 25 July 2005, http://www
.limag.refer.org/Volumes/Mimouni.htm.

Le site Officiel de Rachid Mimouni. Ed. unavailable. 26 Mar. 2005.
Rachidmimouni.net. 25 July 2005, http://www.rachidmimouni.net/.

In addition to the bio-bibliographical information, the site includes audio and
video clips of interviews and extracts from a film version of a Mimouni's work, and
articles by and about him.

Biographies and Criticism

Graebner, Seth. "Mimouni, Rachid." Gikandi, *Encyclopedia of African Literature.*
330–31.

Marx-Scouras, Danielle. "Mimouni, Rachid." Serafin, *Encyclopedia of World
Literature in the 20th Century.* 3:269–70.

Felix Mnthali, 1933–

Web Sites

"Felix Mnthali." *Contemporary Africa Database.* 25 July 2005, http://people.africa
database.org/people/data/person15956.html.

Biographies and Criticism

Roscoe, Adrian. "Mnthali, Felix." Benson and Conolly, *Encyclopedia of Post-
colonial Literatures in English.* 2:1031.

(William) Bloke Modisane, 1923–1986

Web Sites

"Blame Me on History (II)." *The Legacy Project.* Ed. and update unavailable. Legacy-
project.org. 25 July 2005, http://www.legacy-project.org/lit/
display.html?ID=87.
Excerpt from *Blame Me on History* (Dutton, 1963).

"Bloke Modisane." *Introducing South African Writers.* 25 July 2005, http://home
page.oniduo.pt/chacmalissimo/SAfrican/html/bloke_modisane.htm.

"William (Bloke) Modisane." *Contemporary Africa Database.* 25 July 2005. http://
people.africadatabase.org/en/person/15920.html.

Biographies and Criticism

"Exile as a Space of Death: The Individual (William "Bloke" Modisane) and the Organization (The ANC)." Gready, Paul. *Writing as Resistance: Life Stories of Imprisonment, Exile, and Homecoming from Apartheid South Africa.* Langham, Md.: Lexington, 2003. 153–185.

Ngwenya, Thengani. "Modisane, Bloke." Gikandi, *Encyclopedia of African Literature.* 340.

Thomas Mokopu Mofolo, 1876–1948

Websites

"Thomas Mofolo." *Introducing South African Writers.* 25 July 2005, http://home page.oniduo.pt/chacmalissimo/SAfrican/html/thomas_mofolo.htm.

Biographies and Criticism

Ball, Kimberly. "Chaka." Moss and Valestuk, *African Literature and Its Times* (*World Literature and Its Times* 2): 35–46.

Groenewald, H.C. "Mofolo, Thomas Mokopu." Benson and Conolly, *Encyclopedia of Post-colonial Literatures in English.* 2:1033.

Kunene, Daniel. "Thomas Mokopu Mofolo." Cox, *African Writers.* 2:479–93.
Biography, with analyses of Mofolo's works, and a select bibliography of primary and secondary works published between 1907 and 1989.

Moeketsi, Rosemary. "Mofolo, Thomas Mopoku." Gikandi, *Encyclopedia of African Literature.* 341.

"Mofolo, Thomas." Wordworks, *Modern Black Writers.* 479–81.
Excerpts from criticism published between 1931 and 1997.

Swanepoel, C.F. "Thomas Mofolo." Scanlon, *South African Writers* (*Dictionary of Literary Biography* 225). 283–87.

"Thomas (Mokopu) Mofolo." Poupard et al., *Twentieth-Century Literary Criticism.* 22: 243–65.
Excerpts from criticism on Mofolo from 1931 to 1976, with an annotated bibliography.

Tucker, Martin. "Mofolo, Thomas." *Encyclopedia of World Literature in the 20th Century.* 3:281–82.

Tololwa Mollel, 1952–

Web Sites

"Mollel, Tololwa." *African Children's Literature.* 25 July 2005, http://web.uflib.ufl .edu/cm/africana/mollel.htm.

"Tolowa M. Mollel." *Contemporary Africa Database.* 25 July 2005, http://people .africadatabase.org/en/person/3040.html.

"Tololwa M. Mollel." *The Writers' Union of Canada.* Ed. and update unavalable. Writersunion.ca. 25 July 2005, http://www.writersunion.ca/m/mollel.htm.
Brief biography and a list of selected works and awards.

Biographies and Criticism

Jones, Raymond. "Mollel, Tololwa." Pendergast and Pendergast, *St. James Guide to Children's Writers.* 756–57.

"Mollel, Tololwa." *Contemporary Authors.* 137:308–9.

Tierno Monénembo, 1947–

Web Sites

"Tierno Monénembo (Diallo Tierno Saïdou)." *Contemporary Africa Database.* 25 July 2005, http://people.africadatabase.org/people/data/person3044.html.

Biographies and Criticism

Ba, Ousmane. "Monenembo, Tierno." Gikandi, *Encyclopedia of African Literature.* 342.

King, Adele. "L'aine des orphelins." *World Literature Today.* 75.1 (Winter 2001): 94. Review of the English translation (U. of Nebraska, 2004) of Monénembo's novel.

Stephanson, Blandine. "Monenembo, Tierno." Serafin, *Encyclopedia of World Literature in the 20th Century.* 3:286–87.

Bai T(amia) J(ohns) Moore, 1916–1988

Web Sites

"Murder in the Cassava Patch." *Bong Town.* Ed. Robert Kranz. Update unavailable. 25 July 2005, http://www.bong-town.com/Bong_Town/Liberia/Literature/ Murder_in_Casava_Patch.html.
Text of a short story by Moore.

Biographies and Criticism

Gikandi, Simon. "Moore, Bai T. Gikandi," *Encyclopedia of African Literature.* 342.

Atwell Sidwell Mopeli-Paulus, 1913–1960

Web Sites

"A.S. Mopeli-Paulus." *Contemporary Africa Database.* 25 July 2005, http://people .africadatabase.org/people/data/person11466.html.

Biographies and Criticism

Dunton, Chris. "Mopeli-Paulus, Atwell Sidwell." Benson and Conolly, *Encyclopedia of Post-colonial Literatures in English.* 2:1039–40.

Eskia (Ezekiel) Mphahlele, 1919–

Web Sites

"Es'kia (Ezekiel) Mphahlele." *Contemporary Africa Database.* 25 July 2005, http:// people.africadatabase.org/people/data/person3065.html.

"Ezekiel Mphahlele." *Introducing South African Writers.* 25 July 2005, http://home page.oniduo.pt/chacmalissimo/SAfrican/html/ezekiel_mphahlele.htm.

"Ezekiel Mphahlele." *African Writers: Voices of Change.* 25 July 2005, http://web
.uflib.ufl.edu/cm/africana/mphahlel.htm.

Biographies and Criticism

Atwell, David. "Mphahlele, Es'kia." Gikandi, *Encyclopedia of African Literature.*
343–44.

Barnett, Ursula A. "Es'kia (Ezekiel) Mphahlele." Lindfors and Sander, *Twentieth-
Century Caribbean and Black African Writers, Second Series* (*Dictionary of
Literary Biography* 125). 89–108.

"Ezekiel Mphahlele." Hunter et al., *Contemporary Literary Criticism.* 133:124–63.
Criticism on Mofolo from 1960 to 1997.

"Ezekiel Mphahlele." Draper, *Black Literature Criticism.* 3:1446–58.
Biography, list of major works, excerpts from criticsm from 1971 to 1985, and
an annotated bibliography.

Motasapi, Seitlhamo. "Es'kia (Ezekiel) Mphahlele." Scanlon, *South African Writers*
(*Dictionary of Literary Biography* 225). 288–97.

"Mphahlele, Ezekiel." Wordworks, *Modern Black Writers.* 496–501.
Excerpts from criticism published between 1947 and 1993.

Thuynsma, Peter. "Es'kia Mphahlele." Cox, *African Writers.* 2:495–510.
Biography, analyses of Mphahlele's works, and a select bibliography of works
by and about him published between 1946 and 1989.

Tucker, Martin. "Mphahlele, Ezekiel (Es'kia)." Serafin, *Encyclopedia of World
Literature in the 20th Century.* 3:311–12.

Woeber, Catherine. "Mphaklele, Es'kia (Ezekiel)." Benson and Conolly,
Encyclopedia of Post-colonial Literatures in English. 2:1045–47.

Dictionaries, Encyclopedias, and Handbooks

Akosu, Tyohdzuah. *The Writing of Ezekiel (Es'kia) Mphahlele, South African Writer:
Literature, Culture, and Politics.* Lewiston: Mellen, 1995.

Obee, Ruth. *Eskia Mphahlele: Themes of Alienation and African Humanism.* Athens,
Ohio: Ohio University Press, 1999.

Interviews

"Interview: Richard Samin with Es'kia Mphahlele." *Research in African Literatures.*
28.4 (Winter 1997): [182] –200.

Edison Mpina, c.1942–

Web Sites

"Edison Mpina." *Contemporary Africa Database.* 25 July 2005, http://people.africa
database.org/people/data/person15958.html.

Biographies and Criticism

Roscoe, Adrian. "Mpina, Edison." Benson and Conolly, *Encyclopedia of Post-
colonial Literatures in English.* 2:1047.

Samuel Edward Krune Mqhayi, 1875–1945

Web Sites

"In Praise of Dube." *DISA: Digital Imaging South Africa.* 15 June 2005. U. of
    KwaZulu-Natal. 25 July 2005, http://disa.nu.ac.za/
    articledisplaypage.asp?articletitle=Poem%3A+In+praise+of+Dube&filename=
    SeJan82.
    Scanned text of a poem by Mqhayi

Biographies and Criticism

Make, N. P. "Mqhayi, Samuel Edward Krune." Gikandi, *Encyclopedia of African
    Literature.* 345.

"S(amuel) E(dward) K(rune Loliwe) Mqhayi." Poupard et al., *Twentieth-Century
    Literary Criticism.* 25:319–28.
    Excerpts from criticism published between 1943 and 1975, with an annotated
bibliography.

Oswald Mbuyiseni Mtshali, 1940–

Web Sites

"Oswald Mbuyiseni Mtshali." *Introducing South African Writers.* 25 July 2005, http://
    homepage.oniduo.pt/chacmalissimo/SAfrican/html/oswald_mbuyiseni_mtshali
    .htm."Oswald Mbuyiseni Mtshali." *African Poetry.* 25 July 2005, http://www
    .aghadiuno.com/poetry/african/oswald.html.
    Text of "Always a Suspect."

Biographies and Criticism

Locket, Cecily. "Oswald Mbuyiseni Mtshali." Lindfors and Sander, *Twentieth-
    Century Caribbean and Black African Writers, Second Series* (*Dictionary of
    Literary Biography* 125). 109–13.Gaylard, Rob. "Oswald Mbuyiseni Mtshali."
    Scanlon, *South African Writers* (*Dictionary of Literary Biography* 225). 298–304.

Mpe, Phaswane. "Mtshali, Oswald Mbuyiseni." Gikandi, *Encyclopedia of African
    Literature.* 345–6.

"Mtshali, Oswald." Wordworks, *Modern Black Writers.* 503–6.
    Excerpts from criticism published between 1972 and 1991.

Mzamane, Mbuleleo Vizikhungo. "Mtshali, Oswald Mbuyiseni." Benson and
    Conolly, *Encyclopedia of Post-colonial Literatures in English.* 2:1047–48.

Valentin Yves Mudimbe, 1941–

Web Sites

"Valentin Y. Mudimbe." *Contemporary Africa Database.* 25 July 2005, http://people
    .africadatabase.org/people/data/person3080.html.

Biographies and Criticism

Kemedjio, Cilas. "Mudimbe, V. Y." Gikandi, *Encyclopedia of African Literature.*
    346–7.

Hirchi, Mohamed. "Mudimbe, V(alentin) Y(ves)." Serafin, *Encyclopedia of World Literature in the 20th Century.* 3:313.

"Mudimbe. V. Y." Wordworks, *Modern Black Writers.* 506–11.
Excerpts from criticism published between 1985 and 1994.

Micere Githae Mugo, 1942–

Web Sites

"Micere Mugo." *Anglophone and Lusophone African Women's Writing.* 25 July 2005, http://www.ex.ac.uk/~ajsimoes/aflit/MugoEN.html.

"Micere Mugo." *Contemporary Africa Database.* 25 July 2005, http://people.africa database.org/people/data/person3084.html.

"Micere Githae Mugo." *Women's WORLD.* Ed. and update unavailable. Wworld.org. 25 July 2005, http://www.wworld.org/about/board/micere_githae_mugo.htm. Contains bio-bibliographical information.

Biographies and Criticism

Abala, Judith Imali. "Micere M. Githae Mugo." Parekh and Jagne, *Postcolonial African Writers: A Bio-bibliographical Critical Sourcebook.* [305] –11.

"Mugo, Micere Githae." Robinson, *Modern Women Writers.* 3:289–91.
Excerpts from criticism published between 1982 and 1983.

"Mugo, Micere Githae." Wordworks, *Modern Black Writers.* 511–13.
Excerpts from criticism published between 1980 and 1995.

Outa, George Odera. "Mugo, Micere Githae." Gikandi, *Encyclopedia of African Literature.* 347.

Interviews

"Micere Githae Mugo." James, *In Their Own Voices.* 93–101.
Text of a 1986 interview.

"Micere Githae Mugo." Wilkinson, *Talking With African Writers.* 110–20.
Text of a 1984 interview.

Dominic Mulaisho, 1933–

Web Sites

"Dominic Chola Mulaisho." *Contemporary Africa Database.* 25 July 2005, http://people.africadatabase.org/people/data/person3097.html.

Biographies and Criticism

Reed, John. "Mulaisho, Dominic." Benson and Conolly, *Encyclopedia of Postcolonial Literatures in English.* 2:1052–53.

Vambe, M. "Mulaisho, Dominic." Gikandi, *Encyclopedia of African Literature.* 348.

Charles Mungoshi, 1947–

Web Sites

"Charles Mungoshi." *African Writers: Voices of Change.* 25 July 2005, http://web
.uflib.ufl.edu/cm/africana/mungoshi.htm.

"Charles Mungoshi." *Contemporary Africa Database.* 25 July 2005, http://people
.africadatabase.org/en/person/3103.html.

"Charles Mungoshi." *Contemporary Postcolonial and Postimperial Literature in
English.* 25 July 2005, http://www.scholars.nus.edu.sg/post/zimbabwe/
mungoshi/mungoshiov.html.

"Charles Mungoshi." *Zimbabwe: Poetry International.* Ed. and update unavailable.
Poetry Internaional. 25 July 25, 2005, http://zimbabwe.poetryinternational.org/
cwolk/view/17263.
Biography, with the text of some poems and articles by him.

"Walking Still." *LitNet.* 25 July 2005, http://www.litnet.co.za/africanlib/walking.asp.

Biographies and Criticism

Brown, G. R. and T. O. McLoughlin. "Charles Mungoshi." Lindfors and Sander,
Twentieth-Century Caribbean and Black African Writers, Third Series
(*Dictionary of Literary Biography* 157). 209–17.

Chiome, Emmanuel. "Mungoshi, Charles Lovemore." Gikandi, *Encyclopedia of
African Literature.* 348–9.

Thompson, Katrina Daly. Serafin, *Encyclopedia of World Literature in the 20th
Century.* 3:321.

John Munonye, 1929–1999

Web Sites

"John Munonye." *Contemporary Africa Database.* 25 July 2005, http://people.africa
database.org/people/data/person3104.html.

Biographies and Criticism

Dillard, Mary. "The Oil Man of Obanje." Moss and Valestuk, *African Literature and
Its Times* (*World Literature and Its Times* 2). 309–16.

Gikandi, Simon. "Munonye, John." Gikandi, *Encyclopedia of African Literature.* 349.

"Munonye, John." Wordworks, *Modern Black Writers.* 513–17.
Excerpts from criticism published between 1982 and 1998.

Nnolim, Charles E. "John Munonye." Lindfors and Sander, *Twentieth-Century
Caribbean and Black African Writers, First Series* (*Dictionary of Literary
Biography* 117). 247–51.

Okonkwo, Chidi. "Munyone, John." Benson and Conolly, *Encyclopedia of Post-
colonial Literatures in English.* 2:1056.

Interviews

"John Munonye." Ezenwa-Ohaeto, *Winging Words: Interviews with Nigerian Writers
and Critics.* 15–21

Meja Mwangi, 1948–

Web Sites

"Striving for the Wind." *LitNet.* 25 July 2005, http://www.litnet.co.za/africanlib/ striving.asp.

"Meja Mwangi." *Contemporary Africa Database.* 25 July 2005, http://people.africa database.org/people/data/person3125.html.

Biographies and Criticism

Gikandi, Simon. "Meja Mwangi." Lindfors and Sander, *Twentieth-Century Caribbean and Black African Writers, Second Series* (*Dictionary of Literary Biography* 125). 114–20.

———. "Mwangi, Meja." Gikandi, *Encyclopedia of African Literature.* 350–51.

Kabaji, Egara. "Mwangi, Meja." Benson and Conolly, *Encyclopedia of Post-colonial Literatures in English.* 2:1061–62.

Kurtz, J. Roger. "Meja Mwangi." Cox, *African Writers.* 2:511–25.
    Biography, analyses of works by Mwangi, and a select bibliography of works by and about him published between 1973 and 1986.

"Mwangi, Meja." Wordworks, *Modern Black Writers.* 522–26.
    Excerpts from criticsm published between 1976 and 1993.

Mbulelo Vizikhungo Mzamane, 1948–

Web Sites

"Mbulelo Mzamane." *Contemparary Africa Database.* 25 July 2005, http://people .africadatabase.org/people/data/person15960.html.

Biographies and Criticism

Handley, Patricia. "Mzamane, Mbulelo Vizikhungo." Benson and Conolly, *Encyclopedia of Post-colonial Literatures in English.* 3:1067–68.

Mkhize, Jabulani. "Mzamane, Mbulelo." Gikandi, *Encyclopedia of African Literature.* 351–2.

Peter Nazareth, 1940–

Web Sites

"Peter Nazareth." *Contemporary Africa Database.* 25 July 2005, http://people.africa database.org/people/data/person3914.html.

Biographies and Criticism

Kabaji, Egara. "Nazareth, Peter." Benson and Conolly, *Encyclopedia of Post-colonial Literatures in English.* 2:1085–86.

Kurtz, J. Roger. "Nazareth, Peter." Serafin, *Encyclopedia of World Literature in the 20th Century.* 3:354–55.

———. "Peter Nazareth." Parekh and Jagne, *Postcolonial African Writers: A Bio-bibliographical Critical Sourcebook.* [312] –17.

Ojwang, Dan Odhiambo. "Nazareth, Peter." Gikandi, *Encyclopedia of African Literature*. 360.

Interview

"Peter Nazareth." Lindfors, *Africa Talks Back*. [191] – 212.
    Text of a 1986 interview.

Anthony Nazombe, 1955–2004

Web Sites

"Anthony Nazombe." *Contemporary Africa Database*. 25 July 2005, http://people
    .africadatabase.org/people/data/person15971.html.

Biographies and Criticism

Roscoe, Anthony. "Nazombe, Anthony. " Benson and Conolly, *Encyclopedia of Post-colonial Literatures in English*. 2:1086.

Interview

"Anthony Nazombe." Lindfors, *Africa Talks Back*. [213] –25.
    Text of a 1986 interview.

Cheikh Aliou Ndao, 1933–

Web Sites

Herzberger-Fofana, Pierrette. "Un Entretien avec Cheik Aliou Ndao, Écrivain." *Mots Pluriels*. 12 (Dec. 1999). 25 July 2005, http://www.arts.uwa.edu.au/
    MotsPluriels/MP1299ndao.html.
    Transcript of a 1997 interview.

Biographies and Criticism

"Cheik Ndao: *L'Exile d'Albouri*." Conteh-Morgan, *Theatre and Drama in Francophone Africa*. 152–63.
    Brief biography, wiwth a critical analysis of *L'Exile d'Albouri*.

Diop, Samba. "Ndao, Cheik Aliou." Gikandi, *Encyclopedia of African Literature*.
    361–62.

"Ndao, Cheikh Aliou." Serafin, *Encyclopedia of World Literature in the 20th Century*.
    3: 356–57.

"Ndao, Cheikh Aliou." Wordworks, *Modern Black Writers*. 533–37.
    Excerpts from criticism published between 1976 and 1984.

Njabulo Ndebele, 1948–

Web Sites

Manigat, Béatrice. "An Interview with Njabulo S. Ndebele." *Alizés*. 19 (n.d.). 25 July
    2005, http://www2.univ-reunion.fr/~ageof/text/74c21e88-302.html.
    Transcript of a 1998 interview.

"Njabulo Ndebele." *Introducing South African Writers*. 25 July 2005, http://cosmos
    .oninetspeed.pt/chacma/SAfrican/html/njabulo_ndebele.htm.

Biographies and Criticism

Alvarez, David. "Ndebele, Njabulelo S." Serafin, *Encyclopedia of World Literature in the 20th Century.* 3:357–58.

MacKenzie, Craig. "Njabulo S. Ndebele." Scanlon, *South African Writers (Dictionary of Literary Biography* 225). 305–13.

———. "Ndebele, Njabulo Simakahle." Benson and Conolly, *Encyclopedia of Post-colonial Literatures in English.* 2:1086–87.

"Ndebele, Njabulo." Wordworks, *Modern Black Writers.* 537–40.
Excerpts from criticism published between 1989 and 1990.

Nkosi. Lewis. "Njabulo, Ndebele." Lindfors and Sander, *Twentieth-Century Caribbean and Black African Writers, Third Series* (*Dictionary of Literary Biography* 157). 227–34.

Peterson, Bhekizizwe. "Ndebele, Njabulo Simakahle." Gikandi, *Encyclopedia of African Literature.* 362.

Interviews

"Njabulo Ndebele." Lindfors, *Africa Talks Back.* [226] –48.
Text of a 1986 interview.

"Njabulo Ndebele." Wilkinson, *Talking With African Writers.* 146–57.
Text of a 1987 interview.

Marie Ndiaye, 1967–

Web Sites

Boutoulle, Myriam. "Le paradis est infernal." *Lire* (Nov. 2003). 25 July 2005, http://www.lire.fr/entretien.asp/idC=45755/idTC=4/idR=201/idG=.
Interview with Ndiaye, with internal links to related articles.

"Marie Ndiaye." *Reading Women Writers and African Literatures.* 25 July 2005, http://www.arts.uwa.edu.au/AFLIT/NDiayeMarieEng.html.

"Rosie Carpe." *Les Editions de Minuit.* Ed. Philippe Menestret. Update unavailable. Leseditionsdeminuit.fr. 25 July 2005, http://www.leseditionsdeminuit.fr/titres/2001/rosie-carpe.htm.
Publisher's publicity web site with a brief description of Ndiaye's novel anad extracts from press reviews.

Biographies and Criticism

King, Adele. "Papa doit manger." *World Literature Today.* 78.2 (2004):85.
Review of Ndiaye's play.

King, Adele. "Providence." *World Literature Today.* 76.2 (2002): 178–79.
Review of Ndiaye's first play.

Teko-Abgo, K. Ambroise. "En Famille or the Problematic of Alterity." *Research in African Literatures.* 26.2 (1995): [158] –68.
Critical analysis of Ndiaye's novel, *En Famille.*

Tené, Emmanuel. "Ndiaye, Marie." Gikandi, *Encyclopedia of African Literature.* 363.

Pol Nnamuzikam Ndu, 1940–1976

Web Sites

"Pol Nnamuzikam Ndu." *Contemporary Africa Database.* 25 July 2005, http://
people.africadatabase.org/people/data/person15979.html.

"Afa." *African Letters.* 25 July 2005, http://www.bowwave.org/AfricanWriters/
Pol%20Ndu.htm.

Biographies and Criticism

Aiyejina, Funso. "Ndu, Pol Nnamuzikam." Benson and Conolly, *Encyclopedia of
Post-colonial Literatures in English.* 2:1087–88.

Agostinho Neto, 1922–1979

Web Sites

"A. Agostinho Neto." *Contemporary Africa Database.* 25 July 2005, http://people
.africadatabase.org/en/person/3156.html.

"Agostinho Neto." *Poesia Africana de Expressão Portuguesa.* Ed. and update
unavailable. 25 July 2005, http://betogomes.sites.uol.com.br/AgostinhoNeto
.htm.
Biographical sketch, list of works, and the text of twelve poems.

Biographies and Criticism

Burness, Donald. "Agostinho Neto and the Poetry of Combat." Donald Burness. Ed.
Critical Perspectives on Lusophone African Literatures. Washington, D. C.:
Three Continents Press, 1981. [89] –103.
Overview of Neto's poetry.

Martinho, Ferdinand. "The Poetry of Agostinho Neto." Genova, *Companion to
Contemporary World Literature.* 1:315–18.
Gives a general discussion of Neto's poetry.

"Neto, Agostinho." Wordworks, *Modern Black Writers.* 541–43.
Excerpts from criticism published between 1977 and 1991.

Rothwell, Phillip. "Neto, (António) Agostinho." Gikandi, *Encyclopedia of African
Literature.* 366–67.

Pius Ngandu-Nkashama, 1946–

Web Sites

Yuma, Jimi and Robert Levine. *Translations in Progress: Modern French Literature.*
Update unavailable. Boston U. 25 July 2005, http://www.bu.edu/english/levine/
pius.htm.
Text of the English translation of Nkashama's short story "The Children of
Lake Tana" and a partial translation of the novel *Un jour de grand soleil sur les
montagnes de l'Ethiopie.*

Biographies and Criticism

Tcheuyap, Alexie. "Ngandu Nkashama, Pius." Gikandi, *Encyclopedia of African Literature.* 367–68.

Lauretta Ngcobo, 1931–

Websites

"Lauretta Ngcobo." *Contemporary Africa Database.* 25 July 2005, http://people .africadatabase.org/people/data/person3166.html. Thomas, Cornelius. "And the Women…They Survived." *Dispatch Online* (8 July 2000). 25 July 2005, http:// www.dispatch.co.za/2000/07/08/features/WOMEN.HTM.
Provides the text of an interview with Ngcobo.

———. "Not for the Squeamish." *Dispatch Online* (8 July 2000). 25 July 2005, http:// www.dispatch.co.za/2000/07/08/features/BOOK2.HTM.
Review of *And They Didn't Die.*

Biographies and Criticism

Ibrahim, Huma. "Ngcobo, Lauretta." Gikandi, *Encyclopedia of African Literature.* 369.

"Ngcobo,Lauretta." *Contemporary Authors.* 165:282–84.

Ngugi wa Thiong'o (James Ngugi), 1938–

Web Sites

Margulis, Jennifer. "Ngugi wa Thiong'o." *Postcolonial Studies at Emory.* 10 Oct. 2003. Emory U. 26 July 2005, http://www.emory.edu/ENGLISH/Bahri/Ngugi .html.

"Ngugu wa Thiong'o." *African Writers: Voices of Change.* 26 July 2005, http://web .uflib.ufl.edu/cm/africana/thiongo.htm.

"Ngugu wa Thiong'o." *Books and Writers.* 26 July 2005, http://www.kirjasto.sci.fi/ ngugiw.htm.

"Ngugi wa Thiong'o: An Overview." *Contemporary Postcolonial and Postimperial Literature in English.* 26 July 2005, http://www.scholars.nus.edu.sg/landow/ post/poldiscourse/ngugiov.html.

"Ngugi wa Thiongo." *Postcolonial African Literatures in English.* 26 July 2005, http:// www.fb10.uni-bremen.de/anglistik/kerkhoff/AfricanLit/Ngugi/Ngugi.htm.

Ngwenya, Thengani. "Themba, Can." Gikandi, *Encyclopedia of African Literature.* 533.

Biographies and Criticism

Cancel, Robert. "Literary Criticism as Social Philippic and Personal Excorcism: Ngugi wa Thiong'o's Critical Writings." Genova, *Companion to Contemporary World Literature.* 1:346–50.
Analyzes Ngugi's nonfiction writing.

———. "Ngugi wa Thiong'o." Cox, *African Writers.* 2:537–55.
Biography, analyses of Ngugi's works, and a select bibliography of works by and about him published between 1964 and 1990.

Gikandi, Simon. "Ngugi wa Thiong'o." *Encyclopedia of African Literature.* 369–73.

———. "Ngugi wa Thong'o." Schellinger, *Encyclopedia of the Novel.* 3:934–35.

Guzzio, Tracie Church. "Ngugi wa Thiong'o." Parini, *World Writers in English.* 2:407–23.

Hawson, John C. "Ngugi wa Thiong'o." Parekh and Jagne, *Postcolonial African Writers: A Bio-bibliographical Critical Sourcebook.* [318]–31.

Kabaji, Egara. "Ngugi wa Thiong'o." Benson and Conolly, *Encyclopedia of Post-colonial Literatures in English.* 2:1095–97.

Killam, G. D. "Ngugi wa Thinog'o: Writing Down the Barrel of a Pen." Ross, *International Literature in English.* 121–30.
    Survey of major themes and an annotated bibliography of selected critical readings.

Lindfors, Bernth. "Ngugi wa Thiong'o." Serafin, *Encyclopedia of World Literature in the 20th Century.* 3:381–2.

Littleton, Jacob. "Weep Not, Child." Moss and Valestuk, *African Literature and Its Times* (*World Literature and Its Times* 2): 471–80.

Maughan-Brown, David. "Ngugi wa Thiong'o (James Ngugi)." Lindfors and Sander, *Twentieth-Century Caribbean and Black African Writers, Second Series* (*Dictionary of Literary Biography* 125). 145–69.

"Ngugi, James." Mendelson and Bryfonski, *Contemporary Literary Criticism.* 7:70–76.
    Excerpts from criticism published between 1970 and 1976.

"Ngugi wa Thiong'o." Draper, *Black Literature Criticism.* 3:1495–1514.
    Biography, list of major works, excerpts of criticism from 1967 to 1989, and an annotated bibliography.

"Ngugi wa Thiong'o." Wordworks, *Modern Black Writers.* 543–52.
    Excerpts from criticism published between 1964 and 1997.

Dictionaries, Encyclopedias, and Handbooks

Cantalupo, Charles. Ed. *Ngugi wa Thiong'o: Texts and Contexts.* Trenton, N. J.: Africa World Press, 1995.

Cook, David and Michael Okenimkpe. *Ngugi wa Thiong'o: An Exploration of His Writings.* Portsmouth, N. H.: Heineman, 1997.

Gikandi, Simon. *Ngugi wa Thiong'o.* Cambridge: Cambridge University Press, 2000.

Bibliographies

Sicherman, Carol. *Ngugi wa Thiong'o: A Bibliography of Primary and Secondary Sources, 1957–1987.* London: Hans Zell, 1989.

Interviews

"Nguigi wa Thiongo." Jussawalla and Dasenbrock, *Interviews with Writers of the Post-Colonial World.* 25–41.

Rodrigues, Angela Lamas. "Beyond Nativism: An Interview with Ngugi wa Thiong'o." *Research in African Literatures.* 35.3 (2004): [161] –67.

Abioseh (Davidson) Nicol, 1924–1994

Web Sites

"Abioseh Nicol." *Contemporary Africa Database.* 25 July 2005, http://people.africa database.org/people/data/person15988.html.

Biographies and Criticism

Gikandi, Simon. "Nicol Abioseh (Davidson)." Gikandi, *Encyclopedia of African Literature.* 374–5.

Palmer, Eustace. "Nicol, Abioseh." Benson and Conolly, *Encyclopedia of Post-colonial Literatures in English.* 2:1099–1100.

Simon Njami, 1962–

Web Sites

Héric Libong. "You Have To Be Inside Something to Change It." *Africulture.* 39. 25 July 2005, http://www.africultures.com/anglais/articles_anglais/39njami.htm. Interview with Njami.

"Simon Njami." *Contemporary Africa Database.* 25 July 2005, http://people.africa database.org/people/data/person15727.html.

Biographies and Criticism

Ekotto, Frieda. "Njami, Simon." Gikandi, *Encyclopedia of African Literature.* 376.

Rebeka (Rebecca) Njau (Marina Gashe), 1932–

Web Sites

"Marina Gashe." *Contemporary Africa Database.* 25 July 2005, http://people.africa database.org/people/data/person15987.html.

"Rebecca Njau." *Reading Women Writers and African Literatures.* 25 July 2005, http://www.ex.ac.uk/~ajsimoes/aflit/NjauEN.html.

Biographies and Criticism

Bardolph, J. "Njau, Rebecca." Benson and Conolly, *Encyclopedia of Post-colonial Literatures in English.* 2:1103.

Gikandi, Simon. "Njau, Rebeka (Rebecca)." Gikandi, *Encyclopedia of African Literature.* 376.

"Njau, Rebecca." Robinson, *Modern Women Writers.* 3:361–63. Excerpts from criticism published between 1981 and 1985.

Lewis Nkosi, 1936–

Web Sites

Harris, Janice. "On Tradition, Madness, and South Africa: An Interview with Lewis Nkosi." *Weber Studies.* 11.2 (1994). 25 July 2005, http://weberstudies.weber .edu/archive/archive%20B%20Vol.%2011-16.1/Vol.%2011. 2/11.2Harris.htm. Transcript of a 1992 interview.

"Lewis Nkosi." *Contemporary Africa Database.* 25 July 2005, http://people.africa database.org/people/data/person3194.html.

"Lewis Nkosi." *Introducing South African Writers.* 25 July 2005, http://homepage .oniduo.pt/chacmalissimo/SAfrican/html/lewis_nkosi.htm.

Biographies and Criticism

Bose, Brinda. "Lewis Nkosi." Parekh and Jagne, *Postcolonial African Writers: A Bio-bibliographical Critical Sourcebook.* [332] –36.

Coetzee, Paulette. "Lewis Nkosi." Scanlon, *South African Writers (Dictionary of Literary Biography* 225). 314–21.

Graham, Lucy Valerie. "Lewis Nkosi." Parini, *World Writers in English.* 2:425–40.

"Lewis Nkosi." Draper, *Black Literature Criticism.* 3:1515–21.

Biography, list of major works, excerpts of criticism from 1966 to 1987, and an annotated bibliography.

Worsfold, Brian. "Lewis Nkosi." Lindfors and Sander, *Twentieth-Century Caribbean and Black African Writers, Third Series (Dictionary of Literary Biography* 157). 241–50.

———. "Nkosi, Lewis." Benson and Conolly, *Encyclopedia of Post-colonial Literatures in English.* 2:1103–04.

Arthur (Kenneth) Nortje, 1942–1970

Web Sites

"Arthur Nortje." *Contemporary Africa Database.* 25 July 2005, http://people.africa database.org/people/data/person15969.html.

Biographies and Criticism

Bunn, David. "Arthur Nortje." Lindfors and Sander, *Twentieth-Century Caribbean and Black African Writers, Second Series (Dictionary of Literary Biography* 125). 170–77.

Gagiano, A. H. "Arthur Nortje." Scanlon, *South African Writers (Dictionary of Literary Biography* 225). 322–27.

Hacksley, Malcolm. "Nortje, Arthur." Gikandi, *Encyclopedia of African Literature.* 388–89.

Hobsbaum, Phillip. "Arthur Nortje." Parini, *World Writers in English.* 3:441–58.

Klopper, Dirk. "Nortje, Arthur Kenneth." Benson and Conolly, *Encyclopedia of Post-colonial Literatures in English.* 2:1105.

Richard Carl Ntiru, 1946–

Web Sites

"First Rains." *African Letters.* 25 July 2005, http://www.bowwave.org/AfricanWriters /Richard%20Ntiru.htm.

"Richard Carl Ntiru." *Contemporary Africa Database.* 25 July 2005, http://people .africadatabase.org/people/data/person15989.html.

Biographies and Criticism

Kabaji, Egara. "Ntiru, Richard Carl." Benson and Conolly, *Encyclopedia of Post-colonial Literatures in English*. 2:1165–66.

"Ntiru, Richard." Wordworks, *Modern Black Writers*. 552–55.
Excerpts from criticism published between 1973 and 1987.

Outa, George Odera. "Ntiru, Richard." Gikandi, *Encyclopedia of African Literature*. 396.

Nkem Nwankwo, 1936–

Web Sites

"Nkem Nwankwo." *Contemporary Africa Database*. 25 July 2005, http://people .africadatabase.org/en/person/15989.html.

Biographies and Criticism

Aiyejina, Funso. "Nwanko, Nkem." Benson and Conolly, *Encyclopedia of Post-colonial Literatures in English*. 2:1166.

Gikandi, Simon. "Nwankwo, Nkem." Gikandi, *Encyclopedia of African Literature*. 397

Flora (Nwanzuruaha) Nwapa, 1931–1993

Web Sites

"Flora Nwapa." *African Literature in English: Five Women Writers*. 25 July 2005, http://www.fb10.uni-bremen.de/anglistik/kerkhoff/AfrWomenWriters/Nwapa/ Nwapa.html.

"Flora Nwapa." *Anglophone and Lusophone African Women's Writing*. 25 Jul, 2005, http://www.ex.ac.uk/~ajsimoes/aflit/NwapaEN.html.

"Flora Nwapa." *Books and Writers*. 25 July 2005, http://www.kirjasto.sci.fi/nwapa .htm.

"Flora Nwapa." *Contemporary Africa Database*. 25 July 2005, http://people.africa database.org/people/data/person3215.html.

Leisure, Susan. "Flora Nwapa." *Postcolonial Studies at Emory*. 17 Aug. 1998. Emory U. 25 July 2005, http://www.emory.edu/ENGLISH/Bahri/Nwapa.html.

Biographies and Criticism

Carchidi, Victoria. "Nwapa, Flora (Nwanzuruaha)." Serafin, *Encyclopedia of World Literature in the 20th Century*. 3:409–10.

Eko, Ebele. "Nwapa, Flora." Benson and Conolly, *Encyclopedia of Post-colonial Literatures in English*. 2:1166–67.

Emenyonu, Ernest. "Flora Nwapa." Schellinger, *Encyclopedia of the Novel*. 3:951–52.

"Flora Nwapa." Hunter and Moore, *Black Literature Criticism Supplement*. 340–54.
Bio-critical introduction, list of major works, excerpts from criticism on Nwapa's works from 1986 to 1992, and an annotated bibliography.

"Flora Nwapa." Hunter et al., *Contemporary Literary Criticism*. 133:164–249.
Criticism published between 1986 and 1996.

Loflin, Christine. "Flora Nwapa." Parekh and Jagne, *Postcolonial African Writers: A Bio-bibliographical Critical Sourcebook.* [337] – 44.

Loy, Pamela S. and Ernest N. Emenyonu. "Efuru." Moss and Valestuk, *African Literature and Its Times* (*World Litertaure and Its Times* 2). 107–17.

"Nwapa, Flora." Robinson, *Modern Women Writers.* 3:380–90.
Excerpts from criticism published between 1971and 1994.

"Nwapa, Flora." Wordworks, *Modern Black Writers.* 555–59.
Excerpts from criticism published between 1972 and 1992.

Schmidt, Nancy J. "Nwapa, Flora." Pendergast and Pendergast, *St. James Guide to Children's Writers.* 800–1.

Umeh, Marie. "Nwapa, Flora." Gikandi, *Encyclopedia of African Literature.* 397–99.

Wilentz, Gay. "Flora Nwapa." Lindfors and Sander, *Twentieth-Century Caribbean and Black African Wrietrs, Second Series* (*Dictionary of Literary Biography* 125). 178–83.

Dictionaries, Encyclopedias, and Handbooks

Umeh, Marie. Ed. *Emerging Perspectives on Flora Nwapa; Critical and Theoretical Essays.* Trenton, NJ; Africa World Press, 1998.

Bibiliographies

Berrian, Brenda F. "Flora Nwapa (1931–1993)." *Research in African Literatures.* 26.2 (Summer 1995): [124] –29.
Bibliography of primary works, criticism, interviews, and bio-bibliographies published between 1966 and 1994.

Interviews

"Flora Nwapa." Ezenwa-Ohaeto, *Winging Words: Interviews with Nigerian Writers and Critics.* 22–30.

"Flora Nwapa." James, *In Their Own Voices.* 111–17.
Text of a 1985 interview.

Umeh, Marie. "The Poetics of Economic Independence for Female Empowerment: An Interview with Flora Nwapa." *Research In African Literatures.* 26. 2 (1995): 22–29.
Text of a 1992 interview.

Onuora Nzekwu, 1928–

"Onuora Nzekwu." *Contemporary Africa Database.* 25 July 2005, http://people.africa database.org/en/person/15985.html.

Biographies and Criticism

Gikandi, Simon. "Nzekwu, Onuora." Gikandi, *Encyclopedia of African Literature.* 400–1.

Killam, G. D. "Nzekwu, Onuora." Benson and Conolly, *Encyclopedia of Post-colonial Literatures in English.* 3:167–68.

"Nzekwu, Onuora." Wordworks, *Modern Black Writers.* 559–61.
Excerpts from criticism published between 1961 and 1971.

Okello Oculi, 1942–

Web Sites

"Okello Oculi." *Contemporary Africa Database.* 25 July 2005, http://people.africa
database.org/people/data/person16035.html.

Biographies and Criticism

Bardolph, J. "Oculi, Okello." Benson and Conolly, *Encyclopedia of Post-colonial
Literatures in English.* 2:1170.

Okumu, Charles. "Oculi, Okello." Gikandi, *Encyclopedia of African Literature.* [402].

"Oculi, Okello." *Contemporary Authors.* 143:318.

Asenath Odaga, 1938–

Web Sites

"Asenath Bole Odaga." *Anglophone and Lusophone African Women's Writing.*
25 July 2005, http://www.ex.ac.uk/~ajsimoes/aflit/OdagaEN.html.

"Odaga, Asenath Bole." *African Children's Literature.* 25 July 25, 2005, http://web
.uflib.ufl.edu/cm/africana/odaga.htm.

Biographies and Criticism

"Odaga, Asenath (Bole) (Kiyuomba)." *Contemporary Authors.* 124: 331–33.

Schmidt, Nancy J. "Odaga, Asenath (Bole)." Pendergast aand Pendergast, *St. James
Guide to Children's Writers.* 804–5.

Interview

"Asenath Odega." James, *In Their Own Voices.* 123–35.
Text of a 1986 interview.

Grace Emily Ogot, 1930–

Web Sites

"Grace Ogot." *Anglophone and Lusophone African Women's Writing.* 25 July 2005,
http://www.ex.ac.uk/~ajsimoes/aflit/OgotEN.html.

Biographies and Crticism

Berrian, Brenda F. "Grace Ogot." Lindfors and Sander, *Twentieth-Century Caribbean
and Black African Writers, Second Series* (*Dictionary of Literary Biography*
125). 184–87.

Kabaji, Egara. "Ogot, Grace Akinyi." Benson and Conolly, *Encyclopedia of Post-
colonial Literatures in English.* 2: 1171–72.

Kurtz, J. Roger. "Ogot, Grace." Serafin, *Encyclopedia of World Literature in the 20th
Century.* 2: 422–23

"Ogot, Grace." Robinson, *Modern Women Writers.* 3:457–60.
Excerpts from criticism published between 1974 and 1992.

"Ogot, Grace." Wordworks, *Modern Black Writers.* 563–66.
Excerpts from criticism on Ogot's works from 1974 to 1996, with a
bibliography.

Ojwang, Dan Odhiambo. "Ogot, Grace (Emily Akinyi)." Gikandi, *Encyclopedia of African Literature*. 405.

Molara Ogundipe-Leslie, 1949–

Web Site

Molara Ogundipe." *Anglophone and Lusophone African Women's Writing*. 25 July 2005, http://www.ex.ac.uk/~ajsimoes/aflit/OgundipeEN.html.

Biographies and Criticism

Ogede, Ode S. "Molara Ogundipe-Leslie." Parekh and Jagne, *Postcolonial African Writers: A Bio-bibliographical Critical Sourcebook*. [345] –51.

"Ogundipe-Leslie, Molara." *Contemporary Authors*. 154:317–18.

Interview

"Molara Ogundipe-Leslie." James, *In Their Own Words*. 65–73.

(Ola)Wale Ogunyemi, 1939–2001

Web Sites

Banham, Martin. "Wale Ogunyemi." *The Guardian Obituaries*. (14 Feb. 2002). Guardian Unlimited. 25 July 2005, http://www.guardian.co.uk/obituaries/story/0,3604,649747,00.html.

"Wale Ogunyemi." *Contemporary Africa Database*. 25 July 2005, http://people.africa database.org/people/data/person12213.html.

Biographies and Criticism

Dunton, Chris. "Wale Ogunyemi." *Twentieth-Century Caribbean and Black African Writers, Third Series* (*Dictionary of Literary Biography* 157). 251–61.

Killam, G. D. "Ogunyemi, Wale." Benson and Conolly, *Encyclopedia of Post-colonial Literatures in English*. 2: 1172.

Gikandi, Simon. "Ogunyemi, Wale." Gikandi, *Encyclopedia of African Literature*. 406.

Tanure Ojaide, 1948–

Web Sites

"Tanure Ojaide." *Written Word*. Ed. Nkiru Nzegwu. Update unavailable. Africa resource.com. 25 July 2005, http://www.africaresource.com/poe/tanu.htm. Short biography and the text of some poems.

"Tanure Ojaide." *Contemporary Africa Database*. 25 July 2005, http://people.africa database.org/people/data/person13025.html.

"Tanure Ojaide." *Postcolonial African Literatures in English*. 25 July 2005, http://www.fb10.uni-bremen.de/anglistik/kerkhoff/AfricanLit/Ojaide.htm.

"Two Poems: Tanure Ojaide." *Left Curve*. 23 (n.d.). 25 July 2005, http://www.leftcurve.org/LC23webPages/ojaide.html. Text of "Home Song: II" and "Home Song: VIII."

Biographies and Criticism

Alabi, Adetayo. "Ojaide, Tanure." Benson and Conolly, *Encyclopedia of Post-colonial Literatures in English*. 2:1173.

Garuba, Harry. "Ojaide, Tanure." Gikandi, *Encyclopedia of African Literature*. 406–07.

Killam, G. D. "Tanure Ojaide." Cox, *African Writers*. 2:557–65.

Biography, analyses of Ojaide's works, and a select bibliography of works by and about him published between 1973 and 1995.

Nwankwo, Chimalum. "Ojaide, Tanure." Serafin, *Encyclopedia of World Literature in the 20th Century*. 2:425–26.

Interviews

"Tanure Ojaide." Ezenwa-Ohaeto, *Winging Words: Interviews with Nigerian Writers and Critics*. 93–100.

Femi Ojo-Ade, 1941–

Web Sites

"Poetry by Femi Ojo-Ade." *Mots Pluriels*. 7 (1998). 25 July 2005, http://www.arts .uwa.edu.au/MotsPluriels/MP798foj.html.
    Text of three poems.

Biographies and Criticism

"Ojo-Ade, Femi." *Contemporary Authors*. 181:347–48.

Atukewi Okai, 1941–

Web Sites

"Atukwei Okai." *Contemporary Africa Database*. 25 July 2005, http://people.africa database.org/people/data/person13230.html.

Biographies and Criticism

Asante, Yaw."Atukwei Okai." Benson and Conolly, *Encyclopedia of Post-colonial Literatures in English*. 2:1173–74.

Odamtten, Vincent O. "Okai, Atukwei." Gikandi, *Encyclopedia of African Literature*. 407.

Gabriel Imomotimi Gbaingbain Okara, 1921–

Web Sites

"Gabriel Okara." *Contemporary Africa Database*. 25 July 2005, http://people.africa database.org/people/data/person16037.html.

Biographies and Criticism

Garuba, Harry. "Okara, Gabriel." Gikandi, *Encyclopedia of African Literature*. 407.

Gingell, Susan. "Okara, Gabriel." Benson and Conolly, *Encyclopedia of Post-colonial Literatures in English*. 2:1174–75.

King, Bruce. "Gabriel Okara." Lindfors and Sander, *Twentieth-Century Caribbean and Black African Writers, Second Series* (*Dictionary of Literary Biography* 125). 188–99.

Lindfors, Bernth. "Okara, Gabriel." Serafin, *Encyclopedia of World Literature in the 20th Century*. 2:427.

"Okara, Gabriel." Wordworks, *Modern Black Writers*. 566–68.
Excerpts from criticism published between 1965 and 1974.

Parekh, Pushpa Naidu. "Gabriel Okara." Parekh and Jagne, *Postcolonial African Writers: A Bio-bibliographical Critical Sourcebook*. [352]–59.

Zabus, Chantal. "Gabriel Okara." Cox, *African Writers*. 2:567–82.
Biography, analyses of Okara's works, and a select bibliography of works by and about him published between 1963 and 1991.

Christopher Ifeanyichukwu Okigbo, 1932–1967

Web Sites

"Christopher Okigbo." *Books and Writers*. 25 July 2005, http://www.kirjasto.sci.fi/okigbo.htm.

"Christopher Okigbo." *Contemporary Africa Database*. 25 July 2005, http://people.africadatabase.org/people/data/person3759.html.

"Christopher Okigbo: An Overview." *Contemporary Postcolonial and Postimperial Literature in English*. 25 July 2005, http://www.thecore.nus.edu.sg/landow/post/nigeria/okigbo/okigboov.html.

"The Passage." *African Letters*. 25 July 2005, http://www.bowwave.org/African Writers/Chirstopher%20Okigbo.htm.

Web Concordance to the Collected Poems of Christopher Okigbo. Ed. Michael J. C. Echeruo. Copyright 2002. Syracuse U. 25 July 2005, http://echeruo.syr.edu/okigbo/Okigbo.htm.
The four-frame format of the site makes it easy to select items from the list and have them displayed in their specific contexts or situate them within the source poems. The main page of the site also includes a biography and the text of a poem dedicated to Okigbo.

Biographies and Criticism

Aiyejina, Funso. "Christopher Okigbo." Cox, *African Writers*. 2:583–98.
Biography, analyses of Okigbo's works, and a select bibliography of works by and about him published between 1958 to 1991.

"Christopher Okigbo." Draper, *Black Literature Criticism*. 3:1522–30.
Biography, list of major works, excerpts of criticism from 1968 to 1975, and an annotated bibliography.

"Christopher Okigbo." Draper et al., *Contemporary Literary Criticism*. 84. 296–344.
Interview and excerpts from criticism published between 1965 and 1986.

"Christopher Okigbo." Drew Kalasky, *Poetry Criticism*. 7. Detroit: Gale, 1994. 217–57.
Excerpts from criticism published between 1965 and 1986.

Elimimian, Isaac I. "Okigbo, Ifeanyichukwu Christopher." Benson and Conolly, *Encyclopedia of Post-colonial Literatures in English.* 2: 1175–76.

Garuba, Harry. "Okigbo, Christopher." Gikandi, *Encyclopedia of African Literature.* 408–9.

Iyer, Nalini. "Christopher Ifeanyichukwu Okigbo." Parekh and Jagne, *Postcolonial African Writers: A Bio-bibliographical Critical Sourcebook.* [360] –63.

Lindfors, Bernth. "Okigbo, Christopher." Serafin, *Encyclopedia of World Literature in the 20th Century.* 2:427–28.

Nwoga, Donatus Ibe. "Christopher Okigbo." Lindfors and Sander, *Twentieth-Century Caribbean and Black African Writers, Second Series* (*Dictionary of Literary Biography* 125). 200–24.

"Okigbo, Christopher." Wordworks, *Modern Black Writers.* 568–72. Excerpts from criticism published between 1963 and 1986.

Ifeoma Okoye, n.d.

Web Sites

"Ifeoma Okoye." *Contemporary Africa Database.* 25 July 2005, http://people.africa database.org/en/person/16040.html.

Ifeoma Okoye's Web Site. Ed. Ifeoma Okoye. 17 May 2004. Geocities.com. 25 July 2005, http://www.geocities.com/ifeokoye/index.html. A sparsely designed Web site with biographical information and brief excerpts from Okoye's works.

Biographies and Criticism

"Ifeoma Okoye: Maladies, Malaise, and National Recovery." Chikwenye Okonjo Ogunyemi. *Africa Wo/Man Palava: The Nigerian Novel by Women.* Chicago: University of Chicago Press, 1996. 302–7.

Interviews

"Ifeoma Okoye." Ezenwa-Ohaeto, *Winging Words: Interviews with Nigerian Writers and Critics.* 47–52.

Isidore (Chukwudozi Oghenerhuele) Okpewho, 1941–

Web Sites

"Isidore Okpewho." *Contemporary Africa Database.* 25 July 2005, http://people .africadatabase.org/people/data/person16042.html.

Biographies and Criticism

Emenony, Ernest. "The Last Duty." Moss and Valestuk, *African Literature and Its Times* (*World Literature and Its Times* 2). 237–45.

Gikandi, Simon. "Okephwo [sic] , Isidore." *Encyclopedia of African Literature.* 407–8.

King, Bruce. "Okpewho, Isidore." Benson and Conolly, *Encyclopedia of Post-colonial Literatures in English.* 2: 1176–77.

Obiechina, Emmanuel. "Isidore Okpewho." Lindfors and Sander, *Twentieth-Century Caribbean and Black African Writers, Third Series* (*Dictionary of Literary Biography* 157). 262–76.

Interviews

"Isidore Okpewho." Ezenwa-Ohaeto, *Winging Words: Interviews with Nigerian Writers and Critics.* 129–34.

Ben Okri, 1959–

Web Sites

"Ben Okri." *Booker McConnell Prize Pages.* Eds. Bradley C. Shoop and Alice O'Dea. Update unavailable. U. Tennessee at Chattanooga. 25 July 2005, http://www.utc.edu/~engldept/booker/okri.htm.
Bibliography of primary and secondary works and a biographical sketch.

"Ben Okri." *Books and Writers.* 25 July 2005, http://www.kirjasto.sci.fi/okri.htm.

"Ben Okri." *Contemporary Africa Database.* 25 July 2005, http://people.africa database.org/people/data/person3264.html.

"Ben Okri." *Contemporary Postcolonial and Postimperial Literature in English.* 25 July 2005, http://www.scholars.nus.edu.sg/post/nigeria/okri/okriov.html.

"Ben Okri." *Poetry International Web.* Ed. and update unavailable. Poetryinternational.org. 25 July 2005, http://www.poetryinternational.org/cwolk/view/15733.

Biographical information

"Ben Okri." *Writers Talk: Ideas of Our Time.* 25 July 2005, http://www.roland-collection.com/rolandcollection/literature/101/W74.htm.

Smith, Jules. "Ben Okri." *Contemporary Writers.* 25 July 2005, http://www.contemporarywriters.com/authors/?p=auth82.
Provides a biography, list or works, and a critical overview of his writing.

Ball Kimberly. "The Famished Road." Moss and Valestuk, *African Literature and Its Times* (*World Literature and Its Times* 2). 151–61.

"Ben Okri." Eds. Christopher Giroux and Brigham Narins. *Contemporary Literary Criticism* 87. Detroit: Gale, 1995. 312–31.
Excerpts from criticism published between 1980 and 1993.

Bennett, Robert. "Ben Okri." Parekh and Jagne, *Postcolonial African Writers: A Bio-bibliographical Critical Sourcebook.* [364] –73.

Cooper, Brenda. "Okri, Ben." Gikandi, *Encyclopedia of African Literature.* 412–13.

———. "Okri, Ben." Serafin, *Encyclopedia of World Literature in the 20th Century.* 2: 428–29.

Garuba, Harry. "Ben Okri." Lindfors and Sander, *Twentieth-Century Caribbean and Black African Writers, Third Series* (*Dictionary of Literary Biography* 157). 277–85.

Graff, Ann-Barbara. "Ben Okri." Mosely, *British Novelists since 1960, Fourth Series* (*Dictionary of Literary Biography* 231). 200–06.

King, Bruce. "Okri, Ben." Benson and Conolly, *Encyclopedia of Post-colonial Literatures in English.* 2:1177–79.

"Okri, Ben." Wordworks, *Modern Black Writers.* 573–76.
Excerpts from criticism published between 1988 and 1998, with a bibliography.

Quayson, Ato. "Ben Okri." Cox, *African Writers.* 2:599–608.
Biography, analyses of Okri's works, and a select bibliography of works by and about him published between 1980 and 1995.

Warnes, Christopher. "Ben Okri." Parini, *World Writers in English.* 2:459–75.

Dictionaries, Handbooks, and Encyclopedias

Moh, Felicia Okah. *Ben Okri: An Introduction to His Early Fiction.* Enugu, Nigeria: Fourth Dimension, 2001.

Interviews

"Ben Okri." Wilkinson, *Talking With African Writers.* 76–89.
Text of a 1990 interview.

Wilce, Hilary. "My Best Teacher." *Times Educational Supplement.* (29 Sept. 2000): 7.

(Ban)Kole Omotoso, 1943–

Web Sites

"Kole Omotoso." *Contemporary Africa Database.* 25 July 2005, http://people.africa database.org/people/data/person16044.html.

Biographies and Criticism

Aiyejina, Funso. "Omotoso, Kole." Benson and Conolly, *Encyclopedia of Post-colonial Literatures in English.* 2:1180.

Atai, Uko. "Kole Omotoso." Cox, *African Writers.* 2:609–17.
Biography, analyses of Omotoso's works, and a select bibliography of works by and about him published between 1971 and 1988.

Balogun, F. Odun. "Kole Omotoso." Lindfors and Sander, *Twentieth-Century Caribbean and Black African Writers, Second Series* (*Dictioanry of Literary Biography* 125). 238–42.

Motsa, Zodwa. "Omotoso, Kole." Gikandi, *Encyclopedia of African Literature.* 413.

(Nathaniel) Kola(wole) Onadipe, 1922–

Web Sites

"Kola Onadipe." *Contemporary Africa Database.* 25 July 2005, http://people.africa database.org/people/data/person11261.html.

"Onadipe, Kola." *African Children's Literature.* 25 July 2005, http://web.uflib.ufl.edu /cm/africana/onadipe.htm.

Biographies and Criticism

"Onadipe, (Nathaniel) Kola(wole) (Nita Kolon.)." *Contemporary Authors.* 101:353–54.

Osonye Tess (Akaeka) Onwueme, 1955–

Web Sites

"Osonye Tess Onwueme." *Anglophone and Lusophone African Women's Writing.*
    25 July 2005, http://www.ex.ac.uk/~ajsimoes/aflit/OnwuemeEN.html.

Osonye Tess Onwueme. Ed. Osonye Tess Onwueme. Update unavailable.
    Writertess.com. 25 July 2005, http://www.writertess.com/.
    Combining information on her academic and creative careers, the author's
official Web site includes a list of plays and photos of scenes from her stage
productions.

"Osonye Tess Onwueme: An Overview." *Contemporary Postcolonial and
    Postimperial Literature in English.* 25 July 2005, http://www.scholars.nus.edu
    .sg/landow/post/nigeria/tess/onwuemeov.html.

Pierce, Brooke. "The Missing Face." *Theatermania.com.* 21 May 2001. 25 July 2005,
    http://ibs.theatermania.com/content/news.cfm?int_news_id=1405.
    Review of the New Federal Theatre (New York) production of Onwueme's play.

Biographies and Criticism

Chukuma, Helen. "Onwueme, Tess." Benson and Conolly, *Encyclopedia of Post-
    colonial Literatures in English.* 2:1181–82.

Eke, Maureen N. "Onwueme, Osonye Tess." Gikandi, *Encyclopedia of African
    Literature.* 414–15.

Nwankwo, Chimalum. "Onwueme, (Osonye) Tess." Serafin, *Encyclopedia of World
    Literature in the 20th Century.* 2:442–43.

"Onwueme, Tess." Robinson, *Modern Women Writers.* 3:474–77.
    Excerpts from criticism published between 1986 and 1992.

"Onwueme, Tess." Wordworks, *Modern Black Writers.* 576–78.
    Excerpts from criticism published between 1992 and 1998.

Femi Osofisan (Okinba Launko), 1946–

Web Sites

"Femi Osofisan." *Contemporary Africa Database.* 25 July 2005, http://people.africa
    database.org/people/data/person3295.html.

"Femi Osofisan: An Overview." *Contemporary Postcolonial and Postimperial
    Literature in English.* 25 July 2005, http://www.scholars.nus.edu.sg/post/
    nigeria/osofisan/osofisanov.html.

Biographies and Criticism

Elimimiam, Isaac. "Osofisan, Babafemi Adeyemi." Benson and Conolly,
    Encyclopedia of Post-colonial Literatues in English. 2:1183–84.

Gikandi, Simon. "Osofisan, Femi." Gikandi, *Encyclopedia of African Literature.*
    421–23.

Griffiths, Gareth. "Femi Osofisan." Cox, *African Writers.* 2:619–29.
    Biography, analyses of Osofisan's works, and a select bibliography of works by
and about him published between 1975 and 1992.

"Osofisan, Femi." Wordworks, *Modern Black Writers.* 578–82.
Excerpts from criticism published between 1982 and 1997 and a bibliography.

Owoyela, Oyekan. "Osofisan, Femi." *Encyclopedia of World Literature in the 20th Century.* 2:450–51.

Richards, Sandra. "Femi Osofisan." Lindfors and Sander, *Twentieth-Century Caribbean and Black African Writers, Second Series* (*Dictionary of Literary Biography* 125). 243–50.

Savory, Elaine. "Femi Osofisan." Parekh and Jagne, *Postcolonial African Writers: A Bio-bibliographical Critical Sourcebook.* [374] –81.

Interviews

Jeyifo, Biodun. "Interview with Femi Osofisan." *Yearbook of Comparative and General Literature.* 43 (1995):120–32.

Niyi Osundare, 1947–

Web Sites

"Niyi Osundare." *Contemporary Africa Database.* 25 July 2005, http://people.africa database.org/people/data/person11734.html.

Ogoanah, N. F. "'I'm a Humanist: Niyi Ousndare on the Poetry of Niyi Osundare (An Interview)." *West Africa Review.* 4.1 (2003). 25 July 2005, http://www.west africareview.com/vol4.1/ogoanah-osundare.html.
Text of an interview.

Biographies and Criticism

Aiyejina, Funso. "Osundare, Niyi." Benson and Conolly, *Encyclopedia of Post-colonial Literatures in English.* 2:1186–87.

Burness, Don. "Niyi Osundare." Lindfors and Sander, *Twentieth-Century Caribbean and Black African Writers, Third Series* (*Dictionary of Literary Biography* 157). 286–95.

Garuba, Harry. "Osundare, Niyi." Gikandi, *Encyclopedia of African Literature.* 424.

Killam, G. D. "Niyi Osundare." Cox, *African Writers.* 2:631–40.
Biography, analyses of Osundare's works, and a select bibliography of primary and secondary works.

"Osundare, Niyi." Wordworks, *Modern Black Writers.* 582–87.
Excerpts from criticism published between 1986 and 1995.

Dictionaries, Handbooks, and Encyclopedias

Na'Allah, Abdul-Rashid. Ed. *The People's Poet: Emerging Perspectives on Niyi Osundare.* Trenton, N. J.: Africa World Press, 2003.

Interviews

Hogue, Cynthia and Nancy Easterlin. "An Interview with Niyi Osundare." *Contemporary Literature.* 41.2 (Summer 2000): [191]–213.

"Niyi Osundare." Ezenwa-Ohaeto, *Winging Words: Interviews with Nigerian Writers and Critics.* 66–77.

Yambo Ouologuem (Utto Rudolph), 1940–

Web Sites

"Ouologuem, Yambo." *Books and Writers.* 25 July 2005, http://www.kirjasto.sci.fi/ ouolo.htm.

"Yambo Ouologuem." *ChickenBones: A Journal for Literary and Artistic African-American Themes.* Ed. and update unavailable. 25 July 2005, http://www .nathanielturner.com/yamboouologuem.htm.

Biography, extracts from reviews of *Bound to Violence,* and links to selections from two chapters and the text of a 1971 interview.

Biographies and Criticism

Ouédraogo, Jean. "Ouologuem, Yambo." Gikandi, *Encyclopedia of African Literature.* 425.

"Ouologuem, Yambo." Wordworks, *Modern Black Writers.* 587–92.

Excerpts from criticsm on Ouologuem's works from 1974 to 1998.

Dictionaries, Handbooks, and Encyclopedias

Wise, Christopher. Ed. *Yambo Ouologuem: Postcolonial Writer, Islamic Militant.* Boulder, Colo.: Lynne Reinner, 1999.

Ferdinand Oyono, 1929–

Web Sites

Ferdinand Oyono–Une Vie de Boy: Bibliographie Sélective. Ed. Anton Andereggen. Update unavailable. Lewis and Clark C. 25 July 2005, http://www.lclark.edu/ ~anton/b.boy.htm.

Select bibliography of secondary sources on Oyono's novel. Some references lack publication dates.

"Ferdinand Léopold Oyono." *Contemporary Africa Database.* 25 July 2005, http:// people.africadatabase.org/people/data/person4422.html.

Biographies and Criticism

Bishop, Stephen. "Oyono, Ferdinand." Gikandi, *Encyclopedia of African Literature.* 427–28.

Dunton, Chris. "Ferdinand Oyono." Cox, *African Writers.* 2:641–49.

Biography, analyses of Oyono's works, and a select bibliography of works by and about him published between 1956 and 1991.

Everson, Victoria. "Ferdinand Oyono." Parekh and Jagne, *Postcolonial African Writers: A Bio-bibliographical Critical Sourcebook.* [382] –86.

"Oyono, Ferdinand." Wordworks, *Modern Black Writers.* 592–94.

Excerpts from criticism published between 1956 and 1997.

Popkin, Debra. "Oyono, Ferdinand." Serafin, *Encyclopedia of World Literature in the 20th Century.* 2:458–59.

Sams, Victorian and Pamela Loy. Moss and Valestuk, *African Literature and Its Times (World Literature and Its Times* 2).193–202.

Sarvan, C. P. "French Colonialism in Africa: The Early Novels of Ferdinand Oyono." Genova, *Companion to Contemporary World Literature*. 1: 319–24.
Overview of Oyono's early writing.

Guillaume Oyono-Mbia, 1939–

Web Sites

"Guillaume Oyono-Mbia." *Contemporary Africa Database*. 25 July 2005, http://people.africadatabase.org/people/data/person4423.html.

Biographies and Criticism

Bishop, Stephen. "Oyônô-Mbia, Guillaume." Gikandi, *Encyclopedia of African Literature*. 428–29.

"Guillaume Oyono-Mbia: *Trois pretendants...un mari*." Conteh-Morgan, *Theatre and Drama in Francophone Africa*.184–92.
Brief biography and a critical analysis of Oyono-Mbia's play.

Lewis, Tim. "Oyono-Mbia, Guillaume." Chevalier, *Contemporary World Writers*. 386–87.

Okot p'Bitek, 1931–1982

Web Sites

"Okot p'Bitek." *African Writers: Voices of Change*. 25 July 2005, http://web.uflib.ufl.edu/cm/africana/pbitek.htm.

"Okot p'Bitek." *African Poetry*. 25 July 2005, http://www.aghadiuno.com/poetry/african/op.html.

"Okot p'Bitek." *Books and Writers*. 25 July 2005, http://www.kirjasto.sci.fi/pbitek.htm.

"Okot p'Bitek." *Contemporary Africa Database*. 25 July 2005, http://people.africadatabase.org/people/data/person3359.html.

"In My Mother's House." *African Letters*. 25 July 2005, http://www.bowwave.org/AfricanWriters/Okot%20P'%20Bitek.htm.

Biographies and Criticism

Ayodo, Awuor. "Okot P'Bitek." Parekh and Jagne, *Postcolonial African Writers: A Bio-bibliographical Critical Sourcebook*. [397]–99.

Cooke, Michael G. "P'Bitek, Okot." Serafin, *Encyclopedia of World Literature in the 20th Century*. 2:506.

Lindfors, Bernth. "Okot p'Bitek." Lindfors and Sander, *Twentieth-Century Caribbean and Black African Writers, Second Series* (*Dictioanry of Literary Biography* 125). 225–37.

Littleton, Jacob. "Song of Lawino and Song of Ocol." *African Literature and Its Times* (*World Literature and Its Times* 2). 387–96.

"Okot p'Bitek." Draper, *Black Literature Criticism*. 3:1559–80.
Biography, list of major works, excerpts from criticism from 1981 to 1988, and annotated bibliography.

Okumu, Charles. "Okot p'Bitek." Gikandi, *Encyclopedia of African Literature*. 409–11.

"P'Bitek, Okot." Wordworks, *Modern Black Writers*. 595–98.
Excerpts from criticism published between 1967 and 1992.

Pido, J. P. Odoch. "Okot p'Bitek." Cox, *African Writers*. 2:669–83.
Biography, with analyses of p'Bitek's works, and a select bibliography of primary and secondary works published between 1953 and 1993.

Peter K. Palangyo, 1939–1993

Web Sites

"Peter Palangyo." *Contemporary Africa Database*. 25 July 2005, http://people
.africadatabase.org/people/data/person16081.html.

Biographies and Criticism

Ojwang, Dan Odhiambo. "Palangyo, Peter K." Gikandi, *Encyclopedia of African Literature*. [430] –431.

Alan (Stewart) Paton, 1903–1988

Web Sites

"Alan Paton." *African Writers: Voices of Change*. 25 July 2005, http://web.uflib.ufl
.edu/cm/africana/paton.htm.

"Alan Paton." *Contemporary Africa Database*. 25 July 2005, http://people.africa
database.org/people/data/person3332.html.

"Alan Paton." *Introducing South African Writers*. 25 July 2005, http://homepage
.oniduo.pt/chacmalissimo/SAfrican/html/alan_paton.htm.

"Alan (Stewart) Paton." *Books and Writers*. 25 July 2005, http://www.kirjasto.sci.fi/
apaton.htm.

"'The Negro in America Today': South African Novelist Alan Paton Dissects the Racial Situation in the South in the Year of Brown vs Board of Education." *History Matters*. Eds. Pennee Bender et al. Update unavailable. George Mason U. 25 July 2005, http://historymatters.gmu.edu/d/6337/.
Reprint of Paton's article on segregation in the United States, originally published in *Collier's* (15 Oct. 1954).

Biographies and Criticism

"Alan Paton." Draper, *World Literature Criticism*. 4:2640–56.
Excerpts from criticism published between 1948 and 1962.

"Alan Paton." Schmitt et al., *Contemporary Literary Criticism*. 106:276–311.
Excerpts from criticism published between 1948 and 1989.

Alexander, Peter F. "Alan Paton." Cox, *African Writers*. 2:651–67.
Biography, with analyses of Paton's works, and a select bibliography of primary and secondary works published between 1948 and 1992.

———. "Alan Paton." Scanlon, *South African Writers* (*Dictionary of Literary Biography* 225). 328–45.

———. "Paton, Alan Stewart." Gikandi, *Encyclopedia of African Literature*. 432–33.

Johnson, Manly. "Paton, Alan." Serafin, *Encyclopedia of World Literature in the 20th Century.* 2:495–96.

Loy, Pamela. "Cry the Beloved Country." Moss and Valestuk, *African Literature and Its Times (World Literature and Its Times* 2). 57– 65.

Nel, Jo E. "Alan Paton." Parekh and Jagne, *Postcolonial African Writers: A Bio-bibliographical Critical Sourcebook.* [391]–95.

Paton, Jonathan. "Alan Paton: Comfort in Desolation." Ross, *International Literature in English.* 161–69.
    Survey of major themes, and an annotated bibliography of selected criticsm.

Van der Vlies, Andrew. "Alan Paton." Parini, *World Writers in English.* 2:495–514.

Pepetela (Artur Carlos Mauricio Pestana), 1941–

Web Sites

Baer, Eugene M. "The Secret of Yaka: Pepetela and Colonialism." *H–AfrLitCine* (Feb. 1998). Michigan State U. 25 July 2005, http://www.h-net.org/reviews/showrev.cgi?path=8151888342598.
    Review of *Yaka.*

"Pepetela (Artur Pestana)." *Contemporary Africa Database.* 25 July 2005, http://people.africadatabase.org/people/data/person3337.html.

Zimler, Richard (trans.). "From *A Dog in Luanda." The Literary Review: Fiction* (Winter/Spring 1996). 25 July 2005, http://theliteraryreview.org/tlr-p1.htm.
    Text of two short stories, "Tico the Poet" and "Rabies!"

Biographies and Criticism

Ball, Kimberly. "Yaka." Moss and Valestuk, *African Literature and Its Times (World Literature and Its Times* 2). 515–26.

Da Silva, Tony Simoes. "Pepetala." Serafin, *Encyclopedia of World Literature in the 20th Century.* 2:510–11.

Willis, Clive. "Pepetela." Cox, *African Writers.* 2:685–95.
    Biography, with analyses of Pepetela's works, and a select bibliography of primary and secondary works published 1976 to 1993.

Lenrie (Wilfred Leopold) Peters, 1932–

Web Sites

"Lenrie Peters." *Contemporary Africa Database.* 25 July 2005, http://people.africadatabase.org/people/data/person16083.html.

"Parachute Men Say." *African Poetry.* 25 July 2005, http://www.aghadiuno.com/poetry/african/lp.html.

Biographies and Criticism

Knipp, Thomas R. "Lenrie Peters." Lindfors and Sander, *Twentieth-Century Caribbean and Black African Writers, First Series (Dictionary of Literary Biography* 117). 252–57.

"Peters, Lenrie." Wordworks, *Modern Black Writers.* 598–600.
Excerpts from criticism published between 1966 and 1973, with a bibliography.

Priebe, Richard. "Peters, Lenrie." Serafin, *Encyclopedia of World Literature in the 20th Century.* 2:520–21.

Sol(omon) (T)shekisho Plaatje, 1876–1932

Web Sites

"Native Life in South Africa." *LitNet.* 25 July 2005, http://www.litnet.co.za/africanlib/plaatje.asp.

"Sol Plaatje." *Introducing South African Writers.* 25 July 2005, http://homepage.oniduo.pt/chacmalissimo/SAfrican/html/sol_plaatje.htm.

Sol Plaatje: Native Life in South Africa. Ed. Neil Parsons. Update unavailable. History Dept., U. of Botswana. 25 July 2005, http://www.thuto.org/ubh/etext/nlisa/nlcon.htm.
E-text of Plaatje's *Native Life in South Africa.*

"Plaatje, Solomon Tshekisho." *Biographies of Former ANC Leaders and Activists.* Ed. unavailable. 11 May 2004. African National Congress. 25 July 2005, http://www.anc.org.za/ancdocs/history/people/plaatje/plaatje.html.
Biography, with a list of books by and about Plaatje.

"Solomon Tshekisho Plaatje." *McGregor Museum.* Ed. unavailable.3 Mar. 2004. Museumsnc.co.za. 25 July 2005, http://www.museumsnc.co.za/McGregor/departments/history/solplaat/solplaat.htm.
Provides biographical information on Plaatje and his family, with photos included.

Biographies and Criticism

Couzens, Tim. "Plaatje, Solomon Tshekisho." Benson and Conolly, *Encyclopedia of Post-colonial Literatures in English.* 2:1222–23.

Midgley, Peter. "Sol T. Plaatje." Scanlon, *South African Writers* (*Dictionary of Literary Biography* 225). 346–57.

Mpe, Phaswane. "Plaatje, Solomon Tshekisho." Gikandi, *Encyclopedia of African Literature.* 436.

"Sol T. Plaatje." Hunter and Moore, *Black Literature Criticism Supplement.* 387–415.

Bio-critical introduction, list of major works, excerpts from criticism on Plaatje's works from 1930 to 1993, and an annotated bibliography.

Willan, Brian P. "Sol T. Plaatje." Lindfors and Sander, *Twentieth-Century Caribbean and Black African Writers, Second Series* (*Dictionary of Literary Biography* 125). 251–55.

Jean Pliya, 1931–

Web Sites

"Jean Pliya." *Contemporary Africa Database.* 25 July 2005, http://people.africadatabase.org/people/data/person4315.html.

Biographies and Criticism

"Jean Pliya: *Kondo le requin.*" Conteh-Morgan, *Theatre and Drama in Francophone Africa.* 164–73.
Brief biography, with a critical analysis of Pliya's play.

Gabara, Rachel. "Pliya, Jean." Gikandi, *Encyclopedia of African Literature.* 436–47.

William Charles Franklyn Plomer, 1903–1973

Web Sites

"William Plomer." *Introducing South African Writers.* 25 July 2005, http://homepage
.oniduo.pt/chacmalissimo/SAfrican/html/william_plomer.htm.

Biographies and Criticism

Alexander, Peter F. "Plomer, William Charles Franklyn." Benson and Conolly, *Encyclopedia of Post-colonial Literatures in English.* 2:1224–26.

Boxwell, D. A. "William Plomer." Johnson, *British Novelists between the Wars (Dictionary of Literary Biography* 191). 256–65.

Gikandi, Simon. "Plomer, William." Gikandi, *Encyclopedia of African Literature.* 437.

Heywood, Christopher. "William Plomer." Scanlon, *South African Writers (Dictionary of Literary Biography* 225). 358–69.

Lynch, Rachael J. "William Plomer." Rogers, *British Short-fiction Writers (Dictionary of Literary Biography* 162). 293–306.

Martin, Robert K. "William Plomer." Stanford, *British Poets, 1914–1945 (Dictionary of Literary Biography* 20). 280–84.

Noero, Gillian. "Plomer, William." Serafin, *Encyclopedia of World Literature in the 20th Century.* 2:555–56.

"Plomer, William." Riley, *Contemporary Literary Criticism.* 4:405–7.
Excerpts from criticism published between 1964 and 1974.

Powell, Neil. "William Plomer." Cox, *African Writers.* 2:697–706.
Biography, analyses of Plomer's works, and a select bibliography of primary and secondary works published 1925 and 1991.

Thomas Pringle, 1789–1834

Web Sites

"Thomas Pringle." *South African Sonnets.* Ed. E. H. Crouch. Update unavailable. Sonnet Central. 25 July 2005, http://www.sonnets.org/pringle.htm.
Text of eight poems.

Degnan, Tim "Thomas Pringle, 'The Slave Dealer.'" *Editing Anti-Slavery Poems.* Ed. Alan Richardson. 3 Nov. 1999. English Dept., Boston College. 25 July 2005, http://www2.bc.edu/~richarad/asp/tpsd.html.
Text of Pringle's poem, with notes and a short critical introduction.

Biographies and Criticism

Klopper, Dirk. "Thomas Pringle." Scanlon, *South African Writers (Dictionary of Literary Biography* 225). 370–381.

Gikandi, Simon. "Pringle, Thomas." Gikandi, *Encyclopedia of African Literature.* 448–49.

Jean-Joseph Rabearivelo, 1901–1937

Web Sites

"Jean-Joseph Rabearivelo." *Books and Writers.* 25 July 2005, http://www.kirjasto.sci .fi/rabie.htm.

"Jean-Joseph Rabearivelo." *Francophone African Poets in English Translation.* 25 July 2005, http://web.uflib.ufl.edu/cm/africana/rabieri.htm.

Biographies and Criticism

Adejunmobi, Moradewun A. "Jean-Joseph Rabearivelo." Parekh and Jagne, *Postcolonial African Writers: A Bio-bibliographical Critical Sourcebook.* [400] –7.

Adejunmobi, Moradewun A. "Rabéarivelo, Jean-Joseph." Serafin, *Encyclopedia of World Literature in the 20th Century.* 2:[623] –24.

Beckett, Carole M. "Rabéarivelo, Jean-Joseph." Gikandi, *Encyclopedia of African Literature.* [453] –54.

"Rabéarivelo, Jean-Joseph." Wordworks, *Modern Black Writers.* 617–19. Excerpts from criticism published between 1967 and 1988.

Jacques Rabémananjara, 1913–

Web Sites

Compan-Barnard, Magali. "Jacques Rabémananjara." *Ile en île.* 25 July 2005, http:// www.lehman.cuny.edu/ile.en.ile/paroles/rabemananjara.html.

Biographies and Criticism

Adejunmobi, Moradewun A. "Rabémananjara, Jacques." Serafin, *Encyclopedia of World Literature in the 20th Century.* 2:624–25.

Beckett, Carole M. "Rabémananjara, Jacques." Gikandi, *Encyclopedia of African Literature.* 454–56.

Interview

"Jacques Rabemananjara and Christiane Yandé Diop." Bennetta Jules-Rosette, *Black Paris.* Urbana and Chicago: U. of Illinois, 1998. [43] –48. Text of a 1988 interview with Rabemananjara and Diop.

Charlotte Arrisoa Rafenomanjato, 1938–

Web Sites

"Charlotte-Arrisoa Rafenomanjato." *Contemporary Africa Database.* 26 July 2005, http://people.africadatabase.org/people/data/person11628.html.

"Charlotte Arrisoa Rafenomanjato." *Reading Women Writers and African Literatures.* 26 July 2005, http://www.arts.uwa.edu.au/AFLIT/Rafenomanjato.html.

Biographies and Criticism

Beckett, Carole M. "Rafenomanjato, Charlotte Arrisoa." Gikandi, *Encyclopedia of African Literature.* 456–57.

Michèle Rakotoson, 1948–

Web Sites

"Michele Rakotoson." *Reading Women Writers and African Literatures.* 26 July 2005, http://www.arts.uwa.edu.au/AFLIT/RakotosonMicheleEng.html.

"Rencontre avec Michèle Rakotoson." *Echos du Capricorne.* Ed. and update unavailable. 26 July 2005, http://perso.club-internet.fr/cjbenoit/french/MicheleRakotoson.html.
  Transcript of a radio interview and a list of Rakotoson's books.

Biographies and Criticism

Adejunmobi, Moradewun A. "Rakotoson, Michèle." Serafin, *Encyclopedia of World Literature in the 20th Century.* 2:632.

Beckett, Carole M. "Rakotoson, Michèle." Gikandi, *Encyclopedia of African Literature.* 457.

Interview

Gray, Stephen. "Michèle Rakotoson Speaks with Stephen Gray." *Research in African Literatures.* 32.4 (2001):[155] –59.

Angèle Ntyugwetondo Rawiri, 1954–

Web Sites

"Ntyugwetondo Angèle Rawiri." *Reading Women Writers and African Literatures.* 26 Jul 2005, http://www.arts.uwa.edu.au/AFLIT/RawiriAngeleeng%7F%7F%7F.html.

Biographies and Criticism

"Angèle Rawiri: 'I Have Children, Therefore I Am.'" d'almeida, Irene *Francophone African Women Writers: Destroying the Emptiness of Silence.* Gainesville: U. Florida, 1994. 87–98.
  Studies the theme of childlessness in Rawiri's *Fureurs et cris de femmes.*

Ngom, M'bare. "Rawiri, Angèle Ntyugwetondo." Gikandi, *Encyclopedia of African Literature.* 458.

Alifa Rifaat, 1930–1996

Web Sites

"Alifa Rifaat." *Contemporary Africa Database.* 26 July 2005, http://people.africadatabase.org/people/data/person12503.html.

Biographies and Criticism

Sheble, Riham. "Rifaat, Alifa." Gikandi, *Encyclopedia of African Literature.* 462.

Richard Rive, 1931–1989

Web Sites

"Richard Rive." *Contemporary Africa Database.* 26 July 2005, http://people.africa database.org/en/person/16085.html.

"Richard Rive." *Introducing South African Writers.* 26 July 2005, http://homepage .oniduo.pt/chacmalissimo/SAfrican/html/richard_rive.htm.

Biographies and Criticism

Handley, Patricia. "Rive, Richard Moore." Benson and Conolly, *Encyclopedia of Post-colonial Literatures in English.* 2:1369–70.

———. "Richard Rive." Scanlon, *South African Writers* (*Dictionary of Literary Biography* 225). 382–94.

Motsa, Zodwa. "Rive, Richard Moore." Gikandi, *Encyclopedia of African Literature.* 462–63.

"Rive, Richard." Wordworks, *Modern Black Writers.* 631–34.
Excerpts from criticism published between 1976 and 1996.

Trump, Martin. "Richard Rive." Lindfors and Sander, *Twentieth-Century Caribbean and Black African Writers, Second Series* (*Dictionary of Literary Biography* 125). 261–64.

Shaaban Robert, 1909–1962

Web Sites

"Shaaban Robert." *Contemporary Africa Database.* 26 July 2005, http://people.africa database.org/en/person/13163.html.

Biographies and Criticism

Arnold, Stephen N. "Robert, Shaaban." Serafin, *Encyclopedia of World Literature in the 20th Century.* 2:685.

Mbele, Joseph. "Robert, Shaaban." Gikandi, *Encyclopedia of African Literature.* 463–64.

"Robert, Shaaban." Wordworks, *Modern Black Writers.* 634–36.
Excerpts from criticism published between 1971 and 1989.

Sheila Roberts, 1937–

Web Sites

Horn, Annette. "Daughters and Other Dutiful Women. Ed. Peter Horn. 24 Dec. 2001. Iafrica.com. 26 July 2005, http://users.iafrica.com/h/ho/hornpet/Dutiful%20 Women.htm.
Review of Roberts' book originally published in *New Contrast* 96 (1996).

"Sheila Cussons." *Introducing South African Writers.* 26 July 2005, http://homepage .oniduo.pt/chacmalissimo/SAfrican/html/sheila_roberts.htm.

"Sheila Roberts." *Anglophone and Lusophone African Women's Writing.* 26 July 2005, http://www.ex.ac.uk/~ajsimoes/aflit/RobertsEN.html.

"Sheila Roberts." *Contemporary Africa Database.* 26 July 2005, http://people.africa
database.org/people/data/person16086.html.

Biographies and Criticism

MacKenzie, Craig. "Roberts, Sheila." Benson and Conolly, *Encyclopedia of Post-
colonial Literatures in English.* 2:1372–73.

"Roberts, Sheila." *Contemporary Authors.* 102:434.

Daphne (Marie) Rooke (Robert Pointon), 1914–

Web Sites

"Rooke, Daphne." *KwaZulu Literary Map.* Copyright 2005. Kzn.za.org. 26 July 2005,
http://literature.kzn.org.za/lit/59.xml.

   Brief biography, excerpt from *A Grove of Fever Trees,* and a list of Rooke's
works.

Biographies and Criticism

Green, Michael. "Rooke, Daphne Marie." Benson and Conolly, *Encyclopedia of Post-
colonial Literatures in English.* 2:1378–79.

"Rooke, Daphne (Marie) (Robert Pointon.)." *Contemporary Authors.* 53–56:491.

(Emmanuel Gladstone) Ola(wale) Rotimi, 1938–2000

Web Sites

"Ola Rotimi." *Contemporary Africa Database.* 26 July 2005, http://people.africa
database.org/people/data/person16087.html.

Biographies and Criticism

Adedeji, Joel. "Ola Rotimi." Lindfors and Sander, *Twentieth-Century Caribbean and
Black African Writers, Second Series (Dictioanry of Literary Biography* 125).
265–69.

Banham, Martin. "Ola Rotimi." Cox, *African Writers.* 2:707–20.

   Biography, analyses of Rotmi's plays, and a select bibliography of primary and
secondary works published between 1971 and 1993.

Gibbs, James. "Rotimi, Ola." Serafin, *Encyclopedia of World Literature in the 20th
Century.* 2:712.

Gikandi, Simon. "Rotimi, Ola." Gikandi, *Encyclopedia of African Literature.* 464–65.

Okafor, Chinyere G. "Ola Rotimi: The Man, the Playwright and the Producer on the
Nigerian Theate Scene." Genova, *Companion to Contemporary World
Literature.* 1: 359–65.

   Bio-critical analysis of Rotimi and his theatre.

"Rotimi, Ola." Wordworks, *Modern Black Writers.* 636–39.

   Excerpts from criticism published between 1976 and 1990.

Interviews

Uwatt, Effiok B. Ed. *Playwriting and Directing in Nigeria: Interviews with Ola
Rotimi.* Lagos, Nigeria: Apex Books, 2002.

David Rubadiri, 1930–

Web Sites

"David Rubadiri." *African Letters.* 26 July 2005, http://www.bowwave.org/
AfricanWriters/David%20Rubadiri.htm.
Text of four poems.

"Professor David Rubadiri." *Contemporary Africa Database.* 26 July 2005, http://
people.africadatabase.org/people/data/person16088.html.

Biographies and Criticism

Gikandi, Simon. "Rubadiri, David." Gikandi, *Encyclopedia of African Literature.*
465.

Roscoe, Adrian. "Rubadiri, David." Benson and Conolly, *Encyclopedia of Post-
colonial Literatures in English.* 2:1386–87.

"Rubadiri, David." Wordworks, *Modern Black Writers.* 640–42.
Excerpts from criticism published between 1972 and 1987.

Interview

"David Rubadiri." Lindfors, *Africa Talks Back.* [363] –374.
Text of a 1986 interview.

John Ruganda, 1941–

Web Sites

"John Ruganda." *Contemporary Africa Database.* 26 July 2005, http://people.africa
database.org/people/data/person16089.html.

Biographies and Criticism

Bardolph, J. "Ruganda, John." Benson and Conolly, *Encyclopedia of Post-colonial
Literatures in English.* 2:1388.

Imbuga, Francis. "John Ruganda." Lindfors and Sander, *Twentieth-Century
Caribbean and Black African Writers, Third Series* (*Dictionary of Literary
Biography* 157). 323–30.

Outa, George Odera. "Ruganda, John." Gikandi, *Encyclopedia of African Literature.*
466.

Gabriel Ruhumbika, 1938–

Web Sites

"Gabriel Ruhumbika." *Contemporary Africa Database.* 26 July 2005, http://people
.africadatabase.org/people/data/person16091.html.

Biographies and Criticism

Mulukozi, M.M. "Ruhumbika, Gabriel." Benson and Conolly, *Encyclopedia of Post-
colonial Literatures in English.* 2:1388–89.

Ojwang, Dan Odhiambo. "Ruhumbika, Gabriel." Gikandi, *Encyclopedia of African
Literature.* 467.

Manuel Rui (Monteiro), 1941–

Web Sites

"Manuel Rui." *Poesia Africana de Expressão Portuguesa.* Ed. and update unavailable.
26 July 2005, http://betogomes.sites.uol.com.br/ManuelRui.htm.
Brief biography, list of published works, and the text of two poems.

"Manuel Rui Montero." *Contemporary Africa Database.* 26 July 2006, http://people
.africadatabase.org/people/data/person14096.html.

Biographies and Criticism

Gikandi, Simon. "Rui, Manuel." Gikandi, *Encyclopedia of African Literature.* 467.

"Manuel Rui and the Construction of Angolan Regeneration." Niyi Afolabi, *The
Golden Cage: Regeneration in Lusophone African Literature anad Culture.*
Trenton, New Jersey: Africa World Press, 2001. [76] –116.
Critical study of Rui's writing.

Nawal el-Saadawi (Nawal al-Sa'adawi), 1931–

Web Sites

Belton, Brian, and Clare Dowding. "Nawal el Saadawi: A Creative and Dissident
Life." *Infed: The Encyclopedia of Informal Education.* Eds. Mark K. Smith et
al. 30 Jan. 2005. Infed.org. 26 July 2005, http://www.infed.org/thinkers/et-
saadawi.htm.
Biography, with a brief discussion of el Saadawi's views on dissidence and
creativity.

"Dr. Nawal el-Saadawi." *Contemporary Africa Database.* 26 July 2005, http://people
.africadatabase.org/people/data/person2437.html.

"Dr. Nawal el-Saadawi." *The Odyssey: Africa.* Eds. Jeff Golden et al. Update
unavailable. The Odyssey: World Trek for Service and Education. 26 July 2005,
http://www.worldtrek.org/odyssey/africa/nawal/.
Features a biography of el Saadawi, excerpts from some of her works, and a
video clip of an interview.

Graves, Nicola. "Nawal el Saadawi." *Postcolonial Studies at Emory.* 26 July 2005,
http://www.emory.edu/ENGLISH/Bahri/Saadawi.html.

McBride, Jennifer. "Nawal Saadawi." *Women's Intellectual Contributions to the
Study of Mind and Society.* Ed. Linda Woolf. Update unavailable. Webster U.
26 July 2005, http://www.webster.edu/~woolflm/saadawi.html.
Biography of el-Saadawi.

McMillan, Stephanie. "An Introduction to Nawal el Saadawi." *Two Eyes Magazine.* 1
(Fall 2000). 26 July 2005, http://home.earthlink.net/%7Etwoeyesmagazine/
issue1/nesintro.htm.
Biographical sketch, and the transcript of a 1999 interview.

"Nawal El Sadaawi." *Books and Writers.* 26 July 2005, http://www.kirjasto.sci.fi/
sadawi.htm.

Naawal El Saadawi–Sherif Hetata. Ed. Nawal el Saadawi. 15 July 2005.
nawalsaadawi.net. 26 July 2005, http://www.nawalsaadawi.net/.
This official Web site of Saadawi and her husband includes a biography, links to
her books and articles, political statements, and current news about her.

Biographies and Criticism

Booth, Marilyn. "al-Sa'dawi, Nawal." Serafin, *Encyclopedia of World Literature in the 20th Century.* 4:5–6.

"el-Saadawi, Nawal." Robinson, *Modern Women Writers.* 3:[802]–09.
Excerpts from criticism published between 1980 and 1993.

Manisty, Dinah. "Nawal al-Sa'adawi."Cox, *African Writers.* 2:721–31.
Biography, analyses of al-Sa'aadawi's works, and a select bibliography of
primary and secondary works published between 1958 and 1995.

Michel-Mansour, Thérèse. "Nawal al-Sa'dawi." Schellinger, *Encyclopedia of the Novel.* 4:1155–57.

Mikhail, Mona N. "el-Saadawi, Nawal." Gikandi, *Encyclopedia of African Literature.* [469] –71.

Zuhur, Sherifa. "Woman at Point Zero." Moss and Valestuk, *African Literature and Its Times* (*World Literature and Its Times* 2)**.** 493–502.

Dictionaries, Encyclopedias, and Handbooks

Royer, Diana. *A Criticial Study of the Works of Nawal El Saadawi, Egyptian Writer and Activist.* Lewiston, N. Y.: Mellen, 2001.

Tayeb (Al-Tayyib) Salih, 1929–

Web Sites

"Season of Migration to the North." *LitNet African Library.* 26 July 2005, http://www.litnet.co.za/africanlib/north.asp.

"Tayib Salih." *Contemporary Africa Database.* 26 July 2005, http://people.africa database.org/people/data/person3432.html.

Biographies and Criticism

Hassan, Waïl S. "Salih, al-Tayyib." Gikandi, *Encyclopedia of African Literature.* 478–79.Littleton, Jacob. "Season of Migration." Moss and Valestuk, *African Literature and Its Times* (*World Literature and Its Times* 2). 367–375.

Sadgrove, Philip. "Al-Tayyib Salih." Cox, *African Writers.* 2:733–44.
Biography, analyses of Salih's works, and a select bibliography of primary and
secondary works published between 1966 and 1996.

Amadou Lamine Sall, 1951–

Web Sites

"Because I Loved Aurora." *Wells College Express* (Summer 2002). Wells C. 26 July 2005, http://www.wells.edu/pdfs/summer2002_18–19.pdf.
College newspaper article with the text of a poem and a brief biography of Sall.

Biographies and Criticism

Diop, Samba. "Sall, Amadou Lamine." Gikandi, *Encyclopedia of African Literature.*
    479–80.

Tijan M (omodu) Sallah, 1958–

Web Sites

"Tijan Momodou Sallah." *Contemporary Africa Database.* 26 July 2005, http://
    people.africadatabase.org/people/data/person16093.html.

Biographies and Criticism

Jagne, Siga Fatima. "Tijan Sallah." Parekh and Jagne, *Postcolonial African Writers: A
    Bio-bibliographical Critical Sourcebook.* [408]–12.

Nwankwo, Chimalum. "Sallah, Tijan M." Serafin, *Encyclopedia of World Literature
    in the 20th Century.* 4:20.

Ken(ule) B(eeson) Saro-Wiwa, 1941–1995

Web Sites

"Ken Saro-Wiwa." *Books and Writers.* 26 July 2005, http://www.kirjasto.sci.fi/saro
    .htm.

"Ken Saro-Wiwa." *Contemporary Postcolonial and Postimperial Literature in
    English.* 26 July 2005, http://www.scholars.nus.edu.sg/post/sarowiwa/
    sarowiwaov.html.

"Kenule Beeson Saro-Wiwa." *Contemporary Africa Database.* 26 July 2005, http://
    people.africadatabase.org/en/person/3455.html.

"Saro-Wiwa, Ken." *The Literary Encyclopedia.* 26 July 2005, http://www.litencyc
    .com/php/speople.php?rec=true&UID=3937.

Biographies and Criticism

Ezenwa-Ohaeto. "Ken Saro-Wiwa." Lindfors and Sander, *Twentieth-Century
    Caribbean and Black African Writers, Third Series* (*Dictionary of Literary
    Biography* 157). 331–39.

"Ken Saro-Wiwa." Hunter et al., *Contemporary Literary Criticism.* 114:251–81.
    Excerpts from criticism published between 1986 and 1997.

King, Bruce. "Saro-Wiwa, Ken." Benson and Conolly, *Encyclopedia of Post-colonial
    Literatures in English.* 2:1415–16.

"Saro-Wiwa, Ken." Wordworks, *Modern Black Writers.* 650–53.
    Excerpts from criticism published between 1987 and 1998.

Dictionaries, Encyclopedias, and Handbooks

Ojo-Ade, Femi. *Ken Saro-Wiwa: A Bio-critical Study.* Brooklyn, N. Y.: Africana
    Press, 1999.

McLuckie, Craig and Aubrey McPhail. *Ken Saro-Wiwa: Writer and Political Activist.*
    Boulder, Colo.: Lynne Reinner, 2000.

Interviews

"Ken Saro-Wiwa." Ezenwa-Ohaeto, *Winging Words: Interviews with Nigerian Writers and Critics*. 31–40.

Williams Sassine, 1944–1997

Web Sites

"Williams Sassine." *Contemporary Africa Database*. 26 July 2005, http://people .africadatabase.org/people/data/person13161.html.

Biographies and Criticism

Volet, Jean-Marie. "Sassine, Williams." Gikandi, *Encyclopedia of African Literature*. 482–83.

Interviews

Diawara, Manthia "Williams Sassine on Afro-pessimism." *In Search of Africa*. Cambridge, Mass: Harvard University Press, 1998. 39–58.
Narrative of an interview.

Olive (Emilie Albertina) Schreiner (Ralph Iron), 1855–1920

Web Sites

Alig, Daniel. "Olive Schreiner." *Postcolonial Studies at Emory*. 26 July 2005, http:// www.emory.edu/ENGLISH/Bahri/Schreiner.html.

"Olive Schreiner." *Anglophone and Lusophone African Women's Writing*. 26 July 2005, http://www.ex.ac.uk/~ajsimoes/aflit/SchreinerEN.html.

"Olive Schreiner." *Books and Writers*. 26 July 2005, http://www.kirjasto.sci.fi/ schrein.htm.

"Olive Schreiner." *Introducing South African Writers*. 26 July 2005, http://homepage .oniduo.pt/chacmalissimo/SAfrican/html/olive_schreiner.htm.

"Olive Schreiner (Ralph Iron)." *Women and Marxism*. Ed. Sally Ryan. Update unavailable. Marxists.org. 26 July 2005, http://www.marxists.org/subject/ women/authors/schrein/.
Biography and e-texts and transcriptions of selected writing and personal
letters.

"Schreiner, Olive." *Victorian Women's Writers Project Library*. Ed. Perry Willet. 24 Apr. 2003. Indiana U. 26 July 2005, http://www.indiana.edu/~letrs/vwwp/ vwwplib.pl?#schreiner.
Machine-readable texts of eight works by Schreiner.

Biographies and Criticism

Barsby, Tina. "Schreiner, Olive Emilie Albertina." Benson and Conolly, *Encyclopedia of Post-colonial Literatures in English*. 2:1418–20.

Berkman, Joyce Avrech. "Olive Schreiner." Nadel, Ira B. and William E. Fredeman, *Victorian Novelists after 1885* (*Dictionary of Literary Biography* 18). Detroit: Gale, 1983. 270–77.

Birns, Nicholas. "Olive Schreiner." Parekh and Jagne, *Postcolonial African Writers: A Bio-bibliographical Critical Sourcebook.* [413] –19.

Clayton, Cherry. "Olive Schreiner." Cox, *African Writers.* 2:745–63.
    Biography, analyses of Schreiner's works, and a select bibliography of primary and secondary works published between 1883 and 1996.

———. "Schreiner, Olive." Serafin, *Encyclopedia of World Literature in the 20th Century.* 4: 52–3.

———. "Olive Schreiner." Scanlon, *South African Writers* (*Dictionary of Literary Biography* 225). 395–407.

Driver, Dorothy. "Schreiner, Olive Emilie Albertina." Gikandi, *Encyclopedia of African Literature.* 484.

Loy, Pamela S. "The Story of an African Farm." Moss and Valestuk, *African Literature and Its Times* (*World Literature and Its Times* 2). 397–407.

Monsman, Gerald. "Olive Schreiner: A Child on the Farm." Ross, *International Literature in English.* 1–19.
    Survey of major themes and an annotated bibliography of selected critical readings.

"Olive (Emilie Albertina) Schreiner (Cronwright). Poupard et al., *Twentieth-Century Literary Criticism.* 9:392–408.
    Excerpts from criticism published between 1883 and 1980 and an annotated bibliography.

"Schreiner, Olive." Robinson, *Modern Women Writers.* 4:75–84.
    Excerpts from criticism published between 1924 and 1991.

Vance, Sylvia. "Olive Schreiner." Eds. Gary Kelly and Edd Applegate. *British Reform Writers* (*Dictionary of Literary Biography* 190). Detroit: Gale, 1998. 266–72.

Dictionaries, Encyclopedias, and Handbooks

Vivan, Itala. *The Flawed Diamond: Essays on Olive Schreiner.* Sydney: Dangaroo, 1991.

Leila Sebbar, 1941–

Web Sites

"Leila Sebbar." *Clicnet.* Eds. Carole Netter and Anne-Marie Obatjek-Kirkwood. Update unavailable. Swarthmore C. 26 July 2005, http://clicnet.swarthmore .edu/leila_sebbar/.
    Bio-bibliographical information, with extracts from selected works. In French.

"Leila Sebbar." *Contemporary Africa Database.* 26 July 2005, http://people.africa database.org/en/person/11008.html.

Biographies and Criticism

Ekotto, Frieda. "Sebbar, Leïla." Gikandi, *Encyclopedia of African Literature.* 484–85.

Higgins, Ellie. "Sebbar, Leila." Serafin, *Encyclopedia of World Literature in the 20th Century.* 4:64–5.

Ménager, S. D. "Leïla Sebbar." Parekh and Jagne, *Postcolonial African Writers: A Bio-bibliographical Critical Sourcebook.* [420] –24.

"Sebbar, Leila." Robinson, *Modern Women Writers*. 4:91–95.
Excerpts from criticism published between 1988 and 1992.

Mabel Segun, 1930–

Web Sites

"Mabel Dorothy Segun." *Contemporary Africa Database*. 25 July 26, 2005, http://
people.africadatabase.org/people/data/person16094.html.

Biographies and Criticism

Bolden, B. J. "Segun, Mabel." Pamela Shelton. Ed. *Contemporary Women Poets*.
Detroit: St. James Press, 1998. 311–13.

Okediran, Wale. "Segun, Mabel." Benson and Conolly, *Encyclopedia of Post-colonial
Literatures in English*. 2:1433.
Osa, Osayimwense. "Segun, Mabel D(orothy)." Pendergast and Pendergast,
St. James Guide to Children's Writers. 958–60.

Kobina Sekyi, 1892–1956

Web Sites

Sekyi, William Esuman-Gwira [Kobina Sekyi] . "The Future of Subject Peoples."
West Africa Review. 2.2 (2001). 26 July 2005, http://www.westafricareview
.com/vol2.2/sekyi.html.
Reprint of Sekyi's article originally published in *The Africa Times and Orient
Review* (Oct–Dec. 1917).

Biographies and Criticism

Owusu, Kofi. "Sekyi, Kobina." Gikandi, *Encyclopedia of African Literature*. 487.

Francis Selormey, 1927–1983

Web Sites

"Francis Selormey." *Contemporary Africa Database*. 26 July 2005, http://people
.africadatabase.org/people/data/person3479.html.

Biographies and Criticism

Awuyah, Chris Kwame. "Selormey, Francis." Benson and Conolly, *Encyclopedia of
Post-colonial Literatures in English*. 2:1433–34.

Owusu, Kofi. "Selormey, Francis." Gikandi, *Encyclopedia of African Literature*. 487.

Ousmane Sembène (Sembène Ousmane), 1923–

Web Sites

Gadjigo, Samba. "Ousmane Sembene: The Life of a Revolutionary Artist." *California
Newsreel:Articles*. Ed and update unavailable. California Newsreel. 26 July
2005, http://www.newsreel.org/articles/OusmaneSembene.htm.
Outline and filmography based on Gadjigo's book on Sembene.

Malcolm, Derek. "Ousmane Sembene: Xala." *Guardian Unlimited: Film.* 21 Dec. 2000. Guardian.co.uk. 26 July 2005, http://film.guardian.co.uk/Century_Of_ Films/Story/0,4135,414318,00.html.
Review of Sembène's "Xala."

Ndiaye, Serigne. "Ousmane Sembene." *Postcolonial Studies at Emory.* 26 July 2005, http://www.emory.edu/ENGLISH/Bahri/Sembene.html.

Nzegwu, Femi. "Sembène, Ousmane." *The Literary Encyclopedia.* 23 July 26, 2005, http://www.litencyc.com/php/speople.php?rec=true&UID=5016.

Ousmane Sembene. Ed. Samba Gadjigo. Copyright 2002. Mt. Holyoke C. 26 July 2005, http://www.mtholyoke.edu/courses/sgadjigo/.
This comprehensive Web site on Sembène offers bio-bibliographical information and photos from a film shoot.

"Sembene Ousmane." *Contemporary Africa Database.* 26 July 2005, http://people .africadatabase.org/en/person/3314.html.

Biographies and Criticism

Mubara, Khalid Al. "Sembène Ousmane." Cox, *African Writers.* 2:765–74.
Biography, analyses of Ousmane's works, and a select bibliography of his films, writing, and critical studies published between 1971 and 1993.

Murphy, David. "Sembene, Ousmane." Gikandi, *Encyclopedia of African Literature.* 487–90.

Popkin, Debra. "Sembène Ousmane." Serafin, *Encyclopedia of World Literature in the 20th Century.* 4:71–2.

"Sèmbene Ousmane." Draper, *Black Literature Criticism.* 3:1531–50.
Biography, list of major works, excerpts from criticism from 1982 to 1986, and an annotated bibliography.

"Sèmbene Ousmane." Matuz et al., *Contemporary Literary Criticism.* 66:332–51.
Excerpts from criticsm published between 1970 and 1986.

"Sembène, Ousmane." Wordworks, *Modern Black Writers.* 657–65.
Excerpts from criticism (on books and films) published between 1957 and 1993.

Taylor, Anna-Marie. "Ousmane, Sembène." Chevalier, *Contemporary World Writers.* 385–86.

Thompson, Brian P. and Pamela S. Loy. "God's Bits of Wood." Moss and Valestuk, *African Litertaure and Its Times* (*World Literature and Its Times* 2). 183–92.

Dictionaries, Encyclopedias, and Handbooks

Gadjigo, Samba et al., Eds. *Ousmane Sembène: Dialogues with Critics and Writers.* Amherst, Mass.: Five Colleges, 1993.
Critical perspectives on Sembène as a filmmaker. Includes an interview with him.

Petty, Sheila. *A Call to Action: The Films of Ousmane Sembene.* Westport, Conn.: Greenwood, 1996.

Léopold Sédar Senghor, 1906–2001

Web Sites

"Dossier Léopold Sédar Senghor." *African Studies Centre.* Ed. unavailable. 12 Apr.
2005. Leiden U. 26 July 2005, http://www.ascleiden.nl/Library/Webdossiers/
Senghor.aspx.
This site provides a comprehensive overview of Senghor's life and a
bibliography of his academic and political writing, with a selection of external Web
resources.

"In Memoriam." *African Letters.* 26 July 2005. http://www.bowwave.org/African
Writers/Leopold%20Sedar%20Senghor.htm.

"Léopold Sédar Senghor." *Académie française.* Ed. Claude-Marix Durix et al. Update
unknown. 26 July 2005, http://www.academie-francaise.fr/immortels/base/
academiciens/fiche.asp?param=666.
Biography and a chronological list of Senghor's works and awards.

"Leopold Sédar Senghor." *African Writers: Voices of Change.* 26 July 2005, http://
web.uflib.ufl.edu/cm/africana/senghor.htm.

"Léopold (Sédar) Senghor." *Books and Writers.* 26 July 2005, http://www.kirjasto.sci
.fi/senghor.htm.

"Leopold Sedar Senghor." *Contemporary Africa Database.* 26 July 2005, http://
people.africadatabase.org/en/person/3482.html.

"Léopold Sédar Senghor." *Radio France.* Ed. and update unavailable. 26 July 2005,
http://www.radiofrance.fr/parvis/senghor.htm.
Biographical sketch and a brief audio clip of Senghor reading one of his poems.

Biographies and Criticism

Diop, Samba. "Léopold Sédar Senghor." Parekh and Jagne, *Postcolonial African
Writers: A Bio-bibliographical Critical Sourcebook.* [425] –37.

Drame, Kandioura. "Senghor, Léopold Sédar." Gikandi, *Encyclopedia of African
Literature.* 491–92.

Irele, Abiola. "Léopold Sédar Senghor." Cox, *African Writers.* 2:775–89.
Biography, analyses of Senghor's poetry, and a select bibliography of his works
and critical studies published between 1967 and 1993.

"Léopold Sédar Senghor." Draper, *Black Literature Criticism.* 3:1671–87.
Biography, list of major works, excerpts from criticism from 1964 to 1989, and
an annotated bibliography.

"Léopold Sédar Senghor." Hunter et al., *Contemporary Literary Criticism.* 130:231–88
Excerpts from criticism published between 1964 and 1996 and an annotated
bibliography.

"Léopold Sédar Senghor." Marowski and Matuz, *Contemporary Literary Criticism.*
54: 388–410.
Excerpts from criticism published between 1964 and 1996.

"Léopold Sédar Senghor." Wisner-Broyles and Wells, *Poetry Criticism.* 25:223–260.
Excerpts from criticism published between 1973 and 1993.

"Senghor, Léopold Sédar." Levi, *Guide to French Literature*. 2:604–6.
Bio-bibliographical overview.

"Senghor, Léopold Sédar." Wordworks, *Modern Black Writers*. 665–69.
Excerpts from criticism published between 1945 and 1997.

Smith, Christopher. "Senghor, Léoplod (Sédar)." Chevalier, *Contemporary World Writers*. 466–68.

Wake, Clive. "Senghor, Léopold Sédar." Serafin, *Encyclopedia of World Literature in the 20th Century*. 4:77–8.

Dictionaries, Encyclopedias, and Handbooks

Spleth, Janice. Ed. *Critical Perspectives on Léopold Sédar Senghor*. Washington, D. C.: Three Continents, 1993.

Bibliographies

Westley, David M. "A Select Bibliography of the Works of Léopold Sédar Senghor." *Research in African Literatures*. 33.4 (2002): [88] –100.

Sipho Sepamla, 1932–

Web Sites

"Sipho Sepamla." *Contemporary Africa Database*. 26 July 2005, http://people.africa database.org/en/person/3483.html.

"Sipho Sepamla." *Introducing South African Writers*. 26 July 2005, http://homepage. oniduo.pt/chacmalissimo/SAfrican/html/sipho_sempamla.htm.

Biographies and Criticism

Clayton, Cherry. "Sepamla, Sydney Sipho." Benson and Conolly, *Encyclopedia of Post-colonial Literatures in English*. 2:1437–38.

Gray, Stephen. "Sipho Sepamla."Moss and Valestuk, *Twentieth-Century Caribbean and Black African Writers, Third Series* (*Dictionary of Literary Biography* 157). 349–60.

Ngwenya, Thengani. "Sepamla, Sipho." Gikandi, *Encyclopedia of African Literature*. 492–3.

"Sepamla, Sipho." Wordworks, *Modern Black Writers*. 671–74.
Exerpts from criticism published between 1976 and 1990.

Sole, Kelwyn. "Sipho Sepamla." Scanlon, *South African Writers* (*Dictionary of Literary Biography* 225). 408–21.

Mongane Wally Serote, 1944–

Web Sites

"Mongane Wally Serote." *Contemporary Africa Database*. 26 July 2005, http:// people.africadatabase.org/people/data/person3487.html.

Msome, S'thembiso. "The Ashes of War." *Sunday Times* (2 Mar. 2003).
Sundaytimes.co.za. 26 July 2005, http://www.suntimes.co.za/2003/03/02/ lifestyle/life04.asp.
Serote discusses his novel *Scatter the Ashes and Go*.

"Mongane Wally Serote." *Introducing South African Writers.* 26 July 2005, http://homepage.oniduo.pt/chacmalissimo/SAfrican/html/mongane_wally_serote.htm.

"Mongane Serote." *Writers Talk: Ideas of Our Time.* 26 July 2005, http://www.roland-collection.com/rolandcollection/literature/101/W029.htm.

Biographies and Criticism

Attwell, David. "Mongane Wally Serote." Lindfors and Sander, *Twentieth-Century Caribbean and Black African Writers, Second Series* (*Dictionary of Literary Biography* 125). 291–97.

Gardner, Colin. "Serote, Mongane Wally." Benson and Conolly, *Encyclopedia of Post-colonial Literatures in English.* 2:1438–39.

Meihuizen, N. C. T. "Mongane Wally Serote." Lindfors and Sander, *South African Writers* (*Dictionary of Literary Biography 225*). 422– 33.

Mkhize, Jabulani. "Serote, Mongane Wally." Gikandi, *Encyclopedia of African Literature.* 493–94.

"Serote, Mongane (Wally)." Wordworks, *Modern Black Writers.* 674–79. Excerpts from criticism published between 1982 and 1996.

Interviews

Solberg, Rolf. "Interview: Mongane Wally Serote." Eds. Derek Attridge and Rosemary Jolly. *Writing South Africa: Literature, Apartheid, and Democracy 1970–1995.* Cambridge: Cambridge University Press, 1998. 180–86. Transcript of a 1995 interview.

Robert Serumaga, 1939–1980

Web Sites

"Robert Serumaga." *Contemporary Africa Database.* 26 July 2005, http://people.africadatabase.org/people/data/person16098.html.

Biographies and Criticism

Outa, George Odera. "Serumaga, Robert." Gikandi, *Encyclopedia of African Literature.* 494–95.

Bardolph, J. "Serumaga, Robert." Benson and Conolly, *Encyclopedia of Post-colonial Literatures in English.* 2:1439.

"Serumaga, Robert." Wordworks, *Modern Black Writers.* 679–681. Excerpts from criticism published between 1970 and 1984.

Pauline (Janet) (Urmson) Smith, 1882–1959

Web Sites

"Pauline Smith." *Introducing South African Writers.* 26 July 2005, http://homepage.oniduo.pt/chacmalissimo/SAfrican/html/pauline_smith.htm.

Biographies and Criticism

Driver, Dorothy. "Smith, Pauline." Serafin, *Encyclopedia of World Literature in the 20th Century.* 4:133.

———. "Smith, Pauline Janet Urmson." Gikandi, *Encyclopedia of African Literature.* 501.

Clayton, Cherry. "Smith, Pauline Janet." Benson and Conolly, *Encyclopedia of Post-colonial Literatures in English.* 2:1503–05.

"Pauline (Urmson) Smith." Poupard et al., *Twentieth-Century Literary Criticism.* 25: 375–405.
  Excerpts from criticism published between 1925 and 1984, with an annotated bibliography.

Roberts, Sheila. "Pauline Smith." Scanlon, *South African Writers* (*Dictionary of Literary Biography* 225). 434–44.

"Smith, Pauline." Robinson, *Modern Women Writers.* 4:180–83.
  Excerpts from criticism published between 1925 and 1988.

Wilbur (Addison) Smith, 1933–

Web Sites

"Wilbur Smith." Ed and update unavailable. *St. Martin's Press.* 26 July 2005, http://www.wilbursmithbooks.com/wilburindex.html.
  This Web site is designed in part for Smith's fans and publishes a weekly fan mail. For the researcher, it provides a biography, synopses of his books—arranged by series—and related Web links.

"Wilbur Smith." *Contemporary Africa Database.* 26 July 2005, http://people.africa database.org/en/person/12171.html.

Biographies and Criticism

Stotesbury, John A. "Smith, Wilbur (Addison)." Benson and Conolly, *Encyclopedia of Post-colonial Literatures in English.* 2:1506.

Zulu Sofola, 1935–1995

Web Sites

"Zulu Sofola." *Anglophone and Lusophone African Women's Writing.* 26 July 2005, http://www.ex.ac.uk/~ajsimoes/aflit/SofolaEN.html.

"Zulu Sofola." *Contemporary Africa Database.* 26 July 2005, http://people.africa database.org/people/data/person16100.html.

Biographies and Criticsm

Akinwale, Ayo. "Sofola, 'Zulu." Benson and Conolly, *Encyclopedia of Post-colonial Literatures in English.* 2:509–10.

Gikandi, Simon. "Sofola, Zulu." Gikandi, *Encyclopedia of African Literature.* 502.

Obafemi, Olu. "Sofola, Zulu." Berney and Templeton, *Contemporary Women Dramatists.* 228–31.
  Bio-bibliographical overview and a short comment by Sofola on her writing.

Olaniyan, Tejumola. " 'Zulu Sofola." Lindfors and Sander, *Twentieth-Century Caribbean and Black African Writers, Third Series* (*Dictionary of Literary Biography* 157). 361–70.

Interview

"Zulu Sofola." Ezenwa-Ohaeto, *Winging Words: Interviews with Nigerian Writers and Critics.* 78–82.

"Zulu Sofola." James, *In Their Own Voices.* 143–53.
Text of a 1986 interview.

Bode Sowande, 1948–

Web Sites

"Bode Sowande." *Contemporary Africa Database.* 26 July 2005, http://people.africa database.org/people/data/person11554.html.

Biographies and Criticism

Gibbs, James. "Bode Sowande." Lindfors and Sander, *Twentieth-Century Caribbean and Black African Writers, Third Series* (*Dictionary of Literary Biography* 157). 371–80.

Gikandi, Simon. "Sowande, Bode." Gikandi, *Encyclopedia of African Literature.* 519–20.

Okagbue, Osita. "Bode Sowande." Cox, *African Writers.* 2:799–806.
Biography, analyses of Sowande's works, and a select bibliography of his works and critical studies published between 1981 and 1992.

(Olu)Wole (Akiwande) Soyinka, 1934–

Web sites

"Conversation with Nobel Laureate Wole Soyinka." *Conversations with History.* Update unavailable. Institute of International Studies, U. of California, Berkeley. 26 July 2005, http://globetrotter.berkeley.edu/Elberg/Soyinka/ soyinka-con0.html.
The transcript of the conversation provide insights into Soyinka's views about the "gestation of [his creative] ideas," his political activism, and the impact of imprisonment on his writing. The entire conversation, arranged by sections, can be viewed in streaming video.

Reith Lecture 2004. Ed. and update unavailable. BBC Radio 4. 26 July 2005, http:// www.bbc.co.uk/radio4/reith2004/.
Transcript and audio clips of Soyinka presenting the prestigious Reith Lecture on the theme "The Climate of Fear."

"Wole Soyinka." *Africa Writers: Voices of Change.* 26 July 2005, http://web.uflib.ufl .edu/cm/africana/soyinka.htm.

"Wole Soyinka–Biography." *Nobel e-Museum.* 14 Apr. 2005. The Nobel Foundation. 26 July 2005, http://www.nobel.se/literature/laureates/1986/soyinka-bio.html.
This official Nobel Foundation Web site provides a biography, links to the press release announcing Soyinka's award, his presentation speech, Nobel lecture, and other related resources.

"Wole Soyinka." *Books and Writers.* 26 July 2005, http://www.kirjasto.sci.fi/soyinka .htm.

"Wole Soyinka." *Contemporary Postcolonial and Postimperial Literature in English.* 26 July 2005, http://www.scholars.nus.edu.sg/post/soyinka/soyinkaov.html.

"Wole Soyinka." *New York State Writers' Institute.* Update unavailable. State University of New York. 26 July 2005, http://www.albany.edu/writers-inst/soyinka .html.
Biography and an audioclip of Soyinka discussing his writing.

"Wole Soyinka." *Writers Talk: Ideas of Our Time.* 26 July 2005, http://www.roland-collection.com/rolandcollection/literature/101/W29.htm.

Biographies and Criticism

Adeeko, Adeleke. "Death and the King's Horseman." Moss and Valestuk, *African Literature and Its Times* (*World Litertaure and Its Times* 2). 77–85.

Euba, Femi. "Wole Soyinka." Parekh and Jagne, *Postcolonial African Writers: A Bio-bibliographical Critical Sourcebook.* [438]–54.

George, Olakunle. "Soyinka, Wole." Gikandi, *Encyclopedia of African Literature.* 520–22.

Gibbs, James. "Wole Soyinka." Lindfors and Sander, *Twentieth-Century Caribbean and Black African Writers, Second Series* (*Dictioanry of Literary Biography* 125). 298–326.

———. "Wole Soyinka: 'Marrying Earth to Heaven'—A Nobel Laureate at the End of the Eighties." Ross, *International Literature in English.* 461–73.
Survey of Soyinka's major works and an annotated bibliography of selected critical readings.

Lindfors, Bernth. "Soyinka, Wole." Serafin, *Encyclopedia of World Literature in the 20th Century.* 4:177–79.

"Soyinka, Wole." Wordworks, *Modern Black Writers.* 689–700.
Excerpts from criticism published between 1959 to 1999.

"Wole Soyinka." Draper, *Black Literature Criticism.* 3:1703–24.
Biography, list of major works, excerpts from criticism published between 1971 and 1990, and an annotated bibliography.

"Wole Soyinka." Draper, *World Literature Criticism from 1500 to the Present.* 5:3316–33
Includes excerpts from criticism published between 1971 and 1990.

"Wole Soyinka." Bryfonski and Harris, *Contemporary Literary Criticism.* 14:505–10.
Excerpts from criticism and on Soyinka published between 1959 and 1977.

"Wole Soyinka." Marowski, *Contemporary Literary Criticism.* 36:408–18.
Excerpts from criticism published between 1969 and 1985.

"Wole Soyinka." Trudeau et al., *Drama Criticism.* 2:357–84.
Excerpts from criticism published between 1986 and 1988 and an annotated bibliography.

"Wole Soyinka." Wordworks, *Modern Black Writers.* 689–700.
Excerpts from criticism published between 1959 and 1999.

Wright, Derek. "Soyinka's Smoking Shotgun: The Later Satires." Genova,
   Companion to Contemporary World Literature. 1:365–72.
   Discusses new directions evident in Soyinka's post-1960s satires.

———. "Wole Soyinka." Cox, *African Writers.* 2:807–31.
   Biography, analyses of Soyinka's works, and a select bibliography of primary
and secondary works published between 1969 and 1993.

Dictionaries, Encyclopedias, and Handbooks

Gibbs, James, and Bernth Lindfors, Eds. *Research on Wole Soyinka.* Trenton, N. J.:
   Africa World Press, 1993.
   A collection of previously published essays.

Jeyifo, Biodun. Ed. *Perspectives on Wole Soyinka : Freedom and Complexity.*
   Jackson, Miss.: University Press of Mississippi , 2001.

Jones, Eldred Durosimi. *The Writing of Wole Soyinka.* Portsmouth, N. H.:
   Heinemann, 1988.

Msiska, Mpalive-Hangson. *Wole Soyinka.* Plymouth, United Kingdom: Northcote, 1998.

Wright, Derek. *Wole Soyinka Revisited.* New York: Twayne, 1993.

Bibliographies

Gibbs, James, Keith Ketrack, and Henry Louis Gates. *Wole Soyinka: A Bibliography
   of Primary and Secondary Sources.* Westport, Conn.: Greenwood Press, 1986.

Okpu, B. *Wole Soyinka: A Bibliography.* Lagos: Libriservice, 1984.

Interviews

Jejifo, Biodun. *Conversations with Wole Soyinka.* Jackson, Miss.: University Press of
   Mississippi, 2001.
   Collection of interviews with Soyinka from 1973 to 1998.

Wilma Stockenström, 1933–

Web Sites

"Wilma Stockenström." *Anglophone and Lusophone Women's Writing.* 26 July 2005,
   http://www.ex.ac.uk/~ajsimoes/aflit/StockenstromEN.html.

"Wilma Stockenström." *Introducing South African Writers.* 26 July 2005, http://home
   pasge.oniduo.pt/chacmalissimo/SAfrican/html/wilma_stockenstrom.htm.

"Wilma Stockenström." Ed. Rosemarie Breuer. Update unavailable.
   StellenboschWriters.com. 26 July 2005, http://www.stellenboschwriters.com/
   stockenst.html.
   Includes a biography, list of published works, and the text of the poem "Die Eland."

Biographies and Criticism

"Stockenström, Wilma." Robinson, *Modern Women Writers.* 4:283–86.
   Excerpts from criticism published between 1985 and 1993.

Coetzee, Carli. "Stockenström, Wilma." Serafin, *Encyclopedia of World Literature in
   the 20th Century.* 4:225–26.

Efua (Theodora Morgue) Sutherland, 1924–1996

Web Sites

"Efua Theodora Sutherland." *Anglophone and Lusophone African Women's Writing.* 26 July 2005, http://www.ex.ac.uk/~ajsimoes/aflit/SutherlandEN.html.

"Efua Theodora Sutherland." *Contemporary Africa Database.* 26 July 2005, http://people.africadatabase.org/people/data/person16101.html.

"Efua Theodora Sutherland (née Efua Theodora Morgue)." *Books and Writers.* 26 July 2005, http://www.kirjasto.sci.fi/efuasut.htm.

Biographies and Criticism

Ankumah, Adaku T. "Efua Theodora Sutherland." Parekh and Jagne, *Postcolonial African Writers: A Bio-bibliographical Critical Sourcebook.* [444]–59.

Carchidi, Victoria. "Sutherland, Efua." Gikandi, *Encyclopedia of World Literature in the 20th Century.* 4:252–53.

Gibbs, James. "Efua Theodora Sutherland." Cox, *African Writers.* 2:833–49.
Biography, analyses of Sutherland's works, and a select bibliography of primary and secondary works published between 1963 and 1993.

Odamtten, Vincent O. "Sutherland, Efua Theodora." Gikandi, *Encyclopedia of African Literature.* 526–27.

Ogunyemi, Chikwenye Okonjo. "Efua Theodora Sutherland." Lindfors and Sander, *Twentieth-Century Caribbean and Black African Writers, First Series* (*Dictionary of Literary Biography* 117). 284–90.

Sofola, 'Zulu." Sutherland, Efua." Benson and Conolly, *Encyclopedia of Post-colonial Literatures in English.* 2:15048–49.

"Sutherland, Efua." Wordworks, *Modern Black Writers.* 705–8.
Excerpts from criticism published between 1976 and 1992.

Véronique Tadjo, 1955–

Web Sites

"Véronique Tadjo." *Reading Women Writers and African Literatures.* 26 July 2005, http://www.arts.uwa.edu.au/AFLIT/TadjoVeroniqueEng.html.

"Véronique Tadjo." *Contemporary Africa Database.* 26 July 2005, http://people.africadatabase.org/people/data/person3572.html.

Biographies and Criticism

McNee, Lisa. "Tadjo, Véronique." Serafin, *Encyclopedia of World Literature in the 20th Century.* 4:281.

Nyatetu-Waigwa, Wangar wa. "Tadjo, Véronique." Gikandi, *Encyclopedia of African Literature.* [529] –30.

"Véronique Tadjo." Herzberger-Fofana, *Littérature feminine francophone d'Afrique noire.* 467–468.
Biography, with brief analysis of Tadjo's works.

Interview

Gray, Stephen. "Véronique Tadjo Speaks with Stephen Gray." *Research in African Literatures.* 34.3 (Fall 2003): [142] –47.

Sony Labou Tansi (Marcel Ntonsi), 1947–1995

Web Sites

Herzberger-Fofana, Pierrette. "Un entretien avec Sony Labou Tansi, écrivain." *Mots Pluriels.* 10 (May 1999). 26 July 2005, http://www.arts.uwa.edu.au/Mots Pluriels/MP1099slt.html.
Transcript of an interview.

"Sony Labou Tansi." *Books and Writers.* 26 July 2005, http://www.kirjasto.sci.fi/ tansi.htm.

Sony Labou Tansi." *Contemporary Africa Database.* 26 July 2005, http://people .africadatabase.org/people/data/person2812.html.

Biographies and Criticism

Evenson, Brian. "Tansi, Sony Labou." Serafin, *Encyclopedia of World Literature in the 20th Century.* 4:294–95.

Nzabatsinda, Anthere. "Sony Labou Tansi." Gikandi, *Encyclopedia of African Literature.* 504–6.

Thomas, Dominic. "Sony Labou Tansi." Parekh and Jagne, *Postcolonial African Writers: A Bio-bibliographical Critical Sourcebook.* [460]–65.

Dictionaries, Encyclopedias, and Handbooks

Devésa, Jean Michel. *Sony Labou Tansi: écrivain de la honte et des rives magiques du Kongo.* Paris: L'Harmattan, 1996.

Kouakou, Jean-Marie. *La pensée de Sony Labou Tansi.* Paris: L'Harmattan, 2003.

Jean-Baptiste Tati-Loutard, 1938–

Web Sites

"Jean-Baptiste Tati-Loutard." *African Writers: Voices of Change.* 26 July 2005, http:// web.uflib.ufl.edu/cm/africana/tati.htm.

"Jean-Baptiste Tati-Loutard." *Contemporary Africa Database.* 26 July 2005, http:// people.africadatabase.org/people/data/person3584.html.

Biographies and Criticism

Nzabatsinda, Anthere. "Tati-Loutard, Jean-Baptiste." Gikandi, *Encyclopedia of African Literature.* 531.

"Tati-Loutard, Jean-Baptiste." Wordworks, *Modern Black Writers.* 714–15.
Excerpts from criticism published between 1978 to 1989.

Francisco José Tenreiro, 1921–1963

Web Site

"Francisco José Tenreiro." *Contemporary Africa Database.* 26 July 2005, http:// people.africadatabase.org/people/data/person3597.html.

Biographies and Criticism

Gikandi, Simon. "Tenreiro, Francisco José de Vasques." Gikandi, *Encyclopedia of African Literature.* 532.

Can Themba, 1924–1968

Web Sites

"Can Themba." *Contemporary Africa Database.* 26 July 2005, http://people.africa database.org/people/data/person16163.html.

Biographies and Criticism

Van Dyk, Bruno. "Themba, Can." Benson and Conolly, *Encyclopedia of Post-colonial Literatures in English.* 2:1558–59.

Miriam Tlali, 1933–

Web Sites

"Miriam Tlali." *Anglophone and Lusophone African Women's Writing.* 26 July 2005, http://www.ex.ac.uk/~ajsimoes/aflit/TlaliEN.html.

"Miriam Tlali." *Introducing Soth African Writers.* 26 July 2005, http://homepage .oniduo.pt/chacmalissimo/SAfrican/html/miriam_tlali.htm.

Biographies and Criticism

Carchidi,Victoria. "Tlali, Miriam Mesoli." Serafin, *Encyclopedia of World Literature in the 20th Century.* 4:326–27.

Hunter, Eva. "Miriam Tlali." Scanlon, *South African Writers* (*Dictionary of Literary Biography* 225). 445–49.

Ibrahim, Huma. "Tlali, Miriam." Gikandi, *Encyclopedia of African Literature.* 533–34.

Locket, Cecily. "Tlali, Miriam Mesoli." Benson and Conolly, *Encyclopedia of Post-colonial Literatures in English.* 2:1565–66.

Ngcobo, Lauretta. "Miriam Tlali." Lindfors and Sander, *Twentieth-Century Caribbean and Black African Writers, Third Series* (*Dictionary of Literary Biography* 157). 381–88.

"Tlali, Miriam." Robinson, *Modern Women Writers.* 4:376–80.
Excerpts from criticism published betwee 1985 and 1992.

"Tlali, Miriam." Wordworks, *Modern Black Writers.* 722–26.
Excerpts from criticism published between 1983 and 1998.

Interviews

Jolly, Rosemary. "Interview: Miriam Tlali." Eds. Derek Attridge and Rosemary Jolly. *Writing South Africa: Literature, Apartheid, and Democracy, 1970–1995.* Cambridge: Cambridge University Press, 1998. 141–48.

Mohamed A. Toihiri, 1955–

Web Sites

"Mohamed Toihiri." Ed. and update unavailable. *MweziNet.* 26 July 2005, http:// www.comores-online.com/mwezinet/litterature/toihiri.htm.
Text of an article on Toihiri, the first published novelist from the Comoros.

"Mohamed Toihiri." *Ile en île.* 26 July 2005, http://www.lehman.cuny.edu/ile.en.ile/
paroles/toihiri.html.
Biography, bibliography of works by and about Toihiri, and a list of prizes won.

Biographies and Criticism

Beckett, Carole M. "Toihiri, Mohamed A." Gikandi, *Encyclopedia of African
Literature.* 535.

Amos Tutuola, 1920–1997

Web Sites

"Amos Tutuola." *African Writers: Voices of Change.* 26 July 2005, http://web.uflib
.ufl.edu/cm/africana/tutuola.htm.

"Amos Tutuola." *Books and Writers.* 26 July 2005, http://www.kirjasto.sci.fi/tutuola
.htm.

"Amos Tutuola." *Contemporary Africa Database.* 26 July 2005, http://people.africa
database.org/people/data/person3654.html.

"Amos Tutuola." *Postcolonial African Literatures in English.* 26 July 2005, http://
www.fb10.uni-bremen.de/anglistik/kerkhoff/AfricanLit/Tutuola.htm.

Clarke, Bronagh. "Amos Tutuola." *The Imperial Archive.* Ed. Leon Litvack. 23 June
1999. Queens U. of Belfast. 26 July 2005, http://www.qub.ac.uk/english/
imperial/nigeria/amos.htm.
Brief overview of Tutuola's life and writing.

Biographies and Criticism

"Amos Tutuola." Draper, *Black Literature Criticism.* 3:1776–98.
Biography, list of major works, excerpts from criticism from 1952 to 1990, and
an annotated bibliography.

Ball, Kimberly and John Roleke. "The Palm-Wine Drinkard and His Dead Palm-
Wine Tapster in the Deads' Town." Moss and Valestuk, *African Literature and
Its Times* (*World Literature and Its Times* 2). 327–36.

Gikandi, Simon. "Tutuola, Amos." Gikandi, *Encyclopedia of African Literature.* 538–40.

Lindfors, Bernth. "Amos Tutuola." Lindfors and Sander, *Twentieth-Century
Caribbean and Black African Writers, Second Series* (*Dictionary of Literary
Biography* 125). 332–46.

———. "Tutuola, Amos." Serafin, *Encyclopedia of World Literature in the 20th
Century.* 4: 361–62.

Okonkwo, Chidi. "The Palmwine Drinkard by Amos Tutuola." Schellinger,
Encyclopedia of the Novel. 2:972–73

Owomoyela, Oyekan. "Amos Tutuola." Schellinger, *Encyclopedia of the Novel.*
2:1359–60.

———. "Tutuola, Amos." Cox, *African Writers.* 2: 865–78.
Biography, analyses of Tutuola's writing, and a select bibliography of his works
and bio-critical studies published between 1950 and 1988.

Owomoyela, Oyekan. "Tutuola, Amos." Benson and Conolly, *Encyclopedia of Post-
Colonial Literatures in English.* 2:1602–3.

Weinstein, Norman. "Amos Tutuola." Parekh and Jagne, *Postcolonial African Writers: A Bio-bibliographical Critical Sourcebook.* [471]–75.

Dictionaries, Encyclopedias, and Handbooks

Owomoyela, Oyekan. *Amos Tutuola Revisited.* New York: Twayne, 1999

Adaora Lily Ulasi, 1932–

Web Sites

"Adaora Lily Ulasi." *Anglophone and Lusophone African Women's Writing.* 26 July 2005, http://www.ex.ac.uk/~ajsimoes/aflit/UlasiEN.html.

"Adaora Lily Ulasi." *Contemporary Africa Database.* 26 July 2005, http://people .africadatabase.org/en/person/16219.html.

Biographies and Criticism

Gikandi, Simon. "Ulasi, Adaora Lily." Gikandi, *Encyclopedia of African Literature.* 542–43.

"Ulasi, Adaora Lily." *Contemporary Authors.* 167:387–88.

(Gerald Felix) Tchicaya U Tam'si, 1931–1988

Web Sites

"Gerald Felix Tchicaya U Tam'si (Gerald Felix Tchicaya.)" *Francophone African Poets in English Translation.* 26 July 2005, http://web.uflib.ufl.edu/cm/africana/ utamsi.htm.

Biographies and Criticism

O'Grady, Betty. "Tchicaya U Tamsi: Some Thoughts on the Poet's Symbolic Mode of Thought." Genova, *Companion to Contemporary World Literature.* 1:324–29. Discussion of U Tamsi's literary style.

Sellin, Eric. "Tchicaya U Tam'si." Serafin, *Encyclopedia of World Literature in the 20th Century.* 4:303–4.

"Tchicaya U Tamsi: *Le Zulu.*" Conteh-Morgan, *Theatre and Drama in Francophone Africa.* 174–83. Critical analysis of *Le Zulu.*

"Tchicaya U Tamsi." Stanley et al., *Contemporary Literary Criticism.* 101:344–67. Excerpts from criticism published between 1974 and 1995, with an annotated bibliography.

"Tchicaya U Tamsi." Wordworks, *Modern Black Writers.* 715–19. Excerpts from criticism published between 1980 and 1995.

Pieter-Dirk Uys, 1945–

Web Sites

"Pieter-Dirk Uys." *Contemporary Africa Database.* 26 July 2005, http://people.africa database.org/people/data/person10948.html.

Biography and Criticism

Hauptfleisch, Temple. "Uys, Pieter-Dirk." Benson and Conolly, *Encyclopedia of Post-colonial Literatures in English.* 2:1609–10.

Laurens (Jan) van der Post, 1906–1997

Web Sites

Iverson, Stacie Lee. "Laurens van der Post." *E-Museum.* Ed. and update unavailable. U. of Minnesota at Mankato. 26 July 2005, http://www.mnsu.edu/emuseum/ information/biography/uvwxyz/vanderpost_laurens.html.
Biographical information about van der Post.

"Laurens van der Post." *Books and Writers.* 26 July 2005, http://www.kirjasto.sci.fi/ laurens.htm.

"Sir Laurens van der Post." *Contemporary Africa Database.* 26 July 2005, http:// people.africadatabase.org/en/person/16166.html.

Biographies and Criticism

Pottiez, Jean-Marc. "Van der Post, Laurens." Benson and Conolly, *Encyclopedia of Post-colonial Literatures in English.* 2:1611–12.

"Laurens van der Post." Riley and Mendelson, *Contemporary Literary Criticism.* 5:463–64.
Excerpts from criticism published between 1967 and 1974.

Robb, Kenneth A. "Laurens van der Post." Eds. Barbara Brothers and Julia Gergits. *British Travel Writers, 1940–1999* (*Dictionary of Literary Biography* 204). Detroit: Gale, 1999. 297–308.

Smith, Christopher. "Laurens van der Post." Cox, *African Writers.* 2:879–91.
    Biography, analyses of van der Post's works, and a select bibliography of his works and bio-critical studies published between 1953 and 1986.

Yvonne Vera, 1964–2005

Web Sites

Habila, Helon. "Yvonne Vera." *Guardian Books: Obituaries.* 27 Apr. 2005. Guardian Unlimited. 26 July 2005, http://books.guardian.co.uk/obituaries/story/0,11617, 1471421,00.html.

Mutandwa, Grace. "Yvonne Vera: The Person and the Dreamer." *Weaver Press.* Ed. and update unavailable. Weaverpresszimbabwe.com. 26 July 2005, http://www .weaverpresszimbabwe.com/reviews/reviewframeset.htm?yvera020523.htm. Transcript of a 2002 interview.

Soros, Eugene. "Yvonne Vera: Breaking the Silence." *World Press Review Online.* 23 Sept. 2002. Worldpress.org. 26 July 2005, http://www.worldpress.org/Africa/ 736.cfm.
A thematic overview of Vera's works.

"Under the Tongue." *LitNet.* 26 July 2005, http://www.litnet.co.za/africanlib/tounge .asp.

"Yvonne Vera." *African Literature in English: Five Women Writers.* 26 July 2005, http://www.fb10.uni-bremen.de/anglistik/kerkhoff/AfrWomenWriters/Vera/Vera.html.

"Yvonne Vera." *Anglophone and Lusophone African Women's Writing.* 26 July 2005, http://www.ex.ac.uk/~ajsimoes/aflit/VeraEN.html.

"Yvonne Vera." *Contemporary Africa Database.* 26 July 2005, http://people.africa database.org/people/data/person3675.html.

"Yvonne Vera." *Contemporary Postcolonial and Postimperial Literature in English.* 26 July 2005, http://www.scholars.nus.edu.sg/post/zimbabwe/vera/veraov.html.

Biographies and Criticism

Vambe, M. "Vera, Yvonne." Gikandi, *Encylopedia of African Literature.* 545–47.

"Vera, Yvonne." *Contemporary Authors.* 168: 397–99.

Dictionaries, Encyclopedias, and Handbooks

Muponde, Robert, and Mandivavarira Maodzwa-Taruvinga, Eds. *Sign and Taboo: Perspectives on the Poetic Fiction of Yvonne Vera.* Oxford: James Currey, 2003.

José Luandino Vieira (José Vieira Mateus da Graça), 1935–

Web Sites

"José Luandino Vieira." *Contemporary Africa Database.* 26 July 2005, http://people .africadatabase.org/people/data/person3685.html.

Biographies and Criticism

Gikandi, Simon. "Vieira, José Luandino (José Vieira Mateus da Graça)." Gikandi, *Encyclopedia of African Literature.* 557–58.

Hamilton, Russell G. "Vieira, José Luandino." Serafin, *Encyclopedia of World Literature in the 20th Century.* 4:431–32.

Jacinto, Tomás. "The Art of Luandino Vieira." Donald Burness. Ed. *Critical Perspectives on Lusophone African Literatures.* Washington, D. C.: Three Continents Press, 1981. [80] –87.
Biographical information and an overview of Vieira's *Luuanda.*

Peres, Phyllis. "José Luandino Vieria." Cox, *African Writers.* 2:893–901.
Biography, analyses of Vieira's works, and a select bibliography of primary and secondary works published between 1975 and 1991.

Benedict Wallet Vilakazi, 1906–1947

Web Sites

"Benedict Vilakazi." *KwaZulu-Natal Literary Map.* Copyright 2005. Kzn.org. 27 July 26, 2005, http://literature.kzn.org.za/lit/25.xml.
Biography, text of English translation of the poem "Now I do Believe" and a list of his works.

"Dr. Benedict Wallet Vilakazi." *South African History Online.* Ed. and update unavailable. Sahistory.org. 26 July 2005, http://www.sahistory.org.za/pages/people/vilakazi-bw.htm.
Brief biography and the text of one poem.

Biographies and criticism

"Vilakazi, Benedict Wallet." Kepos, *Twentieth-Century Literary Criticism.* 37:396–413.
    Excerpts from criticism published between 1935 and 1986 and an annotated
bibliography.

"Vilakazi, B. W." Wordworks, *Modern Black Writers.* 741–42.
    Excerpts from criticism published between 1935 and 1976.

Abdourahman Waberi, 1956–

Web Sites

"Abdourahman Waberi." *Contemporary Africa Database.* 26 July 2005, http://people
    .africadatabase.org/people/data/person13313.html.
Abdourahman A. Waberi. Ed. Abdourahman Waberi. Jan. 2004. Free.fr. 6 Aug. 2004,
    http://waberi.free.fr/.
    On this official site of the author, Waberi's handwritten welcome note invites
readers to click on links to his biography, bibliography, and other information related
to his works and his country, Djibouti. In French.

"Abdourahman Waberi, Djibouti/France." *Lettres Ulysses Award.* Ed. and update
    unavailable. 6 Aug. 2004, http://www.lettre-ulysses-award.org/jury03/waberi
    .html.
    Biographical profile.

Somali and Djibouti Writers on the Web. Ed. and update unavailable. The Africa
    Centre. 6 Aug. 2004, http://www.africacentre.org.uk/somali%20stories.htm.
    This site, designed for students and teachers, provides a biography of Waberi
and texts of some of his stories (in French, English, and Somali).

Biographies and Criticism

Ekotto Frieda. "Waberi, Abdourahman A." Gikandi, *Encyclopedia of African
    Literature.* [561].
King, Adele. "Rift Route Rails: Variations romanesques." *World Literature Today.*
    75.2 (Spring 2001). 305.
    Review of Waberi's collection of short stories.

Godwin Wachira, 1936–

Web Site

"Godwin Wachira." *Contemporary Africa Database.* 26 July 2005, http://people
    . africadatabase.org/people/data/person16159.html.

Biographies and Criticism

Bardolph, J. "Wachira, Godwin." Benson and Conolly, *Encyclopedia of Post-colonial
    Literatures in English.* 2:1622–23.

Charity Waciuma, 1936–

Web Sites

"Charity Waciuma." *Contemporary Africa Database.* 26 July 2005, http://people
    .africadatabase.org/people/data/person16160.html.

Biographies and Criticism

Bardolph, J. "Waciuma, Charity. Benson and Conolly, *Encyclopedia of Post-colonial Literatures in English*. 2:1623.

"Waciuma, Charity." Robinson, *Modern Women Writers*. 4: [518]–22.
    Excerpts from criticism published between 1983 and 1987.

Timothy Wangusa, 1942–

Web Sites

"Timothy Wangusa." *Contemporary Africa Database*. 26 July 2005, http://people
    .africadatabase.org/people/data/person16175.html.

"A Taxi-Driver on His Death." *African Letters*. 26 July 2005, http://www.bowwave
    .org/AfricanWriters/Timothy%20Wangusa.htm.

Biographies and Criticism

Sicherman, Carol. "Wangusa, Timothy." Benson and Conolly, *Encyclopedia of Post-colonial Literatures in English*. 2:631.

Interview

Sicherman, Carol. "Timothy Wangusa and Contemporary Ugandan Literature." *World Literature Written in English*. 32.3/33.1 (1992–1993): 22–32.

Zoë Wicomb, 1949–

Web Sites

"Zoë Wicomb." *Contemporary Africa Database*. 26 July 2005, http://people.africa
    database.org/en/person/16170.html.

"Zoë Wicomb." *Introducing South African Writers*. 26 July 2005, http://homepage
    .oniduo.pt/chacmalissimo/SAfrican/html/zoe_wicomb.htm.

Biographies and Criticism

Gaylard, Rob. "Zoë Wicomb." Scanlon, *South African Writers* (*Dictionary of Literary Biography* 225). 450–54.

Ibrahim, Huma. "Wicomb, Zoe." Gikandi, *Encyclopedia of African Literature*. 571–72.

Interviews

Willemse, Hein. "Zoe Wicomb in conversation with Hein Willemse." *Research in African Literatures*. 33.1 (Spring 2002): [144] –52.

Daniachew Worku (Dannyacchew Werque), 1936–1995

Web Sites

Daniachew Worku. Ed. Seifu Daniachew. Copyright 2005. Adefris.net. 26 July 2005,
    http://www.adefris.net/.
    This site, still under construction, reproduces reviews of Worku's works and his
non-creative writing.

"The Thirteenth Sun." *LitNet*. 26 July 2005, http://www.litnet.co.za/africanlib/sun
    .asp.

Biographies and Criticism

Molvaer, Riedulf. "Dannyachew Werqu." Gikandi, *Encyclopedia of African Literature*. 135–36.

(Bernard) Zadi Zaourou, 1938– n.d.

Web Sites

"Bernard Zadi Zaourou." *La Maison des Auteurs.* Ed. and update unavailable. Les francophonies en Limousin. 26 July 2005, http://www.lesfrancophonies.com/PAGES/maison/AUTEURS%202002/zadizaourou.htm.
Biographical sketch and a list of Zaourou's plays and various performance dates.

Biographies and Criticism

"Zadi Zaourou: *L'Oeil*." Conteh-Morgan, *Theatre and Drama in Francophone Africa*. 202–10.
Critical analysis of Zaourou's play.

Interviews

Bielmeier, Gunther. "C'est vraiement une forme nationale de theater, le Didiga." *Interviews avec des écrivains africaines francophones* (*Bayreuth African Studies* 8, 1986). 63–77.

Paul Tiyambe Zeleza, 1955–

Web Sites

"Professor Paul Tiyambe Zeleza." *Contemporary Africa Database.* 26 July 2005, http://people.africadatabase.org/people/data/person11733.html.

Biographies and Criticism

Roscoe, Adrian. "Zeleza, Paul." Benson and Conolly, *Encyclopedia of Post-colonial Literatures in English*. 2:1678.

Musaemura Zimunya, 1949–

Web Sites

"Musaemura Zimunya." *Zimbabwe: Poetry International Web.* Ed. and update unavailable. Poetry International Web. 26 July 2005, http://zimbabwe.poetry international.org/cwolk/view/17267.
Biography and links to poems and articles on Zimunya.

"Musaemura B. Zimunya." *Contemporary Africa Database.* 26 July 2005,

"Musaemura B. Zimunya." *Contemporary Postcolonial and Postimperial Literature in English.* 26 July 2005,http://people.africadatabase.org/people/data/person 4906.html. http://www.scholars.nus.edu.sg/landow/post/zimbabwe/zimunya/zimunyaov.html.

"To Mai." *African Poetry.* 26 July 2005, http://www.aghadiuno.com/poetry/african/bonas.html.

Williams, Angela A. "Mother Tongue: Interviews with Musaemura B. Zimunya and Solomon Mutswairo." *Journal of African Travel Writing.* 4 (1998). 26 July 2005, http://www.unc.edu/~ottotwo/mothertongue.html.
Transcript of an interview.

Biographies and Criticism

Msiska, Mpalive-Hangson. "Zimunya, Musaemura." Benson and Conolly, *Encyclopedia of Post-colonial Literatures in English.* 2:1680–81.

Vambe, M. "Zimunya, Bonus [sic] Musaemura. Gikandi, *Encyclopedia of African Literature.* 586.

Senouvo Agbota Zinsou, 1946–

Web Sites

"Senouvo Agbota-Zinsou." *Contemporary Africa Database.* 26 July 2005, http://people.africadatabase.org/people/data/person16771.html.

Biographies and Criticsm

"Senouvo Zinsou: *On joue la comédie.*" Conteh-Morgan, *Theatre and Drama in Francophone Africa.* 193–201.
Critical analysis of Zinsou's play.

Gabara. Rachel. "Zinsou, Senouvo Agbota." Gikandi, *Encyclopedia of African Literature.* 586.

Index

About the Author

MIRIAM CONTEH-MORGAN is the African Studies, Linguistics, and French Bibliographer and an associate professor at The Ohio State University Libraries. She holds a B.A. in English and History from the University of Sierra Leone, an M.A. in Linguistics and English Language Teaching from Leeds University, and an M.L.S. from Kent State University. She is a co-author of *The Undergraduate's Companion to Women Writers and Their Web Sites* (Libraries Unlimited, 2002).